# REVOLUTION AND REBELLION

*State and society in England in
the seventeenth and eighteenth
centuries*

This iconoclastic and satirical book provides a radical reconstruction of the recent historiography of the seventeenth and eighteenth centuries. It creates an alliance between those revisionist historians who have rewritten the received account of the origins of the English Civil War and those historians who have been rethinking the Hanoverian era: *Revolution and Rebellion* is thus a companion volume to the author's *English Society 1688–1832*. This book counters the Marxist interpretation of the 1640s as the 'English Revolution' by deploying our new understanding of the non-revolutionary nature of the world after 1660: it challenges the appropriateness of 'revolution' as a description of events like those of 1688, 1715, 1745, the American Revolution, the Industrial Revolution or the Reform Bill, drawing attention instead to the idea of 'rebellion'. This is the first book so to link English history in the seventeenth and eighteenth centuries: it will be required reading for students and teachers of both eras.

JONATHAN CLARK is a Fellow of All Souls College, Oxford.

# REVOLUTION AND REBELLION

*State and society in England in
the seventeenth and eighteenth
centuries*

J. C. D. CLARK

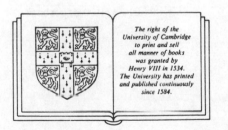

The right of the
University of Cambridge
to print and sell
all manner of books
was granted by
Henry VIII in 1534.
The University has printed
and published continuously
since 1584.

CAMBRIDGE UNIVERSITY PRESS

*Cambridge*

*New York    Port Chester*

*Melbourne    Sydney*

Published by the Press Syndicate of the University of Cambridge
The Pitt Building, Trumpington Street, Cambridge CB2 1RP
40 West 20th Street, New York, NY 10011, USA
10 Stamford Road, Oakleigh, Melbourne 3166, Australia

First published 1986
Reprinted 1987, 1990

Printed in Great Britain at the University Press, Cambridge

*British Library cataloguing in publication data*
Clark, J. C. D.
Revolution and rebellion: state and society in England
in seventeenth and eighteenth centuries.
1. Great Britain – Politics and government – 1603–1714
2. Great Britain – Politics and government – 1714–1820
I. Title
941.06  DA375

*Library of Congress cataloguing in publication data*
Clark, J. C. D.
Revolution and rebellion.
Includes index.
1. Great Britain – Politics and government – 1603–1714.
2. Great Britain – Politics and government – 18th century.
3. England – Social conditions – 17th century.
4. England – Social conditions – 18th century.  I. Title.
JN175.C59 1986  320.941  86–13634

ISBN 0 521 33063 7 hard covers
ISBN 0 521 33710 0 paperback

# CONTENTS

v

# ABBREVIATIONS

| | |
|---|---|
| *BIHR* | *Bulletin of the Institute of Historical Research* |
| *BJECS* | *British Journal for Eighteenth Century Studies* |
| *CHJ* | *Cambridge Historical Journal* |
| *EC* | *The Eighteenth Century: Theory and Interpretation* |
| *ECS* | *Eighteenth Century Studies* |
| *EHR* | *English Historical Review* |
| *HJ* | *Historical Journal* |
| *JBS* | *Journal of British Studies* |
| *JEH* | *Journal of Ecclesiastical History* |
| *JHI* | *Journal of the History of Ideas* |
| *JMH* | *Journal of Modern History* |
| *P&P* | *Past and Present* |
| *SCH* | *Studies in Church History* |
| *THES* | *The Times Higher Education Supplement* |
| *TLS* | *The Times Literary Supplement* |
| *TRHS* | *Transactions of the Royal Historical Society*, 5th series |
| *WMQ* | *William and Mary Quarterly* |

# PREFACE

It will soon become obvious to readers of this book that the debates with which it deals are being described by a participant. I should say therefore that, while I am most grateful to those of my colleagues with whom I have discussed these issues, the views expressed are my personal ones: they are not an authorised statement of the tenets of any school or group. Partly these reflections arise out of self-criticism, in an attempt to improve on some early work on the politics of 1714–60, and to atone for its deficiencies. Partly they are an attempt to give order to a series of confused historical arguments, and so to suggest ways in which those arguments might develop in the future. To encapsulate the views of one's colleagues in a few lines may sometimes be a legitimate aim, but it is intensely difficult to accomplish. At all times my intention is to provide not a substitute for the originals, but an inducement which will provoke the reader to consult for himself the works of those historians whom I discuss. Much can be learned even (or perhaps especially) from those books with which we most disagree: it is only fair that I should record a general indebtedness to those authors who so figure here.

With these appropriate caveats, I can record with gratitude the advice and encouragement of those of my colleagues who read this essay in draft form: Robert Ashton, Jeremy Black, Ian R. Christie, Eveline Cruickshanks, Sir Geoffrey Elton, J. P. Ferris, Anthony Fletcher, J. P. Kenyon, Peter Laslett, Wallace T. MacCaffrey, John Morrill, J. G. A. Pocock, Conrad Russell, Quentin Skinner, John Walsh, Austin Woolrych. To have written a book with which such a diverse group of scholars could all agree was beyond my ambitions: they will, I hope, accept this intervention as a contribution to a living debate rather than as an inscription on the gravestone of a dead one.

The debate is sometimes lively to the point of acrimony. Students approaching these areas for the first time often have difficulty in appreciating what all the fuss is about: why seemingly technical historical arguments over division lists or Jacobite ideology, county government or patronage networks, generated such heat among scholars. This study places those debates in a wider context and emphasises the important issues which were, and are, at stake. Students should bear in mind, too, that this is not a book to be consulted a chapter at a time. Its aim is to give a general view of the shape of the subject, and of the relation of different themes to each other. It should be read as a unity.

It is with particular pleasure that I can dedicate this book to the Warden and Fellows of All Souls College – 'For one day in thy courts : is better than a thousand.'

*February 1986*

# 1

# INTRODUCTION

Among the two most marked characteristics of English historical scholarship are its fixation with the adversary system – its desire to see the past as a debate between two 'sides', and to echo this in the rivalry of scholarly interpretations – and the principle of specialisation, which implicitly shapes so many of the historian's results by confining him to a predetermined chronological field. So great is the volume of new publication that for any century it seems we can only keep up with it by swimming with the current, accepting and working within the framework of explanation which that scholarship contains. Yet it would be useful, and sometimes it seems possible, to stand back from a debate in an attempt to undo the effects of both these imperatives, and to look within a wider perspective at those cross-currents of influence and argument that sway the course of historical scholarship. 'When our ideas on some large historical theme are in a state of disorder', wrote Sir Herbert Butterfield, 'we may find it useful to make ourselves acquainted with the history of the historiography of that particular subject.'[1] Studies of this kind are more commonly undertaken for past generations of historians, as in such deservedly famous works as Sir Herbert's cited below, D. C. Douglas' *English Scholars, 1660–1730* (1939, 1951), J. G. A. Pocock's *The Ancient Constitution and the Feudal Law* (1957), or John Burrow's *A Liberal Descent: Victorian Historians and the English Past* (1981). Here I have sought to pursue these questions in more recent years.

Although the result is much wider both in chronological and thematic range, this book began as an attempt to trace the course of debate over the last decade in two usually quite separate areas: the reigns of the first two Stuarts and the first two Hanoverians. It was conceived as a response to a valuable survey by Professor J. H. Hexter of the impact on scholarship in the former field of the recent writings of Professor Conrad Russell.[2]

---

[1] Herbert Butterfield, *George III and the Historians* (London, 1957), p. 9.
[2] J. H. Hexter, 'The Early Stuarts and Parliament: Old Hat and the *Nouvelle Vague*', *Parliamentary History* 1 (1982), 181–215.

I

Hexter's informality and erudition excused his marshalling of his colleagues into schools or parties; his helpful precedent is my excuse for asking
similarly irreverent questions of the eighteenth century also.

I have borrowed but adapted some of Hexter's terminology, and should
explain my terms. By the 'Old Guard' I mean that cohort of scholars whose
minds were formed in the matrix of inter-war Marxism, and their later
heirs. The 'Old Hat' school in these pages indicates those Whig or liberal
historians, in the tradition of S. R. Gardiner and G. M. Trevelyan,
Wallace Notestein and Sir David Lindsay Keir, who rearranged English
political history into a benign and teleological pattern – the unfolding of
parliamentary liberties, the rule of law, and representative institutions. By
the 'Class of '68' I mean those writers whose world view took shape in
euphoric approval of the radicalism and unrest of the late 1960s and early
1970s. 'Revisionist' and 'revisionism' are labels I inherit from early-Stuart
scholarship in the last decade, and use with more reluctance: each
generation revises the views of its predecessor, and soon post-revisionists,
and *their* successors, will emphasise the inadequacy of those categories. Yet
these are shorthand terms only: little of the argument developed in this
book depends on the infallibility of these categories. Nor do I wish to
imprison particular individuals within them: my ambition, on the contrary, is to abet their escape.

The generation effect, then, is one preoccupation of my discussion.
Another is the effect of those divisions which have grown up within the
historical community. This book arose from the belief that the unit of
production (to borrow an economists' expression) which sets the boundaries of historical enquiry and influences its content is often larger than the
professional historian's avowed 'period' or the range of the student's
textbook. In this case, I wish to suggest that the debate between different
cohorts of historians, well known in the period 1603–42[3] and little known in
the years 1714–60, is part of a wider movement which embraces both
centuries. If those debates are to be clearly understood by the student and
profitably prosecuted by the researcher, the interdependence of academic
arguments in the two areas must be highlighted, and the apparent isolation
of neighbouring groups of historians and of students must be broken down.
This study is a small contribution to that process.

If these two debates can be related more closely, there may be a
consequence for our perception of English history which is both foreseen
and intended in this book. The traditional strategy has posited a decisive

---

[3] Early-Stuart historiography until the mid 1970s may be traced in R. C. Richardson, *The
Debate on the English Revolution* (London, 1977); his helpful study was written before the
appearance of Professor Russell's more recent work, which is the starting point for the
present book.

break at the end of the seventeenth century: 1688 is often taken as the symbolic date. The 'eighteenth century' is consequently coupled to an industrial–democratic engine of change and drawn off into 'the future'. The suggestion here, on the contrary, is that such linkages are very greatly weakened by our new understanding of the nature and chronology of economic growth, and by a proper appreciation of the events of 1828–32. If so, we must explain eighteenth-century English politics and society as a development, not a revolutionary discarding, of their traditional forms in the seventeenth century. Revolution must be located in the realms of politics and ideology, religion and social institutions, and such a redefinition emphasises the large degree of continuity in even these forms. Yet to seek to relate eighteenth-century England to its seventeenth-century origins rather than to its nineteenth-century outcome runs counter to most traditions of English scholarship, and many of the shortcomings of this book will stem from the novelty of the attempt.

Such an enterprise, it is suggested, calls into question a number of historians' long-familiar explanatory categories. Scepticism rather than a new credulity is our aim, however. The elaboration and refinement of definitions is not the business of the historian. We can safely leave it to social scientists to build models of institutions or processes (capitalism, class, party, revolution) and, if they wish, to carry their models back into the past in a search for phenomena which might seem to fit them. The historian should prefer to work more closely with his material and to be more responsive to the content of the categories employed in past time. In contrasting 'revolution' and 'rebellion' in the title of this book I am referring to modern debates: I am not suggesting that those terms carried their present meanings in the seventeenth or eighteenth centuries. Until after 1789 the term 'revolution' indeed often signified a reversion to a previous pattern, as a wheel comes full circle. Clarendon reserved the title 'revolution' for the events of 1660, not 1642; Whigs used the same term of 1688 to signify the repair of the constitution after what they claimed had been James II's innovatory tyranny; and this usage survives in Dr Johnson's *Dictionary*.[4]

Our own meanings are somewhat different. Without wishing to rest much weight on definitions, it might be suggested that we still understand

[4] The various and accumulating meanings of the two words can best be traced in the *Oxford English Dictionary* and its *Supplement*. It is clear that in and before the eighteenth century 'revolution' (apart from its meaning 'a return to origins') was merely used in a sense synonymous with 'successful rebellion', i.e. a 'complete overthrow of the established government'. Not until the nineteenth century did 'revolution' take on the social-structural meanings we now principally give it. Despite the writings of such pioneers as James Harrington (1611–77) or Gregory King (1648–1712), we should not exaggerate the willingness or ability of most seventeenth- and eighteenth-century Englishmen to think about their society in structural terms.

'rebellion' to mean a fundamental challenge to the title to legitimacy of political institutions, often (in the past) a religious title. But this concept now tends to become subsumed in that of 'revolution', since we often take a revolution to be a successful rebellion; and by 'revolution' we now understand, in addition to the political aspects, a fundamental challenge to the legitimacy of social structures, including patterns of hierarchy or stratification, and titles to economic ownership or control. Too much recent writing, it is suggested, rests on this anachronistic sense of 'revolution': the revisionists' preferred category is 'rebellion', and it is one which deserves more exploration.[5]

So to distinguish these two explanatory categories helps us to disengage ourselves from the assumption that revolutions are always 'forward-looking', that they embody the progressive aspirations of 'rising' social classes to speed up developments being impeded by 'the forces of reaction'. Rebellion is a concept more evidently devoid of such implications; it helps our appreciation that many conflicts (like the Civil War or 1688) can better be described as reactions against innovations, a deeply rooted resistance to undesired change. I am not claiming that no revolutions, in the social-structural sense, ever occurred in early-modern societies (though that is a possibility); I am suggesting that we should be far more cautious in applying that category. These modern usages, of course, are not watertight: past events have a way of spilling over into both. The object of any attention to definitions in this book is not to encourage readers to rest content with a new label but to use labels more critically, as a help to understanding the concrete and unique detail of the events themselves.

This study, then, attempts to trace (and, indeed, to reorganise more purposefully) the scholarship of the last decade concerned with England's experience of political and social change over two centuries. It attempts to link both the conceptual formulas and the frameworks of explanation which have been applied in curiously similar ways to those episodes conventionally designated 'revolutions': the Civil War, the events of 1688, of 1776 in America, the 'Industrial Revolution', and the quasi-

---

[5] For a profound and scholarly non-Marxist enquiry into the status and function of the concept of revolution as applied to early-modern Europe see Perez Zagorin, *Rebels and Rulers, 1500–1660* (2 vols., Cambridge, 1982), vol. 1, pp. 3–57. Yet his broadly drawn definition of 'revolution' (vol. 1, pp. 17, 24) subsumes 'rebellion' and confuses social-structural change with discontinuities in the realms of ideology and religion, distinctions which I wish to emphasise. Surveying Britain, France, Spain, the Netherlands and Germany, Professor Zagorin develops a fourfold typology – 'agrarian rebellion', 'provincial rebellion', 'urban rebellion' and 'revolutionary civil war'. Applying the last category to the 'English Revolution' of 1640–60 (vol. 2, pp. 130–86), Zagorin rejects some of the arguments of the revisionist historians which are discussed and partly accepted in the present book. Although I dissent from several aspects of his thesis, Zagorin's able and wide-ranging comparative study is essential reading on the subject.

revolutionary or silently revolutionary upheaval in which the 1832 Reform Act is related to all of the foregoing and to post-1815 'radicalism'.

Such a study, spanning two centuries, must necessarily be a schematic one, and to a large degree a study of the historiography. But lest it should be thought that I am merely postponing 'modern times' and keeping alive 'the world we have lost' until 1789 or 1832, it should be remembered that the same process of revision and reinterpretation has been achieved by François Furet for that most paradigmatic of all revolutions, the French Revolution of 1789. As John Roberts emphasised,

Time and again, the accumulating conclusions of the best scholarly research not merely fail to uphold, but actually undermine, the received conceptual framework within which *bienpensant* narrative of the Revolution is written. That pervading conceptual structure is, in broad terms, progressive and left wing. It has often been summed up as Marxist, or at least *marxisant*, and such terms are understandable – though (as M. Furet from time to time turns from his own argument to show) Marx and Engels themselves provide precious little support for it. Essentially, it is a structure suffused with a commemorative or even celebratory approach to the history of the Revolution. It rests on the presentation of the Revolution as a unitary expression of a supra-historical process of world significance. The Revolution is seen by it as the emergence of a liberating force, organically related to all subsequent 'progressive' social 'movements'. Historians of the Revolution have gone over again and again a narrative which illustrates this basic scenario, stressing the rupture with the past and strengthening the illusion of change. Unfortunately, at the same time solid scholarship was making such views increasingly untenable.[6]

If even the French Revolution now defies incorporation in the *marxisant* schema, we need to look afresh, and to look synoptically, at those English episodes that have been explained as the precursors or counterparts of 1789.

[6] John M. Roberts in *History*, 68 (1983), 168–9, reviewing François Furet, *Interpreting the French Revolution* (Cambridge, 1981).

# 2

# A DISCOURSE ON METHOD

## PERIODISATION: THE EFFECTS OF DIVISION

Few people are more isolated from each other than near neighbours, and among the most effective barriers to historical research are those unwritten rules which have grown up to inhibit scholars from questioning the received orthodoxy in adjacent areas. The result has been the survival of some curiously obsolete opinions. Many historians of seventeenth-century England still seem to believe that Sir Lewis Namier or J. H. Plumb legitimately reigns over the succeeding century; eighteenth-century historians still too often assume a model of the preceding century drawn from the Marxist Old Guard, with perhaps a glance at the somewhat muted critique of it offered by the Old Hat liberals. Even the best scholars sometimes seem up to a quarter of a century in arrears in their understanding of the course of scholarship in adjoining periods which have been designated 'someone else's'.

This does not mean that they are immune from influence, however. Wider movements in opinion show a remarkable ability to produce curiously similar phenomena in apparently unconnected areas of enquiry, and one such coincidence is the occasion of this survey. It took as its starting point the realisation that two debates had been proceeding together, not quite on parallel lines but with strong affinities and similarities, for a decade or more: the reinterpretations of the parliamentary history of the reigns of the first two Stuarts and of the first two Hanoverians. To a small degree, they stimulated and linked up with scholarship in other decades; but the isolation of different groups of historians gave them each a unity and autonomy. Moreover, those two debates, it will be argued, were essentially the same debate. They have, indeed, so far owed little or nothing to an explicit understanding of each other: Conrad Russell's research on the 1620s and Anthony Fletcher's on the 1640s disclosed no recognition of the importance of the eighteenth-century work of the History

6

of Parliament Trust,[1] and when I wrote on the 1750s[2] I failed to see the full significance of the work of the early-Stuart historians discussed here – much to my own loss.[3] But related problems had presented themselves in each area: the attempted answers proved to be strikingly similar, and the orthodoxies which came under attack were essentially the same. The two debates could still learn much from each other, and it is the modest desire to link these two areas more closely which prompts this survey rather than any intention to solve – in so short a book as this – the outstanding problems of either.

By enclosing the common field of English history with those fences termed 'centuries', academic entrepreneurs of a bygone generation prescribed a particular type of agriculture as well as a new pattern of ownership. They did so by preventing the emergence of the English ancien regime, 1660–1832, as an area of study in its own right. It was not only that that area was underpopulated; the numerical dominance of scholars in the 1500–1660 and post-1832 fields,[4] and their high academic calibre, had a disastrous effect on the perceived *substance* of the history of 1660–1832. In one Old Guard model, the years 1660–1760 became an unpleasant hangover after the euphoric revolution of the 1640s, a time when promising libertarian developments were forced 'underground' by oligarchic repression. At the other end of the scale, the combination of Industry, Democracy and Liberalism seemed so appropriate to an equally reified nineteenth century that the period after 1760 was reconstructed as a lead-in to those phenomena which reached maturity only in a later age. The whole experience of England's ancien regime was thus made to seem a temporary aberration from trends naturally successful before 1660 and after 1832.

A periodisation in terms of 'centuries', by fragmenting the continuum 1660–1832, emphasised transitions rather than continuities, cutting his-

---

[1] Namier's research institution, launched in 1951, has produced: Sir Lewis Namier and John Brooke (eds.), *The History of Parliament: The House of Commons 1754–1790* (3 vols., London, 1964); Romney Sedgwick (ed.), *The House of Commons 1715–1754* (2 vols., London, 1970); P. W. Hasler (ed.), *The House of Commons 1558–1603* (3 vols., London, 1981); S. T. Bindoff (ed.), *The House of Commons 1509–1558* (3 vols., London, 1982); B. D. Henning (ed.), *The House of Commons 1660–1690* (3 vols., London, 1983).

[2] Conrad Russell, *Parliaments and English Politics 1621–1629* (Oxford, 1979); Anthony Fletcher, *The Outbreak of the English Civil War* (London, 1981); J. C. D. Clark, *The Dynamics of Change: The Crisis of the 1750s and English Party Systems* (Cambridge, 1982).

[3] Historians have a fair excuse: we need to see each period in the past in its own terms, without papering over the gaps in our knowledge by the devices of hindsight and foresight. But it is also legitimate to use our results to generate a wider perspective, as the historians discussed in this book have done in other writings.

[4] Taking the community of professional historians as a whole, my impressionistic estimate is that for every ten scholars working on the years 1500–1660 there are three for 1660–1832 and thirty for post-1832. And the dividing dates are very sharp: in recent decades only a handful of historians have researched and written on either side of the years 1660 and 1832. Even today, very few do so.

torians off from their neighbours, and this isolation tended to increase as scholars' attention receded from the 'edges' of their subjects. Even quite recently, an outside observer might have been forgiven for supposing that the parliamentary history of 'the nineteenth century' meant mainly Disraelian and Gladstonian manoeuvres in the years between the Second and Third Reform Bills; that of 'the eighteenth century' chiefly meant the conflicts between the accession of George III in 1760 and the crisis of 1782–4; and that of 'the seventeenth century' was largely concerned with the decades immediately preceding the outbreak of the Civil War and with the Interregnum: interest flagged after 1660.

This weighting inevitably had its effect on the substance of the story. Attention was focussed in the seventeenth century on the causes of revolution (historians usually saw their task as the search for 'origins' rather than the balanced depiction of states of existence). Equally, the 'Whig' agenda written by Lord John Russell's generation in the 1830s and 40s for long focussed attention on the apparent stirrings of reform from the 1760s. The years *c.* 1714–60 were *terra incognita*; and in both centuries, new, interesting and dynamic phenomena were rearranged into the pattern of a crescendo. The events of 1642 and 1832 performed a similar role in each scenario.

Nor was there agreement on what 'the eighteenth century' meant: 1700–1800 raised too many problems, and the general answer was 1714–1815; yet the period after 1789 was usually given only perfunctory attention[5] and tacitly abandoned to nineteenth-century historians, reaching back to depict the origins of their world. If 'the eighteenth century' meant, in practice, 1714–89 or even 1760–84, it is less surprising that students concluded that little of importance can have transpired in a period which allowed itself so pusillanimously to be truncated. The vast majority of students, both at school and college level, studied 'Tudors and Stuarts' or 'moderns', and this neglect was by far the most important reason for the amiable tranquillity of eighteenth-century studies compared with the din of academic battle in the seventeenth century and the nineteenth. In particular, the early Hanoverian era was desperately underpopulated: if the units of study were 'the English Revolution [of the 1640s]' and 'Industrial Revolution to the present', then 1714–60 was marginal to everyone's interests.

Only if the unit of study were the English ancien regime, 1660–1832, did the reigns of the first two Georges stand out as conceptually *central* to the viability of the social and political order which prevailed between the Restoration and the Reform Bill. Conversely, the rewriting of the parlia-

---

[5] An honourable recent exception is Ian R. Christie, *Wars and Revolutions: Britain 1760–1815* (London, 1982), which deals in detail with *c.* 1789–1815.

mentary history of the reigns of George I and George II – an enterprise begun as scholarship for scholarship's sake – led to results far more extensive than its initiators ever expected. It led, first, to a fundamental challenge to a ruling orthodoxy; and, second, to a realisation that the challenge posed was the same challenge that was being made in the early seventeenth century also. This book began therefore as an account of a war on two fronts: a large and widely reported battle in a heavily populated area of scholarship, 1603–42, and a small and initially neglected engagement in a thinly populated area, 1714–60. Yet if there was a great imbalance in the forces involved, in strategic terms these two theatres of war proved to be of equal importance.

## REVISIONISM VERSUS ORTHODOXY

When, at last, even the sluggish waters of eighteenth-century scholarship were ruffled by revisionist breezes, the form taken by the arguments in that century had much in common with the structure of the revisionist case in the seventeenth. Partly this was due to the survival in both centuries of an 'Old Hat' liberal account of beneficent constitutional evolution, but the more important reason was the similarity of the models the Old Guard had constructed in each period, and to which authors heavily influenced by 1930s Marxism (if only to the extent of a shared economic reductionism) had given expression.

By the early 1970s, this combined orthodoxy had hardened to such an extent that a certain asperity, even aggressiveness, was found necessary by its critics in both centuries. Many senior scholars evidently felt fragile in 'the new, idol-smashing atmosphere of research on early Stuart politics'.[6] Revisionists in that era, as in the later one, were explicit in announcing that they aimed to revise 'conventional views' and 'received opinions', rejecting 'the present orthodox answer' and 'the traditional interpretation' in favour of a wholly new account of the structure and close texture of parliamentary politics.[7]

There seems no doubt that the Stuart establishment, whether Marxist Old Guard or liberal Old Hat, reacted to such temerity with an indignation matched only by the Hanoverian establishment in their reaction to similar suggestions in the later field. Professor Hexter, in a remarkable peroration, seemed to suggest that the revisionist interpretation of early-Stuart Parliaments was not merely an 'intellectual defect' but 'a moral one' because it

---

[6] The phrase of Theodore K. Rabb, 'Revisionism Revised: The Role of the Commons', *P&P* 92 (1981), 55.
[7] Cf. J. H. Hexter, 'Power Struggle, Parliament, and Liberty in Early Stuart England', *JMH* 50 (1978), 4–5.

did not attend to 'the central importance of liberty and the rule of law in the ordering of human affairs'.[8] If, as Professor Hirst suggested, the *major* concern of revisionist historians has been 'to deny the existence of conflict over issues of principle',[9] it seemed a short step to regarding such historical arguments as themselves *unprincipled*.

Since (as is argued in chapter 3) this orthodox model took a similar form in both the Stuart and Hanoverian periods, economic-reductionist and teleological in respect of political change, it prompted its critics also to adopt similar methodological weapons. The revisionists' 'rallying cry is the declaration that hindsight is dangerous', objected Professor Hirst: it led to the heretical view that 'the causes of the breakdown which led to civil war were essentially short-term', to a renewed attention to the role of chance, accident and disaster, and to a focus on day-to-day manoeuvre for explanations of these things rather than on grand rhetorical announcements of principle lifted out of their specific tactical context and strung together as a spurious chain of causality. Detailed studies of precisely defined tracts of parliamentary history were all very well, warned Hirst, yet 'historians who ignore what comes before and afterwards can fall victim to a myopia as damaging as that suffered by the most teleological Whigs'.[10]

Myopia, teleology and anachronism were the key charges bandied about in all revisionist debates;[11] but they were deliberate practices, not thoughtless slips. What critics denounced as sins, believers defended as self-evident truths. 'Great events do not necessarily have great causes, though it is natural for historians to seek them', noted Anthony Fletcher, explaining the rationale of his detailed and rigorous account of the events of 1641–2. Such care was necessary in the elucidation of this crisis, since

misunderstanding is of its essence. Men's actual intentions must be distinguished from their assumed and alleged intentions. The political debate was conducted in emotional and often highly dramatized terms . . . When war came there were some who were able to articulate the principles and convictions for which they fought. Yet even they, let alone the many who found it impossible to attach themselves steadfastly to one side or the other, had not sought war. This was a war that nobody

[8] *Ibid.*, pp. 48–50.

[9] Derek Hirst, 'Revisionism Revised: The Place of Principle', *P&P* 92 (1981), 79.

[10] Hirst, 'The Place of Principle', pp. 79–80.

[11] Equally, they can be found in analogous debates over the French Revolution, as in François Furet's critique of 'the old tautological proof that deduces causes from results'. Sometimes the method is concealed beneath a category: 'the dominant "concept" of today's historiography of the Revolution, "bourgeois revolution", seems to me to be used less as a concept than as a mask concealing precisely these two presuppositions: that of the inevitability of the event and that of a radical break in time'. Furet, *Interpreting the French Revolution* (Cambridge, 1981), pp. 19, 102.

wanted, a war that left men bewildered and that they marvelled at as it broke out by fits and starts all over England in the summer of 1642.[12]

The subtraction of hindsight from historical explanations is often a laborious and difficult task. Nor was success, when achieved, welcomed by those committed in principle against such an exercise. Christopher Hill, who had announced in 1967 that the 'Whig interpretation of history' was 'the only possible historical attitude',[13] challenged his critics in 1981: 'One of the things "revisionists" most dislike is hindsight: they call it Whiggish to consider what happened next. But in discussing men fumbling with problems which their mental apparatus was incapable of solving, it does not help merely to report on their vain efforts to square the circle.'[14] It does not help the attempt to construct a teleology, certainly; but it may help to rescue past people from the imputation of stupidity in failing so dimly to perceive the answers which the Old Guard so confidently provided.

Professor Zaller maintained that the revisionists' picture of early-Stuart England 'is not so much Whiggery refuted as reversed'.[15] 'Important as it is to correct the teleological pull which the Civil War has exerted over the interpretation of the preceding forty years', added Professor Woolrych, 'we must not make the Civil War itself incredible.'[16] But the problem was to find common ground that did not involve a fudged compromise. Though the methodological questions were explored at length, tenable compromise positions did not emerge: for the Hanoverian period, Old Guard orthodoxies were equally defended against even Lawrence Stone's modest degree of backsliding. E. J. Hobsbawm correctly diagnosed the works of, for example, E. P. Thompson as a more sophisticated restatement of the Marxist position rather than an essential modification of it.[17]

In general, the Old Guard establishment lasted rather longer in the Hanoverian period, though the disintegration, when it eventually came, was more spectacular. In both periods, most of the work of demolition was done through a close (its critics said, a myopic) attention to that long-unfashionable subject: politics. Six early-Stuart revisionists to whom Professor Hexter replied (Christianson, Farnell, Gruenfelder, Kishlansky, Roberts, Russell) were characterised by a particular (and to their critics peculiarly narrow) view of politics – politics as a struggle for power, *rather*

---

[12] Fletcher, *The Outbreak of the English Civil War*, pp. xxix–xxx, 407–8: 'there is no need for political narrative to drain the story of all deep-seated meaning', he felt obliged to protest.

[13] Christopher Hill, *Reformation to Industrial Revolution* (1967; Harmondsworth, 1980), p. 20.

[14] Christopher Hill, 'Parliament and People in Seventeenth-Century England, *P&P* 92 (1981), 122. Hill's attempts, curiously there introduced (pp. 113–14, 123), to justify his opposition to rearmament in the 1930s are interesting in this context.

[15] Robert Zaller, 'The Concept of Opposition in Early Stuart England', *Albion* 12 (1980), 229.

[16] Austin Woolrych, 'Court, Country and City Revisited', *History* 65 (1980), 240.

[17] E. J. Hobsbawm, 'The Revival of Narrative: Some Comments', *P&P* 86 (1980), 3–8.

*than* as the rehearsal of substantive issues which political action expresses,[18] and certainly not as the 'great causes' teleology associated with Trevelyan, with the Marxist vision of Tawney's revolutionary bourgeoisie, or even Stone's sociologising 'multiple dysfunction' of every area of national life.

As with Victorian and later revisionists (Bentley, Cooke, Cowling, Hurst, Jones, Norman, Vincent), and as with some early-Hanoverian revisionists, the early-Stuart revisionists engineered a deliberate narrowing of the historical vision in a search for precise questions and demonstrable answers. As in the later period, the Old Guard and Old Hat historians together stigmatised this as a retrograde step, producing a 'constricted socio-economic range' that was 'curiously old-fashioned', a 'Clarendonian vision' that neglected long-term explanations built around theories of social change. In all three periods, the denunciation of narrative method was peculiarly bitter, indeed instinctive: its critics reacted against it not merely as one among many possible historical methods, but as *the* method in particular which posed a threat to the Old Guard position.

## NAMIER'S GHOST: A CASE OF MISTAKEN IDENTITY

Who was responsible? Derek Hirst detected the influence of 'two spirits' beguiling the revisionists away from the 'high road' of Old Hat orthodoxy: not early-Stuart historians indeed, but men more famous in other fields – Elton and Namier.[19] Theodore Rabb pointed similarly to the work of Professors Elton and Koenigsberger, and to J. R. Vincent and A. B. Cooke's *The Governing Passion: Cabinet Government and Party Politics in Britain, 1885–86* (1974), adding: 'It is striking that this wave of Namierisation has taken place with little, if any, acknowledgement of the influence of Namier himself, perhaps because his star has begun to wane in his own century, the eighteenth.'[20] Professor Rabb meant to challenge the use of narrative, and other scholars also seemed to be labouring under the impression that Namier was an exponent of 'high-political' history: that the sophisticated narratives of, for example, Michael Hurst's *Joseph Chamberlain and Liberal Reunion* (1967), Andrew Jones' *The Politics of Reform 1884* (1972), or Alistair

---

[18] Hexter, 'Power Struggle, Parliament and Liberty', p. 1. Among the historians listed, this may well have seemed a false antithesis. To its authors, the sort of history which has attracted (perhaps needlessly) the label 'high political' was a way of dealing with substantive issues, not a way of denying that issues were involved in politics at all.

[19] Derek Hirst, 'Unanimity in the Commons, Aristocratic Intrigues, and the Origins of the English Civil War', *JMH* 50 (1978), 51–2, 58.

[20] Theodore K. Rabb, 'The Role of the Commons', p. 57.

Cooke and John Vincent's *The Governing Passion* represented a recrudescence of Namierism in another century.[21]

Eighteenth-century revisionists were puzzled to see Sir Lewis Namier, that fine though overrated historian, promoted to the status of bugbear by their seventeenth-century colleagues. Between Namier and the revisionists there are, perhaps, similarities of temperament; of scepticism about the autonomous force of ideas; of hostility to Whig sins of teleology and anachronism. Yet Namier was not, primarily, a narrative historian. His brief narratives, when he wrote them, were clever and highly selective sketches rather than detailed examinations.[22] His relentlessly detailed researches were mainly in the structural analysis of the Commons, and were intended to dissolve Whig generalisations about the course of events at the centre by a series of constituency studies. One could argue that Everitt and Morrill[23] more than Russell and Fletcher are Namier's heirs in the seventeenth century, Aydelotte and Davis[24] rather than Cooke and Vincent in the nineteenth. It might be suggested that what Namier's critics really object to is his caustic and exceedingly effective conservatism, not his historical method. Indeed, his legacy was divided: it did not descend intact.

Lawrence Stone objected:

The two facts about a man's life which most commonly survive are his family connexions and his business interests. The tacit assumption that too often lies behind the 'Namierite' approach is that human beings are primarily motivated by these two factors, an assumption which is then triumphantly demonstrated by assembling the evidence under these headings. This process has its own internal logic, but it has no claim to ultimate validity, since it fails to take cognizance of changes of structure, changes of environment, changes of ideology. It does not examine and explain the material and spiritual needs of humanity: it presupposes them.[25]

---

[21] Cf. the curiously paranoid image of Richard W. Davis, 'Victorian Political Diaries', *Parliamentary History* 1 (1982), 227–32: 'Namierism is like one of those creeping vines, the striking flowers of which gain them a place in a garden they then take over. Rooted out in one place, they spring up and luxuriate in another, where the process of extirpation has to be begun anew', etc. He hailed Rabb and Hirst as allies in this extirpation for the seventeenth century, and (the more respectably reductionist) Plumb, Cannon and Brewer for the eighteenth.

[22] It must be protested that 'high political' history in its recent (and perhaps particularly Cambridge) form derives from Butterfield, not Namier. My own conception of politics and its appropriate narrative expression was worked out as Butterfield's unofficial pupil, and later as his colleague.

[23] See chapter 4 for an account of Provincial history in the Stuart period.

[24] On the strength of W. O. Aydelotte, 'The House of Commons in the 1840s', *History* 39 (1954), 249–62; 'Voting Patterns in the British House of Commons in the 1840s', *Comparative Studies in Society and History* 5 (1962–3), 134–63; 'Parties and Issues in Early Victorian England', *JBS* 5 no. 2 (1966), 95–114, and subsequent work; R. W. Davis, *Political Change and Continuity, 1760–1885: a Buckinghamshire Study* (Newton Abbot, 1972).

[25] Lawrence Stone, *The Crisis of the Aristocracy 1558–1641* (Oxford, 1965), pp. 4–5.

It was a valid complaint. Namier's attention to individual motivation had too often lapsed into a schematic and reductionist formula. Yet, seen from a later perspective, it was by no means clear that even the most open-minded of the Old Guard had freed themselves from this preoccupation with the material and the economic. On the contrary, the reason why that school of thought objected to Namier so bitterly may have been that he drew a quite different conclusion (a politically conservative conclusion) from an essentially shared body of assumptions. A feature of the revisionism discussed in this book was a growing realisation of the extent to which Lawrence Stone and Sir Lewis Namier, Christopher Hill and H. R. Trevor-Roper were arguing within a common nexus of ideas.

How, exactly, was that nexus to be defined? What were the alternatives? The answers to these questions were by no means obvious, and were implicitly worked out in the concrete detail of scholarship over more than a decade. In general terms, Professor Stone himself recognised the extent of the common ground as well as anyone in recording some assumptions which, he believed, because generally shared, could be taken as read:

the view that there must be a direct relationship between social structure and political institutions and that the former tends to dictate the latter, is widely accepted today, even by historians and politicians of a strongly anti-Marxist cast of mind ... The notion that constitutional or administrative history can be studied in a social vacuum, as an isolated story of the growth of liberty or bureaucracy or whatever, is one that few historians are now prepared to countenance ... Marx tended to see [ideology] as a sociologically motivated superstructure and H. R. Trevor-Roper similarly seems to regard religion as economically determined ... Looking back on the controversy [of the 1950s over the supposed 'rise of the gentry'] today [i.e. in 1972], it seems clear that all parties in the early stages were taking an indefensibly narrow view of the causes of revolution.[26]

But although the view was widened, it will be argued in this book that the accepted model was modified very much less than the Old Guard thought. It was scarcely modified because historians' essential framework of explanation, their chosen methodologies, were little changed until the arrival of a new generation of scholars.

When seeking methodological parallels, it must be remembered that the Stuart and Hanoverian debates did not proceed exactly in phase. Nevertheless, for both centuries the impact of Namier had been fully absorbed by *c.* 1960;[27] the characteristic historiography of the next two decades saw a revolt against his influence and a reassertion of the world view of the Old

---

[26] Lawrence Stone, *The Causes of the English Revolution 1529–1642* (London, 1972), pp. 39–40.

[27] The most distinguished examples of early-Stuart parliamentary history in a Namierite idiom were Mary F. Keeler, *The Long Parliament, 1640–1641: A Biographical Study of Its Members* (Philadelphia, 1954), and D. Brunton and D. H. Pennington, *Members of the Long Parliament* (London, 1954).

Guard, latterly through the eyes of the Class of '68. The self-styled revisionism of the 1980s was less a critique of the targets Namier and Butterfield challenged than a critique of their critics. Specifically, the problem was not a somewhat indeterminate Whig interpretation in the hands of historians vaguely Whig,[28] but a politically explicit interpretation in the hands of historians whose present-day practical commitment was closer, more strident and more central to their purposes than that of any other cohort of historians since the 1830s.

### THE REVIVAL OF NARRATIVE

The revival of narrative, then, was not the result of a simple retrojection of Namierite method into the Stuart period. In both centuries, that revival was equally a product of another development, and one much harder to diagnose. Practising historians are generally reluctant to submit their chosen methods to discussion or scrutiny (there are exceptions, notably, in the present context, Professors Hexter and Elton). The methodologies employed by even good scholars are, indeed, often robust rather than philosophically sophisticated: what matters is the result, they might say, not the method. The generality of scholars are only driven to a discussion of method at times of crisis within their subject, when an orthodoxy is threatened or breaking up. Such was the case here: substantive results came first, reflections on method followed. These reflections were, indeed, sometimes a little exotic: one early-Stuart had recourse to T. S. Kuhn's *Structure of Scientific Revolutions* and Werner Heisenberg's *Physics and Philosophy* as well as to Sir Herbert Butterfield's more familiar *The Whig Interpretation of History* in the search for anti-teleological weapons.[29]

Elsewhere, a renewed academic attention to a long-ignored area of national life, religion, was associated with a reconsideration of reductionist assumptions. The full effect of this was evident only from the mid 1980s. In 1972, in a very different intellectual climate, Lawrence Stone had accurately observed that 'Many of the younger generation of historians, in France, in England and in the United States, believe that the future of history lies in a cautious selective cross-fertilisation with the methods and theories of the social sciences, particularly politics, economics, sociology,

28  That loyal Asquithian Herbert Butterfield's *The Whig Interpretation of History* (1931) said many wise and shrewd things; but it did not identify the historians challenged (except by implication) and was distressingly vague about the concrete forms taken by the methodological sins of anachronism and teleology which were so rightly anathematised. Furthermore, it was – as its title made plain – directed against its author's own party. Butterfield (like so many other liberals), did almost nothing to turn his critique against Marxists, to whom it equally applied.

29  See Paul Christianson, 'The Causes of the English Revolution: a Reappraisal', *JBS* 15 no. 2 (1976), 40–75.

social anthropology and social psychology.'[30] Such indeed were the
preoccupations of the Class of '68; but, with complete unanimity, they
ignored one auxiliary discipline which the revisionists were to find of
immense importance in the understanding of early-modern England –
theology. When this changed, an idealist methodology and the narrative
mode were to prove profoundly compatible.

In general, then, it was not Namierite structural analysis but high-political narrative that provided the revisionists with their most effective
weapon aginst Old Guard perspectives. Early-Stuart revisionism got
under way amid explicitly expressed hopes that progress lay through a
modernised version of Gardiner, a scholarly and rigorous narrative 'based
upon a study of day-by-day proceedings and of individual MPs. As the
narrative unfolds, so many of the old assumptions must fall away',
predicted Dr Sharpe.[31] Professor Kishlansky warned of the dangers of
relying on Stuart memorialists, even Clarendon, who 'assess the causes of
events by their consequences, hopelessly muddling their unfolding'. His
chosen themes were ones which, he believed, could 'be explicated only by a
precise narrative – day to day at crucial moments. Narrative history, no
longer the staple it once was, is now thought difficult and "boring" for it
relies on the willingness of readers to familiarise themselves with intricate
detail before they can understand the argument being presented.'[32] In
reality, most early-Stuart scholars were equipped and prepared to make
that effort; yet both they and (to a much greater extent) the early-Hanoverian revisionists met with an unthinking reaction from some historians
unable or unwilling to grapple with serious narrative.

The Old Guard traditionally undervalued political history of any sort,
whether Namierite or narrative. R. H. Tawney had amazingly confessed his
disbelief, before reading Brunton's and Pennington's volume, that any book
on 'a subject at first sight so trite as the parliamentary history of the England
of the early Stuarts' could be interesting or important.[33] It was nothing new:
S. R. Gardiner's first two volumes in 1863 were greeted by a reviewer in *The
Athenaeum* as a product of 'the dry old school of historical writing, in which
facts stood for ideas and dates for pictures ... We do not every day meet an
author with whom we could so easily agree: if, in reading him, we could only
keep awake.'[34] But we expect better things of professional historians today.

[30] Stone, *The Causes of the English Revolution*, p. 31; 'cautious' and 'selective' were, perhaps,
    cosmetic adjectives.
[31] Kevin Sharpe (ed.), *Faction and Parliament* (Oxford, 1978), p. 4.
[32] Mark A. Kishlansky, *The Rise of the New Model Army* (Cambridge, 1979), p. x.
[33] Introduction to Brunton and Pennington, *Members of the Long Parliament* (London, 1954),
    p. xxi.
[34] Roland G. Usher, *A Critical Study of the Historical Method of Samuel Rawson Gardiner*
    (Washington, St Louis, 1915), p. 5. Not until 1875–6 did the reviewers begin to appreciate
    the significance of Gardiner's achievement (pp. 8–9).

The Old Guard, however, by rejecting parliamentary history, had delayed their appreciation of important developments in scholarship. Professor Lawrence Stone, writing in 1979, belatedly recognised a revival of narrative technique, and indeed claimed to welcome that revival. Examined more closely, the works he cited with approval scarcely proved to be 'narrative' in form at all, like E. P. Thompson's *Whigs and Hunters* or E. J. Hobsbawm's and G. Rudé's *Captain Swing*, and Stone was finally compelled to acknowledge the inadequacy of the term to describe these then-fashionable books. It was one thing to imply approval in principle of this alleged revival; when seen in practice, the superb results of real narrative in the works of the early-Stuart revisionists produced only aversion and disparagement: the authors were 'the new British school of young antiquarian empiricists ... chroniclers of the petty event', inspired by Elton, Russell and Kenyon, who were 'busy trying to remove any sense of ideology or idealism from the two English revolutions of the seventeenth century ... Although their premiss is never explicitly stated, their approach is pure neo-Namierism, just at a time when Namierism is dying as a way of looking at eighteenth-century English politics.'[35] It is clear that 'Namierism' was used here as a term of abuse, not of serious description; but a point was made, nevertheless.

Many lesser historians found themselves disliking intensely the products of this narrative revival when they appeared in print over the next few years. Such works tended to be long, complex, heavily footnoted, demanding on author and reader alike, and relatively inaccessible. They called for serious thought about difficult issues, and were little help (indeed the reverse) to the harassed lecturer struggling with his teaching load.[36] Secondly, their substantive results were distinctly uncomfortable to many people, partly because they rendered untenable specific theses with which certain individuals were closely associated (like the early-Hanoverian Court v. Country analysis – for which, see pp. 136–44 below) but more generally because a detailed, rigorous narrative of unfolding events will have a solvent effect on teleological accounts of social evolution: on the idea that societies pursue a steady and beneficent path from *Gemeinschaft* to *Gesellschaft*, on the idea that individual politicians are somehow the embodiment of Great Ideas, on the notion that politics is a rational, purposeful, problem-solving, interest-registering activity in which statesmen, if they defy the logic of events, are soon coerced back into co-

---

35 Lawrence Stone, 'The Revival of Narrative: Reflections on a New Old History', *P&P* 85 (1979), 3–24. A curious feature of this often-cited article is its omission of any serious consideration of historical narratives.

36 The reaction of one reviewer to one such work was to weigh it (2½ lbs) and count all the footnotes (3,075)! Quantifying techniques can sometimes be a substitute for thought rather than an aid to thought.

operation with the forces of progress by 'pressure from without'. A proper
study of the intricacy and uncertainty of human affairs is indeed apt to
reveal values as subservient to situations, and political and ethical norms
and conventions as defined retrospectively, in response to events whose
outcome is often unforeseen or undesired; to show chance, ignorance and
error overriding purposeful endeavour; and to show the values and
intentions of past men, seen at close quarters, as often quite different from
anything which could be fitted into a teleological explanation of English
liberties or a dialectic of social classes.

Professor Stone, then, noticed that a particular group of self-styled
leading historians were increasingly drawn to the study of *mentalité* and of
the individual situation, and deduced in them a revaluation of a modified
form of narrative. Yet he neglected to remark on the continuing hostility of
just such writers to the practice and results of narrative as generally
understood. Such men still accepted the Old Guard model of Westminster
politics as a reflection of 'underlying' phenomena (landownership, trade,
urbanisation); and, since that model served their purposes, they found
little reason to question it closely. Instead, they had often turned from the
study of high politics (which their credulity in these respects had defined as
boring) and revelled in the recreation of the world of the press, public
opinion and mass action.

Seen 'from the outside in', Westminster could be made to seem receptive
to, at times highly responsive to and even coerced by, 'popular politics'. No
more than the Old Guard could the champions of this perspective be
expected to relish the scaling-down in the importance of such phenomena
which followed a modernised account of Westminster affairs, drawn up
with a critical eye to the possible impact there of mobs, ballads, broadsides
or newspapers. In the accounts of the revisionists, that 'nebulous generalisation' public opinion proved to be, as far as St James's and Westminster
were concerned, what the politicians said it was, and though they said
different things this did not give that abstraction an objective, independent
existence. 'Public opinion' was the medium through which the Class of '68
in particular sought to give 'underlying causes' a leverage at Westminster;
narrative historians were increasingly sceptical of such arguments for
reasons both of substance and of method. Politics, to be understood, had to
be seen as itself and not reduced to the reflex of *any* 'underlying'
phenomena.

If a revival of narrative is desirable, however, what are we to revive?
Narrative technique was the natural vehicle for such influential historians
of the two eras as G. M. Trevelyan and Basil Williams, yet whatever their
other professional gifts it is now impossible to examine their *narratives*
without a mounting sense of frustration at the shallowness, the superficia-

lity and glibness of much of their writing, their willingness to skate over ignorance with a commonly received form of words, and to evade important problems with a well-turned generalisation. Narrative can and should mean more than it meant to the Edwardians. Secondly, the evasive nature of this lax narrative mode meant that it had no defences (indeed no very evident understanding of the need to defend itself) against the methodologically disastrous process of abridgement.[37] It was this process which produced the sort of desiccated 'constitutional history' usually held to be classically embodied in the work of Sir David Lindsay Keir,[38] and which formed the staple diet of generations of Oxford undergraduates. It may, of course, be the case that *all* analysis is only an abridgement of narrative, so that inadequacies introduced at the narrative stage are magnified and caricatured by the process of abridgement. If abridgement is a regrettable necessity, only the utmost rigour in its narrative premises can guard against the wildest results: anachronism and teleology can be best disguised in the form of a table of statistics, valuable though quantifying techniques potentially are.

This should not imply that revisionists dealt exhaustively or initially with philosophical problems of method: on the contrary, they offered their abstract suggestions rather as asides. Their main concern was with their positive account of the past. The thrust of the revisionist attack was against the substance of the Old Guard model: one suspects that revisionists were sometimes more committed to their own substantive picture than to their method, wherever it might lead them. Dr Bentley shrewdly noted that the

attitudes of high-political writers readily become self-sealing and suggest no compelling reason for subjecting the overall strategy to review. Many writers interested in the problem of authenticity in political evidence have proved quicker to adduce reasons for deciding what is unacceptable in historical commentary than to provide accounts of what evidence would need to be presented in order to reverse their decisions. If it should turn out, in the house-clearance of some Liberal dowager, that Asquith, Crewe and Grey each wrote a couple of impeccably private letters endorsing the urgency of social reform in terms more naturally associated with Lloyd George and Winston Churchill, would the resistance of high-political writers to the 'progressivist' case change colour? If three cabinet ministers seem insufficient, how many does one need? If two letters seem too few, how many will suffice?[39]

---

[37] The classic denunciation of this practice is, of course, Michael Oakeshott, *Rationalism in Politics and Other Essays* (London, 1962).
[38] Like many such condemnations, this was a little harsh. Lindsay Keir's *The Constitutional History of Modern Britain* (London, 1938) is better than its present reputation.
[39] Michael Bentley, 'Party, Doctrine, and Thought', in Michael Bentley and John Stevenson (eds.), *High and Low Politics in Modern Britain* (Oxford, 1983), p. 152; cf. *idem*, 'What is Political History?', *Durham University Journal* 70 (1978), 133–9.

It is in part because there is no easy answer to this and similar questions that it is profitable to trace the connections between the chosen methodologies of different cohorts of historians and their substantive results, especially at a point of fundamental transition.

## THE WIDER SETTING

The transition discussed here was not a process confined to history, of course: it affected all related areas of scholarly enquiry. By the mid 1980s, one might read remarks like this in a letter to the editor of a periodical aimed at the academic community:

British political science was peculiarly torpid until the electoral shock of 1979. It was dominated by Fabians and Keynesians whose mental set inhibited them from anticipating the upheavals of the 1970s and 1980s. It would be easy to list a succession of books by men who have been left like stranded whales by the ebb of the Keynesian tide ... Too many existing political scientists belong to the generation of 1968 – a provenance that almost disqualifies them from comment on late 20th century politics.[40]

The generation effect, and the intellectual points at issue between generations, were particularly clearly marked in the disciplines of politics, economics and history. Shifts of perspective between generations of historians are nothing new, of course. One such shift had occurred in the late 1950s and early 1960s: in respect of the pre-Revolutionary history of the American colonies, the work of such historical patriarchs as Andrews, Beard, Becker, Gipson, Jameson and Schlesinger were demoted from 'the category of established truths'. 'Liberalism in America has become a subject for analysis rather than celebration', observed an English scholar, 'and with this shift in emphasis there has developed a marked tendency to query the achievements of historians influenced by its assumptions.'[41]

The widespread acceptance of Namierite analysis in England at that time was part of a similar phenomenon. It might be argued that the fate which then overtook liberalism is now overtaking socialism: its role as a scarcely questioned source of historians' assumptions is being progressively scrutinised. In America it was the liberals, in Professor Marshall's categorisation, who were the economic-reductionists; so that a rejection of Beard's analysis of the Constitution in terms of economic self-interest led to a rediscovery of the (admittedly still Whiggish) virtues of Bancroft's massive *History*.[42]

[40] Kenneth Burgin, in *THES*, 3 May 1985, p. 2.
[41] Peter Marshall, 'Radicals, Conservatives and the American Revolution', *P&P* 23 (1962), 44–5.
[42] Marshall, 'Radicals, Conservatives', p. 47; George Bancroft, *History of the United States* (10 vols., Boston, Mass., 1834–74).

Bancroft was America's S. R. Gardiner, and a feature of the early-Stuart revisionists of the last decade has been a similar rediscovery, and renewed admiration, of Gardiner's detailed and scrupulous *histoire événementielle*. Gardiner 'remains *the* authority and *the* indispensable narrative', wrote Dr Morrill: 'returning to it after some years I was amazed by the moderation and carefulness with which Gardiner unfolds the coming of the Puritan Revolution'.[43] Lawrence Stone's *The Causes of the English Revolution 1529–1642* 'must still be read in conjuction with the work of S. R. Gardiner', warned Conrad Russell.[44] Puzzlingly, the Old Guard and the Old Hat historians agreed. 'It is a rash historian who disagrees with Gardiner', commented Christopher Hill.[45] 'Gardiner was one of those inexhaustible nineteenth-century masters whose range and command leave us awestruck', added Theodore Rabb.[46] Gardiner indeed occupied an ambiguous position. Revisionists were drawn to him from a desire to rehabilitate narrative, yet repelled by his irreducibly Whiggish assumption. More work was needed in political history: a simple reversion to a previous narrative was insufficient.[47]

Both sides, then, looked to Gardiner; but they found there different things. The Old Hat school found grand constitutional battles over issues of principle. Revisionists found a scrupulous narrative technique which, they argued, ultimately told against understanding those battles teleologically, as even Gardiner himself was prone to do. Both the Old Hat and *nouvelle vague* historians, too, valued narrative and a close attention to parliamentary matters. But what they narrated was rather different, and so too were the parliamentary matters to which each school attended. The Old Hat school looked to Parliament (in the singular), and in particular to parliamentary debates, for statements of belief, of the principles which, they held, underlay action and which, assembled together, make (as they imagined) a constitution. Such was the emphasis of American scholars especially; it was an approach which came naturally to citizens of a country with a written constitution, in whose universities constitutional lawyers bulked large. The English *nouvelle vague* school looked to Parliaments (in the plural) for *deeds* rather than *words*;[48] like Namier, they were sceptical of grand statements of principle, even (or perhaps especially) when made by politicians. The *nouvelle vague* sought to go behind statements of principle,

[43] J. S. Morrill, *Seventeenth-Century Britain, 1603–1714* (Folkestone, 1980), p. 33.
[44] *EHR* 88 (1973), 861; cf. Kevin Sharpe's compliments to Gardiner in *Faction and Parliament*, pp. 2–4.
[45] Hill, 'Parliament and People', p. 105.
[46] Rabb, 'The Role of the Commons', p. 56.
[47] This idolisation of Gardiner was indeed largely in disregard of the criticisms substantiated by Roland G. Usher, *A Critical Study of the Historical Method of Samuel Rawson Gardiner*. (I owe this reference to Professor Ashton).
[48] I owe this observation to Mr J. P. Ferris.

explaining them by reference to political tactics and parliamentary procedure, and draining them of their apparent teleological force.

This emphasis on deeds rather than words has had its effect. The
principal revisionist weapon against Old Guard model-building has been
the revaluation of detailed narrative studies, both high- and low-political,
of concrete and specific situations. A problem confronting eighteenth-
century revisionists was consequently the absence of a Gardiner-like figure
to whom reference might be made to defend narrative. Lecky never filled
that role, and the more obvious Edwardian exponents of narrative were
intellectually soft-centred. Revisionists asserting the potential of narrative
in an eighteenth-century context met with a hostile reaction from the
entrenched orthodoxy and rather cool encouragement elsewhere.

Yet these minor eddies in one corner of the academic world were more
than offset by a broader and deeper current which swept the participants in
these debates into a new landscape. To historians of Namier's generation,
their choice of explanatory method seemed to lie between two grandiose
schemes of ideas, largely incompatible and mutually exclusive: Freudian
psychology and Marxian socialism.[49] With the deepening bankruptcy of
conventional liberalism, essentially the same choice seemed to present
itself to subsequent cohorts of historians, from Hobsbawm's and Hill's to
the Class of '68. Yet, in the last two decades, the emptiness of these two
grand philosophies has come to seem inescapable; the prophets of their
downfall suddenly seem to be pushing at an open door.[50] First Marx, then
Freud, have emerged as figures who demand explanation in other terms,
rather than as unchallengeable prophets who themselves provide the terms
for explaining others. If Namierism is dying, it is because the psychological
props to the theory of mass biography have dissolved: psychoanalysis no

[49] The most perceptive account of Freud's significance for Namier is Sir Isaiah Berlin, 'L. B.
Namier' (1966), in *Personal Impressions* (London, 1980), pp. 63–82: 'It is not perhaps too
extravagant to classify his essentially deflationary tendency – the desire to reduce both the
general propositions and the impressionism of historians to hard pellet-like "facts", to
bring everything down to brass tacks – to regard this as part of the dominant intellectual
trend of his age and milieu. It was in Vienna, after all, that Ernst Mach enunciated the
principles of "economy of thought" and tried to reduce physical phenomena to clusters of
identifiable, almost isolable, sensations; that Freud looked for "material", empirically
testable causes of psychical phenomena; that the Vienna Circle of philosophers generated
the verification principle as a weapon against vagueness, transcendentalism, theology,
metaphysics; that the Bauhaus with its clear, rational lines had its origin in the ideas of
Adolf Loos and his disciples. Vienna was the centre of the new anti-metaphysical and
anti-impressionist positivism ... this was the world from which Namier came.' Berlin
stresses Namier's dual anticlericalism – '(organised falsification – rabbis were worse than
priests, and lived on and by falsification)'; his conversion to Anglicanism late in life was not
reflected in his work.

[50] Cf. H. J. Eysenck, *Decline and Fall of the Freudian Empire* (London, 1985); Ernest Gellner, *The
Psychoanalytic Movement, or the Coming of Unreason* (London, 1985).

longer seems to us a viable means of insulating historical enquiries from materialist-reductionist claims.[51]

This, indeed, was Namierism's weak point: it damaged liberalism by a strategy which, in an English setting, actually promoted Marxist historiography. Namier's positivism, his deflationary desire to strip away psychological illusions and ideological rationalisations, led in the end to a materialist reductionism even in his own ascription of motives. In other hands, too, psychoanalysis proved too weak a weapon to resist this process. Yet what have survived from Namierite methods, and seem increasingly threatening to the Old Guard, are its *negative* implications: an anti-teleological scepticism, a closeness to sources which could be turned to narrative uses and shield past human conduct from enlistment in present polemical purposes.

The collapse of grand theories originating elsewhere in the academic world has allowed the effective reassertion of scholarly standards generated from within the historical profession: the revival of narrative is an important consequence in respect of method. In respect of substance, historians in several fields have been independently drawn to explain past societies far more in terms of the categories which those societies present to us. Above all, they find themselves talking not about class conflict, economic revolution or democratic representation but about hierarchy, allegiance and authority – concepts articulated within the practice of politics, law and religion. Rebellion rather than revolution is thus the crucial explanatory category for revisionist historians. In their search for modes of conduct which seemed to be paradigms of modes which were inexplicable in terms of something else, historians of periods as far removed as the early Stuarts, the Hanoverians and the mid nineteenth century have been led to an awareness of the centrality of religious issues in the patterns of thought and action of those whom previous cohorts of historians had so resolutely laboured to secularise. Issues of method and issues of substance were inextricably related in the debates discussed in this book.

---

[51] It is remarkable that Namier's chosen methods should have enjoyed such a vogue without any substantial exposition or defence of them by an historian, not even Namier himself. Their credibility was guaranteed by the wider beliefs of the intelligentsia as a whole.

# 3

# SOCIAL CHANGE
# EXPLANATIONS

## THE OLD GUARD MODEL

English history in the period in question was rather exciting: change was in
the air.

New social forces were emerging, new political relationships were forming, and new
intellectual currents were flowing, but neither the secular government nor the
Church was demonstrating an ability to adapt to new circumstances. Thanks to the
growth of the national product, the changing distribution of wealth, the spread of
higher education, the decline of aristocratic political dominance on local affairs, the
formulation of new religious and secular ideals, and the consolidation of new
administrative organizations, in the century after ****, there appeared a growing
body of men of substance, rich property owners, professionals and merchants.
These men – the leading figures among the county squirearchy, the successful
London lawyers, the more eminent **** divines, and the urban patriciates that
dominated the cities – were steadily enlarging their numbers, their social and
economic weight, and their political independence. Behind them loomed far larger
numbers of yeomen and artisans, the respectable, industrious, literate, Bible-
reading, God-fearing lower middle class, many of whose aspirations these leaders
shared, represented and articulated. These men were not only seeking a larger voice
in political affairs and the right to consent to taxation. They were also asking for
change ...

and so on.[1] The author is Lawrence Stone, and his subject the approach to
Civil War; but it might be any conventional Old Guard, Old Hat or Class
of '68 historian from Veitch and Maccoby through Plumb and Cannon to
Brewer and Porter, writing on the eighteenth century. The first deletion is
the date '1540'; it might as well be '1740', and the same model was equally
useful for the conventional account of economic growth and an Industrial
Revolution inevitably producing political change. The second deletion is
the adjective 'Puritan'; it could as well be replaced by 'Nonconformist',

---

[1] Lawrence Stone, *The Causes of the English Revolution 1529–1642* (London, 1972), pp. 114–15. I
was reminded of this passage by Hexter, 'The Early Stuarts and Parliament', p. 188.

and at once we have the late-eighteenth-century bourgeois nexus which is supposed to have transformed traditional patrician hegemony.

The interdependence of political and social history was well demonstrated by Brunton and Pennington's Namierite analysis of the composition of the Long Parliament. It had rendered untenable the old assumption that men's choice of allegiance in the Civil War was determined by class or economic occupation, as R. H. Tawney, incongruously writing an Introduction to their volume, reluctantly but candidly acknowledged:

Royalists and Parliamentarians alike include country gentlemen, lawyers, and merchants. Representatives of old families and new, greater and lesser gentry, conservative and improving landlords, metropolitan and provincial traders and financiers, are found among both ... minorities apart, the two parties appear ... to be economically and socially much of a piece ... It is a question whether the expectation that an Independent will probably be – ambiguous phrase – a *petit bourgeois* is, in fact, better founded than the doctrine that all merchants were Whigs.[2]

But these results were for long neglected by other historians unwilling to consider the implications of parliamentary history.

'Social change' theories eventually proved unsatisfactory on their own ground, however. The emerging problem was not just the arguable *invalidity* of this structural picture but, suspiciously, its *too general* validity: an account so elastic as to fit several periods tells us little of specific value about any of them. On the other hand, so elastic an analysis was unlikely to confront its exponents with sharp discrepancies when compared with the results of new research. It therefore proved peculiarly difficult to remove, despite the outcome of the 'gentry controversy' of the 1950s.[3] Professor Stone continued to say similar things even into the 1980s. 'According to Marxist theory', he acknowledged, 'the Revolution [of the 1640s] opened the way to possessive individualism, a market economy, laissez-faire capitalism, and bourgeois hegemony.' By 1981, Stone still assumed the same eighteenth-century results, and merely argued for a more complex model of the seventeenth-century causes. The effect of the revolutions of 1641 and 1688, he maintained, was 'to shatter the myths of the Divine Right of Kings and Passive Obedience', developing instead that 'individualistic ideology' of 'possessive individualism' which is 'peculiarly associated with an urban middle class and with a squirearchy living off

---

[2] R. H. Tawney, in Brunton and Pennington, *Members of the Long Parliament* (London, 1954), p. xviii. The authors presciently pointed to two subjects for future research which were to achieve much greater prominence in the 1970s and after: localism, and networks of kinship and patronage.

[3] Few would now accept that any of the chief participants in that controversy had succeeded in demonstrating the origins of the Civil War in the economic rise or fall of any 'class': cf. J. H. Hexter, 'Storm over the Gentry', in *Reappraisals in History* (London, 1961), pp. 117–62.

commercialised agriculture'.[4] What shattered this picture was the eventual recognition that these eighteenth-century results, once seemingly so obvious, could no longer be assumed; and a political, social and cultural ancien regime which was markedly indifferent or accommodating towards these 'new' forces demanded a reconsideration of those forces' revolutionary potential.

There had, however, developed a certain diversity in the ways in which the Old Guard model was being cosmetically adapted. Christopher Hill, like Lawrence Stone, continued to defend the notion that the *result* of the events of the 1640s was a 'bourgeois revolution' while modifying his account of *causes*: he went as far as to concede that it was not something intended by, or brought about by, a bourgeoisie. Nevertheless, the 'English Revolution, like all revolutions,[5] was caused by the breakdown of the old society'; so, by definition, the stage *must have been* cleared for the emergence of a new society after 1660. Its form was dictated by economics, for 'by 1640 the social forces let loose by or accompanying the rise of capitalism, especially in agriculture, could no longer be contained within the old political framework except by means of a violent repression of which Charles's government proved incapable'. The years 1660–88 saw 'an uneasy balance'; the 'political supremacy' of the bourgeoisie came in and after 1688, as Marx and Engels said.[6] Christopher Hill thus seemingly handed over to E. P. Thompson and J. H. Plumb: the Old Guard apparently maintained an unbroken front. Indeed, it was essential that their front should be unbroken. The viability of the Old Guard model for the seventeenth century now depended more than ever on its viability for the eighteenth century also.

### THE EIGHTEENTH-CENTURY OUTCOME

It seems certain that few seventeenth-century students traced this analysis forward to the succeeding century. They were, perhaps, sufficiently

---

[4] Lawrence Stone, 'The Results of the English Revolutions of the Seventeenth Century', in J. G. A. Pocock (ed.), *Three British Revolutions: 1641, 1688, 1776* (Princeton, 1981), p. 44. Stone's apt seventeenth-century qualifications on p. 46 are remarkably at odds with the eighteenth-century results he retains: the revolution of the 1640s 'did almost nothing positive to encourage economic laissez-faire and almost nothing to stimulate a more capitalistic and market-oriented approach to agriculture, industry or trade'.

[5] The reification should be noticed: revolution has been transformed from a *category* into a *thing*, objectively existing in the external world. Only on that premiss is it credible to argue that all revolutions are alike in certain respects. Yet revolution (like class, that other favourite) is a descriptive term, not a phenomenon. Studies of revolution as of class are studies of the use of words, not of things.

[6] Christopher Hill, 'A Bourgeois Revolution?' in Pocock (ed.), *Three British Revolutions*, pp. 109–39. For a critique, Robert Ashton, *The English Civil War: Conservatism and Revolution 1603–1649* (London, 1978), chapter 4.

reassured to know that Old Hat, Old Guard and Class of '68 historians were discussing the world which followed 1642 with the common currency of the rise of the bourgeoisie, commercialisation, secularisation, and the relation of political institutions to 'underlying' economic change. Examined more closely, it is now evident that J. H. Plumb was actually saying something rather different from Christopher Hill. Plumb posited exactly the same incipient bourgeois revolution in the 1640s and a curiously similar march of progress for the late eighteenth century, reaching its apotheosis in 1832. But he was able to do so only by an implausible argument that the clock had been put back in fundamental ways in the Glorious Revolution[7] – the 'revolution' which the seventeenth-century Old Guard, abandoning 1642, now wished to claim as the apotheosis of developments in their century.

Plumb's *political* model of the eighteenth century explicitly echoed an inherited model of preceding social change. Where Stone and Hill posited widening social rifts as a cause of the Civil War, Plumb assumed a closing of the same divisions to produce a complacent oligarchy. This could be expressed in a form which concealed its inconsistency with the seventeenth-century model of Christopher Hill. As Professor Pocock summarised it:

The thesis of an electorate large in the seventeenth but restricted in the eighteenth century means that the Whig aristocratic order attacked by American revolutionaries and British reformers was not an *ancien régime* and had no feudal character, but was a recent outgrowth of mercantile and patronage politics instituted in the search for social stability combined with expanding empire. The Whig oligarchs combined with the monied interest and successfully bought off the landed gentry.[8]

This view of early-eighteenth-century developments was soon adopted by Stuart historians. Lawrence Stone duly accepted this social model as the terminal point for his theory of seventeenth-century conflicts,[9] the result of an alliance between an 'economically dynamic ... squirearchy' and 'the merchant elite of the cities'. Consequently his political vision of the Hanoverian era echoed Plumb's: the deliberate restriction of a large, undeferential late-Stuart electorate ('For a brief thirty-year period, England was a genuine participatory democracy'[10]); the political imposition of 'one-party government' after the Tory party had 'succeeded in

---

[7] See below, p. 151.
[8] Introduction, pp. 14–15, in Pocock (ed.), *Three British Revolutions*.
[9] Stone, 'The Results of the English Revolutions of the Seventeenth Century', pp. 23–108, for a reductionist use of geological metaphors to explain religious and political conflict.
[10] *Ibid.*, pp. 79–81, citing the work of Plumb, Cannon, Holmes and Speck on the electoral history of *c.* 1689–1715.

destroying itself by becoming tainted with Jacobitism' in 1713–15.[11] England thus entered a 'spoils system based on patronage, influence, and corruption', so that 'government could only be conducted by a blatant distortion of the constitution as it existed in either Lockeian or neo-Harringtonian theory'.[12]

Because of the Restoration, Stone now maintained (like Plumb), social and economic change forged ahead, but political change was shackled: 'As a result England in the early nineteenth century found herself the first industrial nation of the world, but still saddled with a hopelessly antiquated, inefficient, and unjust set of political and legal institutions'. Reform was aimed at redressing a 'wide discrepancy in 1820 between England's modernised economy and her archaic institutions'.[13] A particular view of the frustration of the achievements of the Civil War dictated a certain view of the lead-in to the Reform Bill. The early-Hanoverian revisionist was thus inexorably drawn forward in time to apply a revisionist interpretation also to the events preceding 1832.

It was an interpretation which necessarily dispensed with this cavalier condemnation of the ancien regime: only on the basis of some privileged access to the past, contended the revisionists, could the Old Guard hand down these *obiter dicta* about a contradiction *in an objective sense* between England's material circumstances in 1820 and the rationales and institutions which co-existed with them. Within the Old Guard, a methodological error and a polemical determination to vilify a certain social order went hand in hand. The ancien regime had been not so much explained, as denigrated; the emergence of industrial society had been not so much quantified, as celebrated. Now, an emancipation from these polemical constraints suggested that the events of 1640–2 as well as 1830–2 were to be explained with the category of rebellion, rather than revolution.[14]

The elucidation of these difficulties had been delayed by a failure to relate the two centuries to each other. Despite the problems highlighted by the early-Stuart 'storm over the gentry', many of the Old Guard had been unabashed in espousing a 'falling gentry' thesis for the early-Hanoverian period; 'Country' ideology was presented as an economically articulate response to a high land tax, a rising monied interest, and stagnant or falling prices for agricultural products. Regardless of our new appreciation of the

---

[11] *Ibid.*, pp. 81–9, citing especially J. H. Plumb, *The Growth of Political Stability in England, 1675–1725* (London, 1967). The importance for this model of minimising the significance of Tory and Jacobite allegiance is further explored below, pp. 111–16 and 136–44.

[12] *Ibid.*, pp. 88, 90, 94–5.

[13] *Ibid.*, pp. 56–60.

[14] J. C. D. Clark, *English Society 1688–1832: Ideology, Social Structure and Political Practice during the Ancien Regime* (Cambridge, 1985), chapter 6, 'The End of the Ancien Regime, 1800–1832'; cf. pp. 155–63, below.

extreme methodological difficulties of proving claims about the economic fortunes of whole social classes in the sixteenth and early seventeenth centuries, such claims were blithely made for the eighteenth and swiftly adopted as the basis for views of political structures and ideological forms. In the later period, however, the need to treat 1688 as a setback meant that the gentry were no longer pictured as the agrarian wing of a bourgeoisie. Instead, historians caricatured a bumbling squirearchy: 'Paternal, reactionary, resisting the growth of market relations, and bent on reform only as a means of turning the tide of "history", these bucolic creatures seem, at least, to have squared ideology and interest and to have behaved as every *Marxisant* historian would wish', wrote John Brewer.[15] The greater gentry, too, were equally helpful: the Black Act (1723), for example, was 'an expression of the ascendancy of a Whig oligarchy, which created new laws and bent old legal forms in order to legitimize its own property and status; this oligarchy employed the law, both instrumentally and ideologically, very much as a modern structural Marxist should expect it to do'. So Mr E. P. Thompson.[16] To the revisionists, this all seemed too convenient to be credible. Sceptical voices began to be heard.

## MODIFYING THE MODEL

In the earlier period, the principal modification of the Old Guard model of 'underlying' socio-economic causes was achieved by an eventual acceptance of the consequences of the discovery that class stratification or economic interest does not provide an explanation of men's choice of allegiance in the Civil War. But although 'class' was deleted, the Old Guard sought to retain the same effects even without it: 'economic developments were dissolving old bonds of service and obligation and creating new relationships founded on the operations of the market ... the domestic and foreign policies of the Stuarts were failing to respond to these

[15] John Brewer, 'English Radicalism in the Age of George III', in Pocock (ed.), *Three British Revolutions*, p. 330. However conformable to *Marxisant* expectations, any such parody of the gentry does not survive the evidence presented in such studies as Philip Jenkins, *The Making of a Ruling Class: The Glamorgan Gentry 1640–1790* (Cambridge, 1983), which records their extensive involvement in agricultural and industrial entrepreneurship. Inconveniently, this was especially the case of the *Tory* gentry, excluded from many areas of public life under the first two Georges. This was true in other parts of the country: Sir Roger Newdigate, 5th Bt (1719–1806), the quintessential example of the Tory attitudes of the 1740s and 50s surviving unreconstructed into the second half of the century, was a leading Warwickshire entrepreneur in coal mining, canals and turnpikes, and a reader of Richard Watson's *Chemical Essays* and the *Encyclopédie* as well as of orthodox Anglican theologians: see John Money, *Experience and Identity: Birmingham and the West Midlands 1760–1800* (Manchester, 1977), p. 2.
[16] E. P. Thompson, *Whigs and Hunters: The Origin of the Black Act* (London, 1975), pp. 260–1.

changing circumstances'.[17] By the 1980s, the stripping away of untenable
elements in the argument had made it clear that the Old Guard picture had
always been essentially a claim of the *internal collapse* (because, they wished
to imply, of its inherent absurdity) of a 'world we have lost': a world of
tradition, service, status, hierarchy, deference, and, above all, orthodox
religion.[18] Provided this thesis of the destruction of the religious nexus of
belief and practice could be salvaged, the Old Guard were now prepared to
waive the idea that it was a pre-existing bourgeoisie which produced that
result. Similarly, as will be seen in chapter 7, provided the teleological Old
Hat account of parliamentary history in the years to 1642 as the apotheosis
of libertarian issues could be salvaged, many historians were prepared to
abandon the idea that it was a coherent grouping, 'the opposition', which
provided the motor of change by championing those issues.

Because these two outcomes could seemingly be salvaged, the Old
Guard continued into the 1980s to employ an apparently similar (but
actually inconsistent) social model for both the Stuart and Hanoverian
eras. If the old order collapsed, the *reasons* for its collapse could be made to
seem more important than the *date* of such an event. Indeed, if the object
was to discredit a certain nexus of values and beliefs, then the more often it
could be shown to be in a state of collapse, the better. This duality was
nothing new, of course. Whig historians of the 1830s and 40s had always
written of the eighteenth century in such terms. S. R. Gardiner similarly
traced the social strains which produced the Civil War to the rise of 'the
people', that is, 'the middle classes'. This was inherited in the work of
Tawney and Hill, for whom the 'rise of the gentry' was essentially the same
phenomenon. 'The peerage nearly vanished from sight and the gentry
appeared increasingly bourgeois', objected a revisionist critic.[19]

Sometimes, indeed, historians tried to disguise the argument in new
clothes. Lawrence Stone, in *The Causes of the English Revolution 1529–1642*, as
he elsewhere explained, had retained his belief in 'the rising gentry and/or
the bourgeoisie' as 'a central feature of the English situation', but sought
rather to escape from the too familiar economic controversy over the
gentry's upward or downward mobility. He tried to salvage a view of the
origin of the Civil War in social change by recasting the debate into one
about 'status inconsistency' *within* the gentry as a result of high social

[17] Stone, *The Causes of the English Revolution*, p. 72; cf. pp. 56–7, 68, 109.
[18] It would not be possible without personal discourtesy to dwell on the extent to which a
character-twisting hatred of orthodox religion was at the heart of the critique devised by
some of the historians discussed here, and by other writers of their generation such as
W. H. Auden, Aldous Huxley and Cyril Connolly. But however closely this vision related
to life at English public schools in the 1920s and 30s, its value as an historical analysis has
proved to be rather less.
[19] Paul Christianson, 'The Causes of the English Revolution: A Reappraisal', *JBS* 15 no. 2
(1976), pp. 44–5.

mobility among their ranks. The 'crisis of the aristocracy' produced, in effect, a rise of some of the gentry, and the outcome of this was friction over status. Competition to become a JP or MP increased, and a 'situation was thus created in which a gentleman who won a Parliamentary seat had a rapidly growing incentive to please yeomen voters or other gentlemen, and a rapidly weakening incentive to please Church or Crown. Mr Stone could have profitably used some of Professor Plumb's work in support of this point', noted Conrad Russell perceptively.[20]

To have done so, however, might have raised doubts whether such a process could have been active in *both* periods, or whether, like the 'rise of the middle class', the idea was so vacuous as to serve the polemical purposes of any historian for any period. Russell validly objected that Stone had failed to demonstrate how his general law of status insecurity determined the political behaviour of particular gentlemen.[21] And if the theory was not received by the early-Stuart revisionists, any such projection of it as Professor Russell envisaged was made problematic by Professor Holmes's discussions of the forces making for openness and flexibility in English society in the half century following 1680.[22] In the field of social history especially, the century 1660–1760 had always been a dark age: it was therefore particularly vulnerable to the desire of political historians to devise 'social cause' explanations which located some crucial but untested and unquantified development within it. Only slowly is this changing: but here again the emphasis of recent scholars is on the stability and persistence of social configurations in the period which a bourgeoisie was supposed to have transformed.

Historians of the Hanoverian era became more cautious of taking up the categories which prevailed in the nineteenth century, or which were already appropriate in France. François-René de Chateaubriand, in exile in London in the 1790s, found England delightfully backward in still adhering to hierarchical, not class, ideals. In the 1820s, as French ambassador to the Court of St James, he drew a contrast with his experience three decades earlier.

Separated from the continent by a long war, the English at the end of the last century preserved their national manners and character. There was still only one people, in whose name the sovereign power was wielded by an aristocratic

---

[20] Russell, review of Stone, *Causes*, in *EHR* 88 (1973), 858–9. In fairness, it should be added that the weaknesses of Plumb's version were not apparent at that date.

[21] Russell pointed to some cases in the 1620s which do fit Stone's model: Sir Robert Phelips, Sir John Savile, Sir Thomas Wentworth. My own scepticism about applying this methodological device in the early eighteenth century prompts me to doubt whether it could be systematically used for the early seventeenth either.

[22] Geoffrey Holmes, 'The Achievement of Stability: the Social Context of Politics from the 1680s to the Age of Walpole', in John Cannon (ed.), *The Whig Ascendancy* (London, 1981), pp. 1–22; Holmes, *Augustan England: Professions, State and Society, 1680–1730* (London, 1982).

government; only two great classes existed in friendship, bound by a common interest: patrons and clients. That jealous class, called the *bourgeoisie* in France, which is beginning to arise in England, did not then exist: nothing interposed between the rich landowners and the men occupied with their trades ... The England of 1688 was, towards the end of the last century, at the apogee of its glory.[23]

Significantly, he did not suppose 1688 to have been a revolution in the social-structural sense; and the 1640s did not figure at all. This perception of a hierarchical order, which was an orthodoxy in England into the early nineteenth century, suddenly seemed far more persuasive once the idea had been abandoned that eighteenth-century England was a peculiarly modern society by European standards, and that it was so not least as a result of the bourgeois revolution of the 1640s.

Together with this deletion of class terminology went a revaluation of an associated nexus of ideas. Class and industry had been inseparable concepts within English historiography. Equally impregnable had been the idea that there was a link between religious Nonconformity and technical, industrial innovation – not so much because of what Dissenters believed in (their religion) as because of what they disbelieved in (Anglican 'social control'). Dissenters, it was once thought, were disproportionately represented in the ranks of entrepreneurs (indeed, it was sometimes believed that *most* entrepreneurs were Dissenters), so that an innovative, progressive spirit was to be traced to the Dissenting nexus, whether labelled Puritanism in the seventeenth century or Nonconformity in the eighteenth.[24] It is this body of assumptions which Dr Rubinstein's important research has now exploded: a properly quantified study of those who profited most from economic growth shows that their religious affiliations mirrored the population as a whole: that is, most were Anglicans.[25]

The putative rise of the 'middle class',[26] or even of the gentry, could only

---

23  François-René, Vicomte de Chateaubriand, *Mémoires d'Outre-Tombe* (ed. Maurice Levaillant, 4 vols., Paris, 1949), vol. I, pp. 524–5. Such phenomena as 'class' are matters of *perception*. Chateaubriand's remark is not evidence for the initial absence and later arrival of a bourgeoisie in an objective sense: in no such sense could it have any existence. What he perceived (and perceived correctly, as I argue elsewhere) was the intellectual hegemony of an alternative way of visualising and describing society, and a later challenge to it.

24  For the same thing, characterised as the 'capitalist/Protestant ethic', see Lawrence Stone, *The Crisis of the Aristocracy 1558–1641* (Oxford, 1965), pp. 8–9 and *passim*. It was inherently anti-aristocratic and ultimately anti-Anglican, believed such historians.

25  W. D. Rubinstein, *Men of Property: The Very Wealthy in Britain since the Industrial Revolution* (London, 1981) and Dr Rubinstein's other work there reported.

26  That ancient *canard*, the 'rise of the middle class', has been sighted in so many periods that one might have expected it to come in for more critical scrutiny. Historians anxious to place it at any time before 1832 might equally have learned caution from J. H. Hexter's classic paper of 1948, 'The Myth of the Middle Class in Tudor England', reprinted with additions in *Reappraisals in History* (London, 1961), pp. 71–116. Peter Laslett, writing a

have been at the expense of the peerage. The prerequisite of a bankrupt, decaying traditional elite had seemingly been established by Lawrence Stone's assiduous and justly famous study.[27] The abolition of the House of Lords in 1649, he wrote, 'was not a mere by-product of the dynamics of war; it was the culmination of a crisis of confidence which had been maturing for well over half a century'. The inflation of honours, the breakdown of deference and respect, the decline in wealth and in military or political power, the rise of a rational, literate and bureaucratic ethic to replace the feudal nexus, the emerging gulf between Court and Country – all these things were argued to have eroded the position of the peerage and brought about a 'general weakening of the hierarchical framework of upper-class society in the early seventeenth century'. 'If it came to the crunch, the English nobles would be ground to pieces between the millstones of King and Commons.'[28] The crunch came in the 1640s, according to the Old Guard. The adversary system divided English society into these two 'millstones', according to Old Hat assumptions.

It seems fair to say that rather few historians of Hanoverian England felt eager to grapple with Stone's weighty and statistically buttressed text. Had they done so, they might have found curiously familiar many of the laments about the dilution and decline of the peerage which he recorded from the early-Stuart age: they formed, in fact, a staple of moralists throughout the eighteenth century and into the early nineteenth.[29] They might also have found curiously unsatisfactory Professor Stone's determination (like Harrington) to end his story neatly with a precise date and a definitive destruction of the English peerage in the Civil War. The House of Lords was, after all, restored in 1660: and though nothing was ever quite the same again, this is a truism which applies (usually irrelevantly) to all human affairs. Aristocratic hegemony thereafter took a *different* (but no less effective) form. To many Hanoverian historians, especially those unaware of the line which academic fashion required them to take, the eighteenth century had always seemed a *quintessentially* aristocratic age. What, after all, was the fuss about in 1828–32 if it was not about breaking the

Foreword to that volume, suggested (p. xii) that 'More than any other historian of the present day [Hexter] must be held responsible for the breaking of a circle of explanation, one which had prevailed for three or four generations and which had come to constrict imagination and intellect alike. This was the convention which demanded that all historical change must be referred to the rise and fall of social classes, and most of English history to the rise of the middle classes, especially what happened in Tudor and Stuart times.' Such a convention was not so easily abolished, however.

[27] Lawrence Stone, *The Crisis of the Aristocracy 1558–1641*.

[28] *Ibid.*, pp. 749, 752.

[29] Perhaps even beyond: I do not pretend to settle this question. It might be suggested, however, that the real cultural and financial bankruptcy of the traditional landed elite came in the 1920s and 30s – when the Old Guard historians were young, and were struck by it.

aristocracy's grip on Church and Commons? And what did the agrarian history of the nineteenth century demonstrate other than the substantial survival of the great estates in *c.* 1830–80, an Indian summer in *c.* 1880–1914, and 'eclipse' only in the years after 1914?[30]

To some historians these things had always seemed so obvious that they hardly needed to be said. To the Old Guard and to the Class of '68, such matters were uncongenial: the rising entrepreneur or the Wilkesite radical offered themes more in tune with the spirit of the age as they defined it. Even the *History of Parliament* concerned itself directly with the House of Commons: peers played only supporting roles in its volumes. So many sorts of historian had strong reasons for not dealing with the peerage that in the mid 1980s it suddenly occurred to the profession that a major theme had been almost unanimously neglected.[31] Yet the power and survival of the Hanoverian peerage could rather easily be traced in ways which left little room for any notion of their prior collapse. 'The identification of a "bourgeois revolution" in the mid-seventeenth century has, in my view, caused Marxists to postulate a vast chronological misplacement, anticipating developments by two hundred years or so, and ignoring the nature of the eighteenth-century political regime', argued Professor Cannon.[32]

Professor Stone himself returned to the same theme in an attempt to quantify the survival of the elite over time.[33] When quantified, it is on the contrary the traditional landed elite's strength and independence of transfusions of new money which is apparent. Moreover, the patterns of mobility and marriage do not bear out the idea of a self-aware, united bourgeoisie: between the lawyer or banker and the manufacturer or

---

[30] F. M. L. Thompson's masterly *English Landed Society in the Nineteenth Century* (London, 1963) would alone have refuted the thesis of Lawrence Stone's *Crisis of the Aristocracy* about the eclipse of the peerage in the 1640s; but the two books were addressed to different groups of scholars, and were evidently never placed side by side. The same isolation extended to G. E. Mingay's *English Landed Society in the Eighteenth Century* (London, 1963) and *The Gentry: The Rise and Fall of a Ruling Class* (London, 1976).

[31] Since the pioneering but pedestrian books of A. S. Turberville, *The House of Lords in the Reign of William III* (Oxford, 1913); *The House of Lords in the Eighteenth Century* (Oxford, 1927); *The House of Lords in the Age of Reform, 1784–1837* (London, 1958).

[32] Marxists 'are inexorably attracted to the proposition that the English Civil War must have been of decisive significance, since it is the grandest upheaval in sight, despite much evidence that it decided very little': John Cannon, *Aristocratic Century: The Peerage of Eighteenth-Century England* (Cambridge, 1984) (attacking Hill, 'A Bourgeois Revolution?', in Pocock (ed.), *Three British Revolutions*) and Cannon, 'The Isthmus Repaired: the Resurgence of the English Aristocracy, 1660–1760', *Proceedings of the British Academy* 68 (1982), 431–53; Clark, *English Society 1688–1832*; Michael W. McCahill, *Order and Equipoise: The Peerage and the House of Lords 1783–1806* (London, 1978); M. L. Bush, *The English Aristocracy: A Comparative Synthesis* (Manchester, 1984).

[33] Lawrence Stone and Jeanne C. Fawtier Stone, *An Open Elite? England 1540–1880* (Oxford, 1984); cf. W. D. Rubinstein, *Men of Property: The Very Wealthy in Britain since the Industrial Revolution* (London, 1981).

tradesman was a great gulf fixed. Cultural assimilation inhibited or prevented the emergence of the theory of a distinct, self-aware urban middle class until the 1830s.

These investigations of the degree of mobility of new money into land had wide implications. The untested but mutually reinforcing ideas of a bourgeoisie, of the triumph of Locke, of the prevalence of capitalist values, of the sweeping aside of divine right and of Toryism had fused together in an Old Guard interpretation the more strictly parliamentary components of which could be reconciled with the views of Old Hat historians also. It was this combined model which failed to survive the recent revisionist demonstration of the persistence of a Tory party after 1714, and refutation of the idea of a democratic pressure from below, established by pollbook research. The narrative reconstruction of a workable account of political realities showed the futility of condemning them by appeal to any text in the traditional canon of political thought, let alone Locke or Harrington, as if those texts provided convenient abridgements or epitomes of a tediously complex and inherently confused tactical reality. Revisionist initiatives in the diverse realms of high politics, psephology, social structure, ideology and economic history were therefore essentially the same phenomenon: they can best be understood together.[34]

If 'underlying social cause' explanations had broken down, they had not *ipso facto* been swept aside. The continuing circulation of the textbooks of the Old Guard still gave their ideas a spurious currency into the 1980s. Yet the flaws in those theories were now evident, and revisionists in both areas were henceforth free to focus on politics to widen those fissures still further. As Professor Elton had observed:

> If we are to get further, we need at this present no essays on the causes of the civil war, but studies of the political behaviour of all sorts of men in all sorts of institutions, unaffected by the historian's foreknowledge of the later event. In that way we may ultimately perhaps arrive at an explanation of the mid-seventeenth-century breakdown, but it will be less well tailored, less readily reduced to a list of preconditions, precipitants and triggers, less satisfactory to theorists of revolution. On the other hand, it might be real.[35]

Anthony Fletcher, for example, was able to explain the polarisation of Lords and Commons in the first two years of the Long Parliament, and the outbreak of war, without recourse to long-term causes, underlying social stresses, the rise of the gentry or the bourgeoisie, or a grab for power by the Commons: 'Now it is plain there was no high road to civil war', he wrote in 1981: 'There was not bound to be a struggle between King and Parliament

---

[34] Clark, *English Society 1688–1832*, chapters 1–3, and the works there discussed, especially those of Cruickshanks, Dunn, Kenyon, Laslett, Lindert, McCloskey, Moore, Perkin, Phillips, Schochet, Straka and Williamson.

[35] *HJ* 16 (1973), 208.

in order that the balanced constitution of the eighteenth century could be its outcome.'[36] (Scepticism about the latter might have reinforced this insight still further.)

Detailed studies of politics too often revealed the leadership of the elite, not spontaneous action from village communities: in one case, 'Where Christopher Hill detected class conflict, what we in fact find is the rhetoric of gentry factionalism and the skilful manoeuvring of an intensely ambitious county politician ... it was always the gentry who took the lead.'[37] To Hill, the fact that the Civil War was unintended still meant that it must have been the result of the impersonal forces of social change.[38] But do such forces have any existence outside the historian's study? It seemed, then, that to ask the question, 'why was there a revolution in the 1640s?' was first to reify the notion, then to beg the question: we had been drawn to explain not so much *what happened*, as *the reification itself*. The idea of the Civil War as a revolution was breaking down.

It may be that the most appropriate explanation of a reification is an abstract social force. But such arguments, convincing until challenged, seem suddenly vulnerable both to the micro-structural demonstrations, associated above all with Dr Peter Laslett, that none of the grand revolutions beloved of recent historiography[39] are to be observed in the quantifiable data of seventeenth-century society, and also to the Hanoverian revisionists' excision of categories like 'bourgeois' and 'class' from the armoury of authentic analytical terms. This research in quantified, structural social history had indeed been ready to hand for an embarrassingly long period; at last the parliamentary revisionists realised its relevance, and sought to integrate it into their vision of the wider consequences of their tactical political reinterpretations.[40]

Recent scholarship has concerned itself with method as well as substance. Both in political and in social history, the origin of historians' categories deserves more scrutiny than it has normally received. It was not

---

[36] Fletcher, *Outbreak of the English Civil War*, esp. pp. 407–8.

[37] A. J. Fletcher, 'Parliament and People in Seventeenth-Century England', *P&P* 98 (1983), 153–4.

[38] C. Hill, 'A Rejoinder', *ibid.*

[39] The Bourgeois Revolution, the Puritan Revolution, the Scientific Revolution, the Educational Revolution, the Protestant Revolution, the Revolution in Government, the Revolution of the Saints, the Financial Revolution.

[40] Cf. especially Peter Laslett's demolition of Christopher Hill in *The World we Have Lost further Explored* (London, 1983), chapter 8, 'Social Change and Revolution in the Traditional World': 'It does not follow that the more dramatic the crash and important its consequences the more profound its causes must be and the more likely to be the climax of some perennial "process".' 'It has been complained that this suggestion reduces everything to the status of an improbable misfortune, but there is no point in denying the contingency even of epoch-making historical occurrences' (pp. 199, 334). The mere political historian seizes on such remarks with delight.

an Englishman but a Frenchman, François Guizot, whose *Histoire de la Révolution d'Angleterre* (Paris, 1826–7) was the first to apply the term 'revolution' to the Civil War in place of the traditional 'rebellion'.[41] Guizot had been struck by an analogy between England in the 1640s and the events of 1789 in France, and developed the comparison at length: 'both are victories in the same war', he believed.

Created by the same causes, the fall of the feudal aristocracy, the church, and kingly power, they both laboured to obtain the same result, the dominion of the public in public affairs. They struggled for liberty against absolute power, for equality against privilege, for progressive and general interests against stationary and individual interests. [The revolution of the 1640s] though disappointed in its premature hopes ... caused English society to take a wide step from the monstrous inequality of the feudal system. In a word, the analogy of the two revolutions is such, that the first would never have been understood had not the second taken place.[42]

Equally, the term 'Industrial Revolution' was not an English but a French invention, again of about the same time, and again inspired by an analogy with the upheaval of 1789. The idea of a *'révolution industrielle'* gained currency in France only in the 1820s. In 1837, the economist Jérôme Blanqui claimed in his *Histoire de l'Économie Politique en Europe*: 'While the French Revolution was making its great social experiments over a volcano, England was beginning hers on the solid ground of the industries ... hardly was the industrial revolution born from the brain of those two men of genius, Watt and Arkwright, when it took possession of England.'[43] Yet such a concept, even when formulated, was not self-evidently valid in

---

41 Others since have followed him, of course. Cf.: 'the English Revolution of 1640–60 was a great social movement like the French Revolution of 1789. An old order that was essentially feudal was destroyed by violence, a new and capitalist social order created in its place. The Civil War was a class war, in which the despotism of Charles I was defended by the reactionary forces of the established Church and feudal landlords. Parliament beat the King because it could appeal to the enthusiastic support of the trading and industrial classes in town and countryside', etc., etc.: Christopher Hill, *The English Revolution 1640* (London, 1940), p. 9. It is the simplistic nature of such writing which now seems even more astonishing than the tenuousness of its claims to accuracy.

42 François Guizot, *History of the English Revolution* (2 vols., Oxford, 1838), vol. 1, pp. x, xx–xxi. English historians had not yet understood their revolution, argued Guizot; only modern Frenchmen, seeing the events of the 1640s in the light of 1789, grasped their full significance. In due course, 1917 was to perform the same function for the Old Guard historians discussed here. The effect of the Russian Revolution was, of course, even stronger on twentieth-century French interpretations of 1789: see François Furet, *Interpreting the French Revolution* (Cambridge, 1981), pp. 81–131.

43 Jérôme Blanqui, *History of Political Economy in Europe* (2 vols., Paris, 1837; trans. E. J. Leonard, London, 1880), pp. 430–1. Yet Blanqui gave almost no attention to the specific effects of manufacturing industry or its associated technologies. His vision was both more theoretical, and more melodramatic: 'Markets have become battle-fields ... it is from that vast encyclopaedia, which dates from 1789 and ends in 1830, that political economy has drawn its most valuable materials and the most solid bases of its doctrines' (pp. 433, 441).

English eyes: not until the 1880s and after was the phrase naturalised in England.[44]

Despite its dubious ancestry, the word 'revolution' by now has a Pavlovian effect on some historians: applied to any event, it leads at once to eager expectations of radical structural change, profound discontinuity, a sweeping away of the old order. We may indeed wonder whether England has ever experienced revolution in the extensive terms of the social scientists' definitions[45] in the 1640s, 1688 or 1714, or even under the later impact of 'Industry'. How much was destroyed in the Civil War? Apart from the large extent to which royalist peers and gentry retained their estates, local studies suggest the widespread and deeply rooted survival of Anglican religious loyalties and practices, even reinvigorated by the experience of persecution. 'The strength of the Anglican reaction of 1660 lay not exclusively, or even principally, in the response of a gentry who craved the return of a hierarchical Church which would shore up a hierarchical government and society, but in the popularity of traditional religious forms at all levels of society', suggested one historian.[46] As a materialist–reductionist world view weakened its hold, historians became increasingly unwilling to define 'social structure' in economic terms alone: ideology and, especially, religion began to play a new role in historical explanations.

The most heavily reified of all historical categories was that which Hanoverian revisionists had to confront: the concept of an Industrial Revolution (with invariable capitals). Yet Dr Laslett's methods, carried to their logical conclusion, entail a serious questioning of this revolution also and the replacement of the romantic notion of a sudden and dramatic metamorphosis by a serious scholarly picture of a range of complex and lengthy transitions. Such a reinterpretation, it might be suggested, adds the Industrial Revolution to the list of spurious revolutions which are deleted from our accounts of social change by the act of quantifying. The revisionist in the field of parliamentary history here allies also with the

---

[44] Anna Bezanson, 'The Early Use of the Term Industrial Revolution', *Quarterly Journal of Economics* 36 (1922), 343–9; Sir George Clark, *The Idea of the Industrial Revolution* (Glasgow, 1953). Although he was effectively sceptical about the status of this category, Sir George displayed no premonition of the immense weight about to be placed on it by the Old Guard in England during the next three decades.

[45] Discussed in Stone, *Causes of the English Revolution*, pp. 3–25. There are countless studies by social scientists of the concept of 'revolution'; they have not shown a similar eagerness to recover the early-modern meanings of 'rebellion'.

[46] J. S. Morrill, 'The Church in England, 1642–9', in John Morrill (ed.), *Reactions to the English Civil War 1642–1649* (London, 1982), pp. 89–114, at 91; *idem*, 'The Attack on the Church of England in the Long Parliament, 1640–1642', in Derek Beales and Geoffrey Best (eds.), *History, Society and the Churches: Essays in Honour of Owen Chadwick* (Cambridge, 1985), pp. 105–24.

'new' economic history:[47] an Industrial Revolution which, when quantified, proves to have been neither very industrial nor very revolutionary
allows us to dispense with Whiggish (and Marxist) assumptions about an
industrial–technological Prometheus bursting the constraints of Plumb's
socially monolithic oligarchy in the latter part of the eighteenth century.
(To discover how the ancien regime in England broke down, in 1828–32 as
in 1640–2, we must return to the study of politics.)

This is, perhaps, to anticipate the developing consensus of scholarship.
It is still sometimes difficult to obtain a fair hearing for the thesis that
English society before 1832 did not experience an industrial revolution, let
alone an Industrial Revolution. Even today, traditional economic historians can react with indignation to the suggestion that those two words
have been misused, indeed elevated to the status of a polemical category, at
the same time as they accept the unchallengeably quantifiable aspects of
the revisionist argument: 'the gradual evolutionary character of British
industrialisation', the general absence of technological transformations
before c.1850, the rarity of factory organisation until the late nineteenth
century, and so on.[48] Yet all these insights emphasise to us that the
Industrial Revolution was an historical category, not an event. We may
doubt whether it was even a *process*, if by that we are to understand a single,
unified and thematically coherent development.

The first reaction of most scholars is to seek to fit the results of new
research into the old conceptual framework. Only when the wider significance of their indignation is understood will recent conceptual and
empirical advances be more welcome, yet it seems safe to say that recent
scholarship is tending to a similar conclusion: it is hardly surprising that
historians had such difficulty in agreeing on the causes of the Industrial
Revolution if the Industrial Revolution never took place. English society
was not *revolutionised*: and it was not revolutionised *by industry*. The
statistical aspects of the question are by now established with sufficient
accuracy: we now know how much more cotton was spun, how much
more coal was mined, how many canals were dug. None of this establishes
the validity of the polemical category or the reality of a sudden and
profound discontinuity in social structures. If a profound discontinuity is to
be diagnosed, it is better located in 1828–32, and (like the events of 1776 in
America or 1798 in Ireland) more profitably analysed under the category
'rebellion'. In all of these respects, a decade of work in economic history

---

[47] The classic summary of recent work in this idiom is Roderick Floud and Donald
McCloskey (eds.), *The Economic History of Britain Since 1700, I. 1700–1860* (Cambridge, 1981).
For arguments on method, see Michael Fores, 'The Myth of a British Industrial
Revolution', *History* 66 (1981), 181–98.
[48] Cf. A. E. Musson, 'The British Industrial Revolution', *History* 67 (1982), 252–8.

had the most profound consequences for the Old Hat and Old Guard models – consequences which other historians were slow to grasp.

## THE TWO PHASES OF THE ENGLISH PAST

Theorists of social change, then, had often lazily employed a two-phase model of past time: the world we have lost, followed by the world we now have. Even those revisionist scholars whose researches rescued the world we have lost from the parodies of past generations too often highlighted their results by accepting, as a contrast, the capitalist–individualist or the (in this respect not dissimilar) Marxist model of the world we now have. The first stage in a process of rewriting history therefore carried a new vision from the early Stuarts to *c.* 1688 or 1714 (as in the work of Dr Laslett and Professor Kenyon). The next stage carried a similar process forward to *c.* 1828–32. Once arrived at that point, Hanoverian revisionism was able to join hands with its natural allies in the field of Victorian history – as represented, for example, by Professor D. C. Moore. The point was not merely the structure of society before 1832 as an ancien regime but, granted that conceptualisation, its relevance in many respects for decades thereafter.[49]

What, after all, was capitalist man? Had Jeremy Bentham and James Mill correctly described the atomised individual, the felicific calculator who bought and sold in the Victorian labour market? Or was that model a gross misdescription of their assumptions? It seems fair to say that many academic theorists had understood industrial society through the categories of economic analysis – a process which projected onto the past the very things which were now called in doubt. The modern bourgeois intelligentsia too often betrayed a monumental ignorance of what the daily life of the working man had actually been like.[50] Seen less dogmatically, even the culture of the factory (that paradigmatically individualised world) can best be explained with the concepts of status, deference, paternalism, community and religious affiliation now so familiar to historians of the world before 1832.[51]

The emphasis of the revisionists, here as elsewhere, was on the remarkable degree of continuity which was apparent to historians not bent on

---

49 A similar perspective is re-emphasised for Europe, with some sidelights on England, in Arno J. Mayer, *The Persistence of the Old Regime* (London, 1981). Whether Professor Mayer has overstated a good case is another question.

50 Cf. Harold Perkin, ' 'The Condescension of Posterity': Middle-Class Intellectuals and the History of the Working Class', in *The Structured Crowd* (Brighton, 1980).

51 Patrick Joyce, *Work, Society and Politics: The Culture of the Factory in Later Victorian England* (Brighton, 1980); J. M. Golby and A. W. Purdue, *The Civilisation of the Crowd: Popular Culture in England 1750–1900* (London, 1984); Robert Glen, *Urban Workers in the Early Industrial Revolution* (London, 1984).

celebrating discontinuity. The problem with uncovering long-term 'preconditions' of revolution in Lawrence Stone's formulation is exactly their long persistence without generating revolution of any sort; the problem with J. H. Plumb's preconditions of oligarchic *stability* in the early eighteenth century is similarly that of explaining away the transformations which nearly did occur (1715, 1745) and of redefining profound recastings of politics (1688, 1714) as not revolutions at all, but counterrevolutions averted. Semantic shifts are easier to bring about than scholarly reinterpretations; but it was the latter which the revisionists worked for.

In general, suggested one socialist historian, Britain had avoided violent revolutions only by rephrasing them as 'peaceful' or 'silent' revolutions: Old Hat strategies had been effective. British traditionalism was consequently superficial, consisting of, first, a 'preference for maintaining the *form* of old institutions with a profoundly changed content' and, second, the willingness 'never to resist irresistible changes, but to absorb them as quickly and quietly as possible'. Revolutions cannot be resisted; they can, at most, be delayed or disguised, suggested Professor Hobsbawm. Whigs thus had a star role to play in the Marxist scenario. In the crisis of the years 1830–2, 'something like a revolutionary situation might actually have developed'; it was, of course, defused, and socio-economic change forged ahead.[52] The world we have lost was inevitably and irreversibly lost, suggested such historians (even though they blamed the world we now have for its curious unwillingness to accept its socialist destiny).

In Lawrence Stone's account, revolution 'becomes possible when a condition of multiple dysfunction meets an intransigent elite'.[53] The 'underlying social cause' theory thus linked hands with the traditional Whig prescription for constitutional evolution in and after 1832: compromise, concession, retreat. Such a model could, of course, imply that after the 1640s there were no revolutions which *might* have happened, but which were prevented by a resolute or intransigent resistance. Stone's typology of preconditions, precipitants and triggers (implying that the triggers were insignificant, that inevitable events are easily triggered) was one which systematically understated the significance of revolutions which might have happened but never materialised, whether the Jacobite risings of 1715 and 1745, or, later, Sir Herbert Butterfield's suggestion about the crisis of 1779–80:

not only in Ireland but in England the situation must be described as quasi-revolutionary to a degree which the world has since forgotten ... It would even be perhaps not too far-fetched if we were to say that the real 'revolutionary moment' in

[52] E. J. Hobsbawm, *Industry and Empire* (Harmondsworth, 1969), pp. 18–19, 73.
[53] Stone, *The Causes of the English Revolution*, p. 10. Such a view naturally led to a 'winning of the initiative' perspective on a House of Commons (pp. 93ff) powered by a clearly-defined

this whole period of English history is the moment at which catastrophe loomed threatening, but was circumvented – was escaped by a fairly narrow margin. Our 'French Revolution' is in fact that of 1780 – the revolution that we escaped.[54]

These were options which political, not social, historians now sought to reopen by reverting to the category of 'rebellion'.

Which was the English Revolution – 1642 or 1688? Sometimes it seemed possible to blur the problem and have it both ways, e.g. 'In Britain the resistance to capitalist development had ceased to be effective by the end of the seventeenth century. The very aristocracy was, by continental standards, almost a form of "bourgeoisie", and two revolutions had taught the monarchy to be adaptable.'[55] But, if challenged to be more precise, the Old Guard unhesitatingly confined the label 'revolution' to the events of the 1640s. And, of course, to those economic developments which they dated in the 1780s.

The unchallenged use of the term 'revolution' to cover many very different phenomena was one reason why old prejudices died hard. Even in 1981, a 1930s Marxist could be found inveighing against Professor Elton because, 'failing to appreciate the underlying socio-economic issues', he had chosen to study political complexities.[56] Those who believed that this jargon of 'socio-economic' (meaning economic–reductionist) or 'underlying' (meaning the same thing) had been superseded were a little premature. Hill even suggested a new social schism explanation in terms of the frictions generated by 'the emerging new rich' – some yeomen, merchants and artisans who flourished while the 'mass of the poor were getting relatively and absolutely poorer'. It was 'the emerging new rich' who coerced the poor in the name of 'a new work ethic' (it was highly reminiscent of the eighteenth-century Old Guard), suspicious of 'clerical defenders of arbitrary taxation' who posed 'a threat to property' and, at parish level, 'encouraged junketings harmful to labour discipline', and so on.[57]

It seemed as if the seventeenth-century reductionist model was now to be reinforced by a transposition of the eighteenth-century model of E. P. Thompson *et al.* It was a little late at a time when that model itself was progressively threatened.[58] In *any* period, as we now see, we have been asked to

opposition, a development finding its culmination after 1688 (p. 147 – a passage which might have been written by J. H. Hexter or J. H. Plumb).

54 Herbert Butterfield, *George III, Lord North and the People 1779–80* (London, 1949), p. vi.

55 Hobsbawm, *Industry and Empire*: 'the grandees of Britain ... were a post-revolutionary elite, the heirs of the Roundheads' (pp. 16, 32).

56 Christopher Hill, 'Parliament and People in Seventeenth-Century England', *P&P* 92 (1981), 108.

57 *Ibid.*, pp. 118–24. For a critique, see Fletcher, 'Parliament and People', pp. 151–5, and Hill, 'A Rejoinder', pp. 155–8.

58 For challenges concerned with the political significance of criminality, see J. Langbein, '*Albion*'s Fatal Flaws', *P&P* 98 (1983), 96–120, and P. J. R. King, 'Decision-Makers and

believe that the rich are always getting richer, the poor always getting poorer, the middle class always rising, the aristocracy always about to disintegrate. The old scenario no longer convinces: it fails to identify and date the real transformations which *did* occur. Revisionist historians of the ancien regime in England, 1660–1832, being aware that 'class' emerged as a terminology only in the last decade or so of their period, and then only as a minority dialect, looked back with incredulity and amazement on the Old Guard in the early-Stuart period, labouring to explain the English Revolution in terms of class conflict, of rising or declining classes, or the aspirations of a bourgeoisie.

Such interpretations had something to commend them, but it seems probable that they will be progressively bypassed. Their problem is not only that they look increasingly implausible, but also that they look increasingly dated. Genres of scholarship do fall into desuetude for reasons not wholly indicative of their intellectual merits. Fifty years ago, classical diplomatic history occupied a large and distinguished place in history courses in many universities. It provided an excellent training in the accurate use of evidence; it dealt with momentous issues within a wide frame of reference, both geographical and chronological. Despite these claims to academic attention, the subject is now itself an historical phenomenon. For reasons of which we are only now becoming aware, the same fate may well be overtaking the characteristic idioms of some of the schools of thought discussed here: less denounced as false, more neglected as slightly quaint.

There was a legacy, however, in the pattern of rethinking that had been inspired. In terms of our categories, 'underlying social cause' explanations and Whig constitutional–teleological explanations had both assumed the same scenario for the 1640s: first revolution, then rebellion. First the government collapsed, subverted by social change, then fighting broke out. Revisionists explored a variety of explanations, but they all tended to their own scenario: first rebellion, then revolution (if revolution can be diagnosed at all). The political system had its problems, but it was still viable, and the desire in all quarters to make it work was great; but once the Scottish and Irish rebellions compelled a recourse to arms, conflict moved with its own logic, and descended into the frenzy and antinomian fanaticism of the late 1640s. It was, of course, a revolution largely contained by Cromwellian military power and the substantial dominance of the gentry, and a rebellion reversed in 1660.

In 1688 sufficient care was taken that a minimal measure of revolution followed the rebellion which overthrew James II. In the absence of

Decision-Making in the English Criminal Law, 1750–1800', *HJ* 27 (1984), 25–58; with ideology and social structure, Clark, *English Society 1688–1832, passim.*

quantifiable social-structural transformation, the debate over the nature of what happened in 1688 was pursued chiefly in the context of Jacobite and Nonjuror ideology, where it has failed to grasp the imaginations of more than the revisionist historians. Within a secular and materialist frame of reference, rebellion has long seemed a matter of only minor importance. The issues it raised were seldom explored in an English context. Yet exactly the same alternative between scenarios has (to simplify) emerged from the debate over the 'American Revolution', for here rebellion may indeed have been associated with revolution in a wide extent, and their sequence has been a question running through much profitable argument.[59] In England, the debate took a different form. Some revisionists sought to replace 'underlying' causes with overlaying (i.e. high-political) ones. Others sought to replace 'underlying' causes with, in effect, circumambient ones: the varied reactions of local communities to the grand issues of Whig or Marxist battles. It is to these two types of revisionism that we now turn.

[59] See the typology of rebellion developed by Dr Penry Williams, 'Rebellion and Revolution in Early Modern England', in M. R. D. Foot (ed.), *War and Society: Essays in Honour of John Western* (London, 1973), pp. 223–40, and Williams, *The Tudor Regime* (Oxford, 1979), chapter 10, 'Protest and Rebellion'.

# 4

# THE CASE OF THE PROVINCES

One of the most influential developments in the historiography of the last two decades has been the emergence of local history as a fully fledged academic *genre*, and its practitioners as a distinct school of thought. Dr Morrill explained the main themes of Provincialism:

The new tradition has been built upon the following arguments: (a) That the social, institutional and political arrangements in most counties by 1600 were so distinctive, inward-looking and semi-autonomous that they require to be treated separately. England at this period is more like a federated state than a unitary national state. (b) Effective control over the social, political and (to a lesser extent) religious institutions of each county lay with a fairly self-evident and largely self-sustaining group of gentry families, distinguished from the rest of the community by their wealth, by their interconnections of blood and marriage, by a distinctive educational background. The crown at any moment chose the actual governors from among the very restricted number of families making up these *county communities*. (c) The crown could only govern (in particular, could only raise money, enforce its social and economic policies, maintain law and order) through establishing an identity of interest with these county governors. This meant operating an elaborate system of quid-pro-quos, itself a combination of sticks and carrots. It has been argued by local historians that the early Stuarts failed to operate this system as skilfully as Elizabeth I had done. Most have preferred to see this as a lack of skill on the crown's part rather than the collapse of the system itself from wider forces. (d) National issues did not impinge as directly on provincial squires and others as historians have assumed. Rather, national issues took on different resonances in each local context and became intricately bound up with purely local issues and groupings. Local studies have thus tended to emphasise the uniqueness of each county's response to the crises of the mid-seventeenth century and have also found that much parliamentarianism grew out of an experience of centralist encroachment, and was deeply conservative in nature.[1]

Some qualifications were accepted: ecclesiastical history had yet to be properly integrated into local studies; we need examinations of urban areas, as well as the counties, and of social strata wider than the gentry; very little has been done after 1660, still less after 1688. Yet the main thesis

[1] J. S. Morrill, *Seventeenth-Century Britain, 1603–1714* (Folkestone, 1980), p. 125.

was still maintained: 'The art of politics in the seventeenth century largely consisted in harmonising the discrepant political expectations and aspirations of central government and provincial political nations.'[2]

'What made the provincial gentry so formidable and united them in their opposition to the Crown in 1640 was their *lack* of understanding of royal policies', Dr Morrill had written. The upper gentry knew 'a good deal that was distasteful and unpleasant about the Court', but knew and understood 'less about the real constitutional issues, leaving that to the experts'. The King's right to levy Ship Money was 'rarely questioned in the provinces': it was 'hated for its costliness and its disruptive effects on the social and political calm of the communities, but remarkably few references to Hampden's case can be found in the records'. 'What produced the collapse of co-operation in 1639–40 was not a growing awareness of the great constitutional issues raised by Hampden's lawyers, but a growing fear of the consequences of Ship Money for the economic and social stability of each county community.'[3]

## PROVINCIALISM: A DIFFERENT MODEL IN TWO CENTURIES?

It may well have surprised its authors that such a cautious and carefully researched picture should have become so controversial. To the far left, however, the initial Provincialist outlook may have appeared virtually Namierite in its scepticism about high-flown metropolitan constitutional and legal arguments as trimmings on a reality which was basically local, fiscal, administrative and unrevolutionary: 'Of course the elections of 1640 were about Ship Money, religious innovations and other royal policies. But this does not mean that the elections were about the opposition leaders' constitutional case against those policies. They were against the *effects* of royal policy on the local community.'[4]

If the Old Guard found such arguments objectionable, another problem was evident, from the opposite political standpoint, to the high-political revisionists. They did not deny that much valuable and illuminating

[2] *Ibid.*, pp. 30, 126; cf. the new Preface to the 2nd edn of John Morrill, *The Revolt of the Provinces* (London, 1980).

[3] Morrill, *Revolt of the Provinces*, pp. 21, 23–4, 26; cf. p. 28: 'The constitutional propriety of Ship Money was not the main reason for the opposition to it'; 'The gentry were less concerned with the theoretical implications of Charles's use of his prerogative than with the unacceptable consequences of his actions.' Professor Kenyon has suggested an additional administrative reason for the unpopularity of the new tax. Each county was obliged to produce a centrally determined sum, by whatever means. The old system of subsidies had endeavoured to collect a percentage: county totals were allowed to fall short of estimates.

[4] Morrill, *Revolt of the Provinces*, p. 30. It might not be fanciful to detect in these arguments one form of reaction against the Oxford 'constitutional history' of Lindsay Keir, Costin and Watson *et al.*, though a very different form from that being worked out by high-political historians.

rcscarch resulted from an attention to the local dimension. But the localist explanatory framework did not, in the later period, offer a viable account of its unique political characteristics. Although the forms of local government – JPs, Quarter Sessions, Assizes, Lieutenancies, militias – which had given structure to the early-Stuarts' accounts were clearly present in the eighteenth century, the political consequences of these things were rather different.

An explicitly Namierite study of the personnel of the Long Parliament, published in 1954 by two of Sir Lewis Namier's former colleagues, clearly uncovered the importance of local concerns and local networks of power and influence for those MPs: the phenomena of provincial introversion and cohesion were important enough to impress themselves upon the parliamentary historian.[5] Yet in the succeeding century no such lessons were drawn by members of the same school of historians. As political consciousness, as a tactical unit, it seems that the 'county community' almost nowhere survived into the Hanoverian era: careful and detailed studies of every county constituency between 1715 and 1790 failed to suggest such a concept to the History of Parliament team. Sir Lewis Namier, who above all might have been expected to seize on the notion of a 'county community', notably failed to do so. What there was of county coherence in the Hanoverian era had a different source: Cumberland derived its sense of being a place apart in the reign of George III from the tyrannical grip of that arch-boroughmonger Sir James Lowther, 5th Bt, on its parliamentary representation.[6]

Provincial studies in the seventeenth century and (in so far as there were any) the eighteenth had been conducted in substantial isolation from each other. The year 1660 was initially as impenetrable a barrier for early-Stuart Provincial scholars as for other historians, and this barrier for long prevented Provincialism from integrating its case with that of eighteenth-century revisionists. Consequently, the nature and timing of the profound transitions which seem to have robbed the early-Stuart 'county community' of its political weight had usually escaped investigation.[7] One pioneering study of Glamorgan pointed, importantly, to the social and cultural impact of a demographic crisis among the landed elite in the years *c.* 1720–60 as a cause of a deep divide between the Welsh-oriented, often Welsh-speaking patriarchs of the past and a new generation, a united elite of English-educated, Westminster-oriented patricians evident from the

---

[5] D. Brunton and D. H. Pennington, *Members of the Long Parliament* (London, 1954).
[6] See B. Bonsall, *Sir James Lowther and Cumberland and Westmorland Elections 1754–75* (Manchester, 1960).
[7] This is not among the questions dealt with, for example, in G. C. F. Forster, 'Government in Provincial England under the Later Stuarts', *TRHS* 33 (1983), 29–48.

accession of George III.[8] Was this the case elsewhere in Wales? Was it true of some or all English counties? We need more research on these questions, which recent studies of mobility into the peerage have not really addressed. Nevertheless, the priority of social, cultural, political and religious considerations in a study like that of Dr Jenkins suggests a strategy for countering an older approach in which 'local' too often meant 'economic–reductionist'.

This strategy has not yet been systematically pursued, however. The most famous and influential early-Hanoverian study in an idiom recognisably similar to that of the early-Stuart Provincial historians was not framed as a critique of the Old Guard. Its author was, indeed, none other than E. P. Thompson,[9] and it took the form of a painstaking study of crime and putative political repression in the forests of Windsor and east Hampshire during the reign of George I. The skill and originality of this research earned it some fame in the circles of eighteenth-century scholars, but it also incurred considerable unfriendly criticism. Professor Cannon, in a controversial review, appeared, as Mr Thompson thought, to imply 'that I am a shoddy historical craftsman throughout ... capable of fabricating and falsifying evidence, changing the grounds of my argument to suit my whim, and subordinating the evidence to the "interests of progressive history"'.[10] If these remarkable hostilities have cooled somewhat,[11] it might be possible to place Mr Thompson's work more dispassionately in the context of the work of the early-Stuart Provincial scholars.

Equally with the Provincials, Mr Thompson had seen his study as a critique of the Old Hat school:

As the last imperial illusions of the twentieth century fade, so preoccupation with the history and culture of a small island off the coast of Europe becomes open to the charge of narcissism. The culture of constitutionalism which flowered here, under favoured conditions, is an episode too exceptional to carry any universal significance. If we judge it in terms of its own self-sufficient values we are imprisoned within its own parochialism.

---

8  Philip Jenkins, *The Making of a Ruling Class: The Glamorgan Gentry 1640–1790* (Cambridge, 1983). Professor Jenkins' idea that Glamorgan can stand as a microcosm of England (p. xix) is perhaps a little optimistic.

9  E. P. Thompson, *Whigs and Hunters: The Origin of the Black Act* (London, 1975).

10  Quoted from the Postscript to the Peregrine edition, dated February 1977, in which Mr Thompson replied to his critics.

11  The heat generated in these critical exchanges seems in retrospect quite astonishing, and comparable only with the early-Stuart 'gentry controversy'. I must confess that one of those moved to excessive wrath was a youthful and intemperate research student, myself. I did indeed inhabit one of the 'comfortable and well-endowed places' of which Mr Thompson disapproved: I now find it mildly ironic that *both* of us are alumni of that bastion of early-eighteenth-century establishment Whiggery, Corpus Christi College, Cambridge. It is quite true that that profoundly conservative society has 'contributed almost nothing to the history of "ordinary people"', as Mr Thompson points out.

Instead, he invited readers to see British history 'within the perspective of the expansion of European capitalism', which was not at all what the early-Stuart Provincials had in mind (indeed quite the opposite).[12]

Equally with the History of Parliament team, Mr Thompson had not detected a 'county community' in Berkshire or Hampshire. His study was meant to demonstrate a rather contrary conclusion: that the local implementation of the criminal law was intended to, and did in fact, defend the material self-interest of the ruling class, the Whig oligarchy. Patricians were increasingly restrictive in preserving their deer and their timber (both lucrative 'crops' as well as props in the theatre of gentry hegemony) against proletarian attempts to retain both within a diverse subsistence economy, defended by customary rights. The operation of the criminal law to this end, far from showing gentry in a paternalist relationship with their locality, defending it against the intrusions of the centre, showed a keen co-operation of provincial and metropolitan patricians (who were often indeed the same people) in the suppression of a local proletarian culture which challenged patrician profit and pleasure.

Instead of a gentry community, Mr Thompson perceived a ruling class. His account of the working of the law was supposed to reveal, secondly, the priority of self-interest in the politics of that class. The involvement of Jacobites in the disorders which led to the Waltham Black Act was consequently minimised, and this denial of Jacobitism was to be a keynote in the Old Guard's resistance to early-Hanoverian revisionism.[13] The Black Act was, instead, the work of men

for whom property and the privileged status of the propertied were assuming, every year, a greater weight in the scales of justice, until justice itself was seen as no more than the outworks and defences of property and of its attendant status ... there is a

---

[12] *Whigs and Hunters*, pp. 258–9. The section on 'The Exercise of Law', pp. 245–69, contains a partial retraction. One must 'resist any slide into structural reductionism': the law *did* have a certain autonomy and value, independent of class purposes. This was due to 'the immense capital of human struggle over the previous two centuries against royal absolutism'; 'The work of sixteenth- and seventeenth-century jurists, supported by the practical struggles of such men as Hampden and Lilburne, was passed down as a legacy to the eighteenth century ...' (pp. 264, 269) – which brings us back to Notestein and Trevelyan, the Old Hat model of insular constitutionalism which the author had just denounced. Hence, however, Mr Thompson's insistence that Jacobitism *cannot* have commanded popular support in the early eighteenth century: the seventeenth-century 'legacy' was a legal–constitutional–libertarian one, he believed.

[13] 'No single Black was proved in the courts to have Jacobite associations. (But did the Jacobites ever organize seriously among common people?)'; instead we see 'the symptoms of something close to class warfare': *Whigs and Hunters*, pp. 166, 191. It now seems clear that Jacobitism played a much larger part in these events than Mr Thompson was aware of: cf. Eveline Cruickshanks and Howard Erskine-Hill, 'The Waltham Black Act and Jacobitism', *JBS* 24 no. 3 (1985), 358–65. Mr Thompson was caught in a dilemma: wishing to argue that there was widespread popular disaffection to an odious Hanoverian Whig regime, but unwilling to concede that the common man could entertain a positive allegiance to anything as 'nostalgic and anachronistic' (p. 258) as Jacobitism.

sense in which this elevation of property above all other values was a Whig state of mind ... This is a recognised phase of commercial capitalism when predators fight for the spoils of power and have not yet agreed to submit to rational or bureaucratic rules and forms.[14]

Mr Thompson's exceedingly reductionist analysis, despite its cosmetic qualifications, thus went considerably further than an earlier Provincial study in an Old Guard idiom. E. J. Hobsbawm's and George Rudé's account of widespread unrest and violence in southern and eastern counties in the early nineteenth century was intended to record the consequences of 'the full triumph of rural capitalism', but it had also uncovered much evidence, if not of the solidarity of any 'county community', at least of the solidarity of the hierarchical social order: the 'rising' of 1830 in 'some counties', they admitted, had 'something of the air of a general manifesto of county against town, of past against future, carried by the labourers but signed also by farmers and even gentry. The most extraordinary aspect of this solidarity between the labourers and their employers and rulers was the surprising support these gave to the Luddism of the poor'.[15]

It was Mr E. P. Thompson's attempt to advance a much more extreme case in ante-dating the triumph of the cash nexus by almost a century which made his analysis so controversial in and after 1975, and which made it particularly regrettable that no native school of Hanoverian Provincial historians was able to offer resistance. Moreover, his analysis was eagerly seized on and developed in other areas. His theory of the class function of law was more fully expounded by an acolyte,[16] and taken up and endorsed by other historians.[17] It dovetailed neatly with assumptions, derived from political historians such as Plumb, that the Whig oligarchy was equipped with a political philosophy the main aim of which was to safeguard and promote the material self-interest of men of property – chiefly, that is, the county gentry.[18]

As a reductionist methodology this was, of course, simplistic in the

[14] *Whigs and Hunters*, p. 197; cf. pp. 206–8.

[15] E. J. Hobsbawm and George Rudé, *Captain Swing* (Harmondsworth, 1973, first publ. 1969), p. xxiii. (An armed mob received a remarkably civil hearing from the Rev. Sir John Filmer, Bt, of East Sutton Park, Kent, the descendant of the early-Stuart political theorist: pp. 76–7).

[16] Douglas Hay, 'Property, Authority and the Criminal Law', in Douglas Hay *et al.* (eds.), *Albion's Fatal Tree: Crime and Society in Eighteenth Century England* (London, 1975), pp. 17–63.

[17] E.g. H. T. Dickinson, *Liberty and Property: Political Ideology in Eighteenth Century England* (London, 1977), pp. 160–2.

[18] The classic statement of this position, which now looks amazingly dated, is C. B. Macpherson, *The Political Theory of Possessive Individualism: Hobbes to Locke* (Oxford, 1962). Cf. an extended review by Peter Laslett, 'Market Society and Political Theory', *HJ* 7 (1964), 150–4, and J. G. A. Pocock, 'Authority and Property: The Question of Liberal Origins', in *Virtue, Commerce and History* (Cambridge, 1985), pp. 51–71.

extreme. Consequently it was seldom overtly examined and defended; it was, rather, conveyed by the repetition of phrases which were meant *not* to be scrutinised: divine right monarchy was 'beneficial and expedient for men of property', that is, those concerned to defend 'the privileges and property of the governing classes': men who championed a 'hierarchical and authoritarian' social order to safeguard 'the privileged position of the propertied elite' – both 'the property-conscious Tories' and also the Whigs, who wanted an orderly society which would 'protect the privileges and property of the wealthy and influential', 'a world in which men of property would be safe'. 'When the Whigs spoke of defending the liberties of the people this invariably meant protecting the privileges of men of substance', and so on. In such accounts, the ideological forms of the 'old society' were redescribed in terms of the cash nexus. To the large extent to which they could *not* be so redescribed, they were forgotten. An Industrial Revolution seemed a natural outcome in such a society: Hanoverian Provincialism seemed to play into the hands of the Old Guard.[19]

By contrast, the point of a gentry-centred localist analysis for the early-Stuart parliamentary historian was that it seemed to offer an exactly documented, concrete set of occurrences as an explanation for those breakdowns in government which otherwise might have to be termed revolutions: an explanatory model which *appeared*, at least, to pursue a middle way, avoiding both grand teleologies and the categorisation of 'underlying' causes. Russell's preliminary account of the breakdown in English government in the early seventeenth century pointed to two main reasons. Partly it was the consequence of incompetent kingship, in the daily business of politics and administration. Principally, however, the breakdown was to be explained in terms of the 'permanent tension between the centre and the localities' which had been so ably discussed in the work of Professor Alan Everitt.[20] Metropolitan revisionists thus appeared to join hands with the Provincials. A geographically defined social malaise was substituted for Christopher Hill's and Lawrence Stone's economic one. 'To accept this is not to turn members of the Commons back into representatives of an embattled "Country"', warned Professor Russell,[21] and it is worth stressing of the backbench MPs of 1714–60 also that geographical origin did not determine a political stance (however much it seems to do that in modern England).

---

[19] Dickinson, *Liberty and Property*, pp. 28–9, 41, 43, 50, 52, 57, 59, 69, 77, 88ff. This revealing turn of phrase should not distract our attention from much of value in Professor Dickinson's book, though it does suggest that the title may be a publisher's misprint and that the author probably believed he was writing *Liberty or Property*.

[20] Alan Everitt (ed.), *Suffolk and the Great Rebellion 1640–60* (Ipswich, 1961); *The Community of Kent and the Great Rebellion, 1640–60* (Leicester, 1966); *Change in the English Provinces* (Leicester, 1969).

[21] Conrad Russell, 'Parliamentary History in Perspective, 1604–1629', *History* 61 (1976), 25.

The Provincial model, therefore, seemed to work for the early-Stuart period. It appeared *not* to work for the Hanoverian period, and its invalidity seemed to let in the Old Guard. Nevertheless, its invalidity seemed to be vouched for by Namierite analysis. How could this situation be resolved? Could the seventeenth and eighteenth centuries be integrated in Provincial terms?

## PROVINCIALISM: TRUE BUT UNIMPORTANT? THE LONG SURVIVAL OF LOCALIST PHENOMENA

How many of the early-Stuart localist insights remained valid in the later period? In the absence to date of any significant number of Hanoverian Provincial studies, a possible route to an answer might be to compare the high-political consequences of localist phenomena. Russell had explicitly appealed to the work of two decades on the local dimension of early-Stuart politics and administration.[22] Far from revealing a Whiggish crusade on libertarian principles, a 'pressure from below', that research had, he believed, revealed a pattern of local reticence and compromise in the daily conduct of administrative business. The mental horizon of most of the gentry, as far as practical affairs were concerned, was bounded by their county. Peers and MPs, too, moved in a local political context as well as a national one, and these pressures often conflicted. Instead of deep structural (i.e. material) tensions in society generating two parliamentary 'sides', Russell saw, local studies show a complex and intricate pattern which failed to induce such a simple polarity at the centre.

Equally, a better understanding of Court and Country as rival cultures shows how rarely individuals can be assigned only to one category: 'the worlds of Court and Country were inextricably intertwined', as Professor Ashton observed. 'Historians have paid, and are paying, too much attention to the imagined dichotomy between the local and the national, as opposed to studying the process whereby the latter emerged out of the former.'[23]

An examination of the local priorities of early-Stuart parliamentarians reveals their overriding preference for defending the localities against efficient central administration and realistic central taxation, rather than for using parliamentary privileges for an assault on the powers of the Crown. Most of these inferences could equally well be drawn from the 1715–54 and 1754–90 volumes of the *History of Parliament* (revisionists saw a different origin for Whig v. Tory divisions). That they had never been

---

[22] Conrad Russell, *Parliaments and English Politics 1621–1629* (Oxford, 1979), p. 8.
[23] Robert Ashton, *The English Civil War: Conservatism and Revolution 1603–1649* (London, 1978), pp. 41, 70.

emphasised was due probably to the relative neglect of the monarchy in the eighteenth century: MPs' behaviour was assessed in relation to the question of parliamentary party: the absence of a localist-inspired Commons attempt to diminish the powers of the Crown went unremarked because of the long-unchallenged assumption that those powers had been reduced to a negligible level in 1688–9.

In many ways, however, much in the localities remained the same for generations. The slightly ramshackle but remarkably resilient system of local government through unpaid gentry elites which was under threat in its own eyes in the early-Stuart period was triumphantly reinstated in 1660 and survived, despite an apparent challenge to it in the reign of James II,[24] until the rise of a modern bureaucracy in the nineteenth century: what kept taxes on land so low as to make this possible in an era of warfare after 1688 was a relatively heavy indirect tax burden on commodities,[25] the healthy growth of the customs revenue with the increase of overseas trade, and the vast expansion of the national debt.

Once the early-Hanoverian ideological conflict had been superseded in the 1750s, this system of national finance kept in being the pattern of gentry rule which Everitt, Barnes, Morrill and others have described until the triumph of the bureaucrats in the decades following 1832. Russell's 'permanent tension between the centre and the localities' was, in concrete terms, the failure of the gentry to pay for central government. But this was not some inherent, objective, structural characteristic of the social order; the refusal was political. The commissioners of the subsidy under the early Stuarts persistently and absurdly underrated themselves and their gentry neighbours, and got away with it. Something not dissimilar continued throughout the eighteenth century: land tax valuations bore less and less relation to the real value of property, while, in wartime, other tax revenues raced ahead. Yet, in an age in which wars were significantly financed by massive expansions of the national debt and by indirect taxes on an increasingly prosperous society, this became after 1688 less and less of a constraint.[26]

[24] The theme of 1688 as a response to Charles II's and James II's threats to the autonomy of the county elites re-established in 1660 is explored in D. H. Hosford, *Nottingham, Nobles and the North* (Hamden, Conn., 1976). Dr John Morrill is working on the same subject.

[25] That parliamentarian innovation, the excise, was 'retained at the Restoration, in *lieu* of fiscal feudalism and contentious charges like ship money'; it was 'John Pym's most enduring monument': Ivan Roots, *The Great Rebellion 1642–1660* (London, 1966), pp. 72, 269. I owe this reference to Professor Conrad Russell.

[26] See W. Kennedy, *English Taxation 1640–1799* (London, 1913); W. R. Ward, *The English Land Tax in the Eighteenth Century* (Oxford, 1953); Peter Mathias and Patrick O'Brien, 'Taxation in Britain and France, 1715–1810', *Journal of European Economic History* 5 (1976), 601–50; Peter Mathias, 'Taxation and Industrialisation in Britain, 1700–1870', in Mathias, *The Transformation of England* (London, 1979), pp. 116–30. By contrast Plumb's pupil Dr Colin Brooks, in 'Public Finance and Political Stability: the Administration of the Land Tax,

Localist independence of central government, then, made for a strong gentry, a powerful cultural hegemony by a traditional landed elite, a society relatively resistant to *revolution*. But it also meant, in the seventeenth century, a State weak in relation to foreign powers and a State prone to *rebellion* and civil war. A weak militia and a monarchy starved of funds were related phenomena.[27] The extreme military and financial fragility of the Elizabethan regime is only now coming into clear focus:[28] it is not just the survival of Parliaments which is remarkable but England's avoidance of foreign conquest in the sixteenth century and, after 1689, its rise to a position of military and, above all, naval strength (rebellions like the '15 and the '45 toppled earlier governments.).

In the revisionist account, the years 1603–42 in England witnessed no social revolution, no proletarian or bourgeois upsurge, but military failure and political collapse in the face of a Scots rebellion and invasion. Any revolution which followed civil war in the 1640s, and especially from about 1646, was revolution largely contained by military dictatorship. Domestic politics therefore continued to turn on the chance of war: a successful Dutch invasion and conquest[29] in 1688–9, unsuccessful Scots invasions in 1715 and 1745, an Irish rebellion in 1798, various unsuccessful French invasion attempts throughout the century. If Hanoverian historians are increasingly localists, it is above all in their attempts to gauge the extent of popular disaffection – partly in London, more importantly along the routes of the invading Jacobite armies, to an extent in Wales, and most importantly of all in Scotland. These rebellions failed; the local social upheavals were consequently minimised. Where local rebellion succeeded (again because of foreign military intervention) in the American colonies after 1776, the result (it might be argued) was, once more, revolution in a sense akin to that of the 1640s. For these later analogies to early-Stuart Provincials, eighteenth-century specialists look mainly to their colleagues in Scotland and America.

Yet here the early-Stuart Provincialist thesis did not find strong confirmation in one important respect. The most important revisionist account

1688–1720', *HJ* 17 (1974), 281–300, interprets the absence of conflict over the Land Tax after 1688 as evidence of national unity in shouldering a burden necessary to the continuance of J. H. Plumb's political stability. This notion seems doubtful in the light of the profound idéological divisions, momentarily focussing on an issue of taxation, ably discussed by Paul Langford, *The Excise Crisis: Society and Politics in the Age of Walpole* (Oxford, 1975).

[27]  See Austin Woolrych, 'Court, Country and City Revisited', *History* 65 (1980), 241.

[28]  See Joel Hurstfield, *The Illusion of Power in Tudor Politics* (London, 1979). Penry Williams, *The Tudor Regime* (Oxford, 1979), esp. pp. 457–67, qualifies this thesis; citing Russell, 'Parliamentary History in Perspective', Dr Williams argues against a steady weakening of the State in the fifty years to 1642.

[29]  In part, it was discussed as such: cf. M. P. Thompson, 'The Idea of Conquest in Controversies over the 1688 Revolution', *JHI* 38 (1977), 33–46.

of the American 'revolution' traced a breakdown in government to changes at the periphery, not the centre.[30] Such an argument made those events seem much less like the cautious, virtuous, conservative, localist reaction against centrist innovation and advancing monarchical tyranny that had been the norm in American historiography for the last two decades. To accept American complaints of centrist encroachments is merely to endorse a self-interested account of what the normal constitutional relations between colonies and mother country were, argued the authors. So, in turn, the Irish rebellion of the 1790s is hardly to be portrayed in terms of introverted provincial resistance to metropolitan innovation.[31]

In these cases it was a national or supra-national political perspective which led historians to look sceptically on local claims of innocent, conservative attachment to the *status quo*: much depended on whose definition of the *status quo* was accepted as the valid yardstick. The question was not so much the survival of localist colonial *forms*, as their political *use*. The structure of county government in England also survived little changed from the early-Stuart into the Hanoverian period. But in each period the idea of a rebellion of the periphery against the centre took on renewed appeal.

In this sense, too, early-Hanoverian Provincialism was more a consequence than a cause of the high-political revaluation of Jacobitism and religious issues. In the other direction, Hanoverian Provincialism was relatively little help in revising the old orthodox model of Westminster politics: the outdated fixation with that most reified category, the 'Industrial Revolution', continued to produce numbers of local studies of the North, the West Midlands and other areas of initial industrial growth: but this long-familiar genre generated few original insights to aid the parliamentary historian. It may have been the case that 'rebellion' sometimes led to 'revolution'. But it was by no means clear, on a Provincial level, that putative 'revolutions' in the structure of economic ownership and production produced 'rebellions' in the sense discussed in this book. This long-familiar thesis began to lose its force.

Thus John Money's splendidly researched *Experience and Identity: Birmingham and the West Midlands 1760–1800* (1977) was supposed to illustrate the interaction of locality and centre, so demonstrating the process by which 'the world beyond Westminster' (a phrase evocative of many historians' antipathy to the values of a more recent establishment) 'from the 1760s onwards, began to challenge the conventions and alter the fabric

---

[30] Robert W. Tucker and David C. Hendrickson, *The Fall of the First British Empire: Origins of the War of American Independence* (Baltimore, 1982).

[31] Marianne Elliott, *Partners in Revolution: The United Irishmen and France* (New Haven, Conn., 1982).

of existing political society' (p. vi), in the familiar Old Hat and Old Guard manner. It was pertinently observed by a reviewer[32] that Dr Money had not established that the West Midlands *was* an entity which could be discussed in localist terms: the Old Guard scenario would seem to require that the provinces not be introverted at this time, in order that they should exercise that legendary 'pressure from without' of which we once heard so much.[33]

A test of the validity of Provincialist analysis was indeed the central or national results it seemingly entailed. For the eighteenth century, Provincial studies were encouraging when (though rarely) they seemed to offer a revision of the familiar Old Guard account of an Industrial Revolution, but they produced little for the parliamentary historian. Early-Stuart Provincialism proved far more helpful in this respect. If 'Court' and 'Country' were not clear-cut identities or parties, as Professors Elton, Ashton and Hirst argued (see below, pp. 136–44), there was less room for an equation of Country with Provincial. Material concerns like taxation and militia did not of themselves create a distinct, self-aware body, separate from and defined over against the Court. It was a conclusion worth applying in 1714–60 also, and here the early-Hanoverian revisionist provided powerful confirmation. Gentry hegemony obviously persisted in a very similar form during the period 1714–60 (the problems involved in turning the militia into an effective force during the Seven Years' War were immense).[34] Equally, there was no provincially initiated campaign to shackle the monarchy.[35]

Yet localism in its eighteenth-century form was obviously not inconsistent with the existence of a national ideological polarity, Whig v. Tory, which was fully comprehended in the county gentry community, which meshed intimately with religion, and which bore demonstrably on the gentry's local administrative activities.[36] Early-Hanoverian revisionists who sympathise with much of what Conrad Russell and others have to say about high politics will be more cautious of agreeing that those insights are *necessarily premised* upon localism. Anthony Fletcher's high-political narrative *The Outbreak of the English Civil War* (1981) largely accepted Professor

---

[32] John Brewer, in *Social History* 4 (1979), 137–9.

[33] Significantly, the burden of this critical review seemed to be that Dr Money's excellent book was *insufficiently* reductionist in failing to relate social change closely enough to the local economy; that it was 'bourgeois history' which said too little of the 'labouring poor', etc., etc.

[34] J. R. Western, *The English Militia in the Eighteenth Century* (London, 1965).

[35] I assume here the 'revisionist' emphasis on the interpretation of Bolingbroke's 'Country' opposition as an uneasy and finally unsuccessful alliance of two opposites, Tories and Whig extremists.

[36] L. K. J. Glassey, *Politics and the Appointment of Justices of the Peace 1675–1720* (Oxford, 1979); Norma Landau, *The Justices of the Peace, 1679–1760* (Berkeley, 1984).

Clive Holmes' critique of the Provincial case.[37] Provincialist and high-political schools of thought were allies in many respects, but it is not clear that either was dependent on the other. In method and purpose, claims about the introversion and autonomy of the 'county community' were related to claims about the introversion and autonomy of the realm of 'high politics'. In both cases, the object was to restore an autonomy to past individuals, to free their decisions and beliefs from the spurious determinism of 'underlying' social causes. But what the individual was assumed to wish to do with his newly restored autonomy depended on which school of revisionism was consulted.

## PROVINCIALISM: IMPORTANT BUT UNTRUE? THE OLD HAT AND OLD GUARD CRITIQUE

Provincialism, suggested Professor Hirst, was the new insight of an age reacting against central planning: 'While we lose the ability to appreciate the religious preoccupations' of the seventeenth century, 'we gain in the understanding of such other areas as law-enforcement'[38] and local phenomena. We might add some other analogies. With our intelligentsia emphasising the harmless virtues of localism, and in an age whose key terms are 'community', 'environment', 'gentrification', 'conservation', and – its *reductio ad absurdum* – 'nuclear free zone', historians have responded to past efforts of small men to avoid involvement in mighty national issues and to resist central bureaucratic dictation: Provincialism was to this extent an historiographical echo of the value-nexus of the SDP. 'There is a danger of sentimentalising "the county community" of the gentry', noted that hard liner Christopher Hill acutely.[39]

This localist position was indeed a negation of socialist centralism: a rejection both of 'underlying social cause' explanations in terms of a rising manufacturing interest or gentry, and of centralist ideology – the grand Whig scenario which pictured the parliamentarian cause striding forward to a victory whose rationale established the (rather abstract) liberties of (mainly metropolitan) man. Equally, however, it was a negation of royalism: such Tory virtues as dynastic allegiance and a religion which validated divine right politics were not allowed to have motivated the common man to fight for the King. Provincialism was, instead, an affirmation of the values of what was depicted as the centrist majority – not

---

[37] Anthony Fletcher, *The Outbreak of the English Civil War* (London, 1981), p. 374; for Holmes (1980), see below, pp. 58–61.

[38] Derek Hirst, 'Court, Country and Politics before 1629', in Kevin Sharpe (ed.), *Faction and Parliament* (Oxford, 1978), pp. 105–37, at p. 105.

[39] Christopher Hill, 'Parliament and People in Seventeenth-Century England', *P&P* 92 (1981), 103.

apathetic, but sensibly cultivating their Provincial gardens, and combining in community action groups to resist the pressures of both of the major parties alike. Provincialism had, indeed, been around for some time,[40] especially in the pioneering work of Professor Everitt. But it became fashionable only from the late 1970s, harmonising with an emerging agenda in national life (just as Namierism, invented in the 1920s, was raised to the status of a fashion only in the ideologically favourable 1950s). This does not mean that either set of ideas is any the less true, of course, and Provincialism also must be looked at on its merits.

It was on its merits that it was seriously challenged, however. If the Crown's conduct in 1604–42 is to be explained in terms of its estrangement from local elites, the gentry leaders of the county communities on whose active co-operation efficient government depended, there would seem to be two main alternatives. Did county slackness, inertia and introversion provoke new royal bureaucratic experiments? Or was it chiefly a matter of incompetent administration at the centre – an incompetence derived not least from the unsuitable channels into which governmental business was diverted by the King's unconstitutional measures? Professor Hirst plausibly suggested the second: recalcitrance in the counties was a response to the unpopularity of royal *measures*, not just to rusting administrative machinery, even though the archives reveal 'few cases locally of people standing on the principles that were to be enshrined in the Petition of Right'. Indeed, the Privy Council was sometimes lax in part through unwillingness to provoke principled provincial resistance, and it was 'inconsistency on the part of the central government' which 'allowed local particularism to develop into the force it was'.[41]

Professor Holmes went further in emphasising that early-Stuart localist phenomena are quite consistent with a provincial appreciation of the constitutional issues traditionally enshrined in the Whig canon. The scarcity of local challenges to the King's *right* to act 'unconstitutionally' could be explained as prudence and reticence in the face of the efficient persecution of dissidents (an argument that has seemed to revisionists a powerful one in respect of early-Hanoverian Jacobitism), and local delays and evasions explained as a safer and more effective response to unacceptable measures than ringing but futile declarations of principle.[42] Collisions

---

40 Surprisingly, its central ideas can be found set out in so early a work as the Introduction to Keith Feiling's *A History of the Tory Party 1640–1714* (Oxford, 1924).

41 Derek Hirst, 'The Privy Council and Problems of Enforcement in the 1620s', *JBS* 18 no. 1 (1978), 46–66.

42 Clive Holmes, 'The County Community in Stuart Historiography', *JBS* 19 no. 2 (1980), 54–73. Professor Holmes provides the most effective critique of a Provincialist case, though possibly by first stating it in a stronger form than most of its proponents would wish to accept.

between Liverpool's Trotskyite councillors and a Conservative government at the time this survey was written, or the similarly induced antics of the Greater London Council, illustrate some of the ways in which more profound ideological issues can be deliberately expressed in the limited idiom of administrative squabbles between local and central government.

The argument that Ship Money was challenged locally only 'rarely' on a level of high principle and generally because it was 'hated for its costliness and its disruptive effects on the social and political calm of the communities ... Above all' because the tax 'exemplified the government's insensitivity toward localist sentiment and belief' is doubtless true as far as it goes, but any implication that this is a complete account of political motivations invites a charge of reductionism.[43] It must be added that Dr Morrill disavowed the argument that 'provincialism excluded concern for general ... political or constitutional issues', but there is a danger that such able scholarship will be read as evidence for the provincialist argument in the stronger form propounded by Professor Everitt, that localism was 'normally ... more powerful' than a national consciousness.[44] Other models of localism might profitably be explored in addition to Everitt's county community, suggested Professor Underdown, especially ones which focussed less exclusively on the elite: Holmes on the Eastern Association, Morrill on Cheshire, Peter Clark on Kent and Underdown himself on Somerset have all read more variegated meanings into local conflicts.[45]

Was it true, moreover, that administrative interactions of central and local government were not expressive of ideological issues? Official correspondence between the Council and local administrators was scarcely the place to look for sweeping assertions of principle, argued Dr Lake: indeed the Council itself sought to confine disputes to a localist idiom in order to avoid arguments on general issues. Nevertheless, Dr Lake's tactical (one might almost call it high political) study of the manoeuvres which surrounded the collection of Ship Money in Cheshire revealed much more than 'a mere reflex reaction to the local effects of royal policy ... It may be that Ship Money, by placing the King's authority at the centre of a claim for extra-parliamentary taxation, played a key role in forcing opposition to royal policy out of conventional, localist forms into more general, ideological modes of expression.'[46]

[43] Morrill, *The Revolt of the Provinces*, pp. 22–9; quoted Holmes, 'The County Community', p. 54.
[44] Holmes, 'The County Community', p. 54.
[45] David Underdown, 'Community and Class: Theories of Local Politics in the English Revolution', in B. Malament (ed.), *After the Reformation: Essays in Honour of J. H. Hexter* (Manchester, 1980), pp. 147–65.
[46] P. Lake, 'The Collection of Ship Money in Cheshire during the Sixteen-Thirties: A Case Study of Relations between Central and Local Government', *Northern History* 17 (1981), 44–71.

Did the local gentry articulate these more general ideological matters? A search of private, rather than official, correspondence suggested that at least some of them did. The papers of Sir Roger Twysden offer an insight into opinion in Kentish society:

the content of the discussion, ranging from the belief that the legality of Ship Money could be settled only by a Parliament, to the view that the tax was a financial device to make future Parliaments superfluous, must question a recent interpretation that Ship Money was resented primarily because of the administrative disputes and antagonism it engendered locally ... Nevertheless, this anxiety over the constitutional implications of Ship Money remained largely tacit until the general collapse of the King's personal rule following the Scottish wars of 1639 and 1640.[47]

Professor Holmes sought more directly to challenge Everitt's model. Marriage alliances, and education, broadened gentry horizons and produced an articulate and informed, but *divided*, local elite, he argued.[48] The importance of the county as an administrative unit and a focus of gentry consciousness had been exaggerated: for most gentry, the local unit was much smaller than the county, and county gatherings emphasised, rather, gentry links with central government. Assizes and county elections were often the occasion for the formulation of local aims at Westminster. 'Everitt's account of the March 1640 Kentish election rivals Sir Lewis Namier in its insistence upon the politics of deference', objected Holmes, appealing to Plumb's work to establish the existence of 'an independent electorate to be wooed'.[49]

The early-Hanoverian revisionist can carry this argument in another direction, however, particularly in the case of Kent: sufficiently detailed studies reveal not a floating, independent electorate, but voters profoundly influenced at parochial level by the choices on national issues of a local elite which was, and remained, divided.[50] Eighteenth-century historians have gone much further in the refinement of psephological studies, eliminating

47 Kenneth Fincham, 'The Judges' Decision on Ship Money in February 1637: The Reaction of Kent', *BIHR* 57 (1984), 230–7.
48 It should be remembered that among the earliest research which drew attention to a county consciousness was that which led to a serious study of the ideologue and county squire Sir Robert Filmer, and an appreciation of gentry awareness of national ideological (even divine right) issues: Peter Laslett, 'The Gentry of Kent in 1640', *CHJ* 9 (1948), 148–64; 'Sir Robert Filmer: The Man Versus the Whig Myth', *WMQ*, 3rd ser., 5 (1948), 523–52.
49 Holmes, 'The County Community', p. 72 and *passim*; J. H. Plumb, 'The Growth of the Electorate in England from 1600 to 1715', *P&P* 45 (1969), 90–116. A similar objection to Everitt's reliance on the concept of deference is made by Underdown, 'Community and Class', pp. 150–1.
50 Norman Landau, 'Independence, Deference, and Voter Participation: The Behaviour of the Electorate in Early-Eighteenth-Century Kent', *HJ* 22 (1979), 561–83; J. C. D. Clark, *English Society 1688–1832: Ideology, Social Structure and Political Practice During the Ancien Regime* (Cambridge, 1985), chapter 1.

any easy equation of deference and localist unresponsiveness to issues, but reconstructing in detail the undemocratic, elite-dominated electoral world which prevailed until the rise of mass political allegiances based on Dissent at the end of our period.[51] Derek Hirst's work on the electorate[52] could be used to argue that MPs represented, and were responsive to, a much wider constituency than the gentry community alone, and the theme of independent proletarian 'radicalism' could therefore once again be plugged into the Westminster model. It was a process which early-Stuart Provincialism was less than fully effective in resisting: if a teleological picture of the seventeenth-century electorate is not to gain renewed credence, the Hanoverian revisionist account of psephology will have to make a contribution to the earlier period also.

If Professor Holmes' critique of Provincialism is to be accepted, it must be qualified by the realisation that the crucial fissures within the county elite came late, in 1642, and were substantially reunited by the early 1660s; the Whig v. Tory conflicts from the 1690s onwards had another origin (see below, pp. 136–55). Eighteenth-century psephological research consequently raises important questions about political behaviour within the seventeenth-century county. Deference, the Hanoverian revisionist would observe, does not imply localist oblivion of national issues. The theme of county neutralism in the Civil War should not be overstressed: it must be set against emerging evidence of widespread voluntary proletarian identification with King or Parliament – some areas decidedly for one side, some for the other.[53] Moreover, the easiest analysis of regional variations seemingly proved to be one related not to the complexion of the 'county community' but to economic configurations overlapping county boundaries: Christopher Hill delightedly took up the implications of a score of localist studies and brought the debate back into the old channel of 'underlying' social conflict, this time between gentry-royalist champaign

---

[51] See D. C. Moore, *The Politics of Deference: A Study of the Mid-Nineteenth Century English Political System* (Hassocks, 1976); Frank O'Gorman, 'Electoral Deference in "Unreformed" England: 1760–1832', *JMH* 56 (1984), 391–429.

[52] Chiefly in *The Representative of the People? Voters and Voting in England under the Early Stuarts* (Cambridge, 1975). Professor Hirst's illuminating research on seventeenth-century psephology should as yet be accepted with some caution. In particular, Professor Kishlansky's work on the same subject is awaited. Arguing against Professors Derek Hirst and Lawrence Stone, John K. Gruenfelder's *Influence in Early Stuart Elections 1604–1640* (Columbus, Ohio, 1981) provides a thoroughly researched argument for the continuing importance of the electoral influence of the nobility and gentry – a theme which, as he observes, is also largely missing from such parliamentary accounts as Wallace Notestein, *The House of Commons, 1604–1610* (New Haven, Conn., 1971) and Robert Zaller, *The Parliament of 1621: A Study in Constitutional Conflict* (Berkeley, 1971).

[53] Cf. David Underdown, 'The Chalk and the Cheese: Contrasts among the English Clubmen', *P&P* 85 (1979), 25–48; *idem*, 'The Problem of Popular Allegiance in the English Civil War', *TRHS* 31 (1981), 69–74.

areas and the less subservient, and therefore parliamentarian, areas of forest, fen or pasture. 'What threatened to become an orthodoxy has disintegrated before it congealed', he noted with evident satisfaction.[54]

Observers might be more cautious of dismissing the localist reinterpretation, however. Certainly, valid points have been made against the Provincial thesis in its 'hard' form; but the note of *schadenfreude* in Holmes' and Hill's powerful critiques signals a warning. Old Guard orthodoxy certainly perceives in Provincialism a threat to over-arching explanations which are premised on an easy (and usually undemonstrated) link between local patterns and central alignments. Yet if the Provincialist case has to date proved not as strong as it once promised to be, this is in large part the result of its failure to mesh more closely with the political world of Westminster (perhaps this was inevitable: proving a succession of negatives is a thankless task). Indeed, the links between these two schools have not always been what they might be: if Provincialism was a reaction against vulgar (or even polite) Marxism, it disclosed an equally instinctive reticence about allying with the high-politics school.

High-political revisionism, too, took more account of localist studies than localist studies took of high politics. The great majority of Provincial works, objected Professor Hexter, adopted as their chronological starting point the summoning of the Long Parliament; 'Such works avoid an anachronistic perception of nine tenths of the Parliaments of the Stuarts by the foolproof device of not seeing them at all.' Secondly, he objected, such studies treated Parliament as epiphenomenal, a superstructural register or index of basic, structural, *local* conflicts.[55] Both the early-Stuart and the early-Hanoverian high-political revisionists find much in common with Professor Hexter in one respect at least – his insistence on close attention to Parliament in its own right, and to the significance of what is actually said in Lords' and Commons' debates.

Localist studies refuted the idea that the divisions of the Civil War were rooted in economic change – Parliamentarians as an entrepreneurial vanguard, Royalists as backwoodsmen, overtaken by a tide of innovation. Exactly the same conclusion has emerged from a study of eighteenth-century Jacobitism: G. P. Insh's reductionist picture of the risings as a conservative, localist Highland reaction against the encroachment of a modernising, materialistic commerical nexus has been convincingly replaced by Dr Bruce Lenman's picture of the Highland aristocracy who

---

54 Hill, 'Parliament and Peope'. Hill's polite debate with parliamentary historians contrasts markedly with his bitter dismissal of localist scholars.
55 J. H. Hexter, 'The Early Stuarts and Parliament: Old Hat and the *Nouvelle Vague*', *Parliamentary History* 1 (1982) 195. For a restatement of the Provincial case, see Anthony Fletcher, 'National and Local Awareness in the County Communities' in H. Tomlinson (ed.), *Before the English Civil War* (London, 1983), pp. 151–74.

took arms in the '15 as 'conspicuously anglicised and indeed rather cosmopolitan', pursuing a realistic political option for reasons of hard advantage as well as of credible ideological commitment – reasons which they shared with their counterparts in the Lowlands.[56]

Early-Stuart Provincial scholars, then, successfully disposed of the Old Guard's social change models. But the Provincials' initial preference was to offer little of a positive nature to replace those models. Thus the Provincials stressed the theme of populist neutralism – the reluctance of the common man to fight for either side – and, of the gentry elite, their constitutional conservatism: their resistance to what they saw as the innovations of the metropolis and the tyrannical misuse of royal power.

The skill with which these theses were demonstrated distracted attention from another argument, fully consistent with them, which identified a *positive* initiative to rebellion in sources quite different from the *negative* localist desires to take no steps towards revolution. We must not make the mistake of accepting small minorities of extremists as spokesmen for 'Parliament', 'the people', 'the gentry' or 'the middle class' as a whole; but the State *was* led into rebellion and war (as again in 1685, 1688, 1715, 1745, 1776 and 1798) by minorities whose beliefs were more extreme and more strongly held than their neighbours'; historians' explanations must be able to account for the rise and influence of these minorities, and even place them at the centre of our picture. That most men most of the time were peaceful, provincial and law abiding is true enough, and an important corrective to over-dramatisation; if offered as a *complete* account, it would often be lacking in explanatory power.

### REBELLION AND RELIGION: A NEW DIRECTION FOR THE PROVINCIAL MODEL?

Provincialist scholars had valuably recovered the practical and institutional causes of *stability*. But this did not preclude those forms of turmoil which were not initially caused by structural change: in our terminology,

---

[56] G. P. Insh, *The Scottish Jacobite Movement: A Study in Economic and Social Forces* (Edinburgh, 1952); Bruce Lenman, *The Jacobite Risings in Britain 1689–1746* (London, 1980). I differ from Dr Lenman's important study in his suggestion that early-Hanoverian England was (in J. H. Plumb's sense) far more stable than Scotland: that it saw an 'age of oligarchy, patronage and non-ideological politics dominated by a struggle between "ins" and "outs" for political office' whose 'midwife was probably Sir Robert Walpole' (p. 110). Since Dr Lenman plays down English political and ideological divisions, he is led to explain support for the '15 *in England* partly in terms of 'deep-seated regional discontent' (p. 114), an unpersuasive argument and one which seems inconsistent with his far more coherent account of the supra-local sources of Jacobite allegiance north of the Border. Yet by 'regional' seems really to be meant 'religious', and this distances his analysis from the earlier approach of the early-Stuart Provincials. Dr Lenman does not in fact use the concept of the 'county community' in his account of northern England.

rebellion rather than revolution. The point was aptly anticipated in 1961 by the most successful English pioneer of structural social history, Peter Laslett, in praising Hexter's undermining of Old Guard accounts of the Civil War in terms of rising or falling classes: 'All societies, even English society at its stablest, are liable to break down into conflict, even armed conflict. Conflict is a common enough form of social interaction: there is nothing special about the things which bring it about.'[57] At the time, this may have seemed heretical. By 1981 the spectres of proletarian and racial urban violence were reminding many other scholars 'how fragile is domestic tranquillity, how thin the veneer of civilisation, how little obedience to the law can be taken for granted'.[58] If political stability was not the secure reward of Attlee-esque social engineering, then the calm of an earlier age was even less to be taken for granted, whatever the vast inertia of immemorial forms of social life, or the introverted patterns of authority and leadership in the county community.

A *structural* account of the local community, argued Holmes, had led to 'a failure to recognise ideological divisions, as against superficial rivalries for local status and prestige among the county gentry'. It was a line of argument familiar to critics of Namierism. In eighteenth-century scholarship, the 1950s and 60s witnessed a similar wave of local studies – a cluster of PhD theses, and even a few articles, on constituency politics at a grassroots level.[59] They, too, were animated by the worthy hope that local research would yield a new interpretation of politics at the centre. The world of Westminster was indeed being reinterpreted in structural terms, classically in John Brooke's Introduction to the first volumes of the *History of Parliament*.[60]

Yet it might be suggested that this was not a simple case of cause and effect. A vision of politics had been devised by metropolitan historians on the basis of Westminster, and carried into the localities in a search for supporting evidence. Evidence which seemingly supported this picture was indeed found; but a genuine interaction of local and central studies was not achieved. Once the work of the History of Parliament team on the years 1715–90 was complete, the genre of constituency studies for that period ran out of steam; A. N. Other's PhD thesis on 'Politics and Administration in Namierborough, 1760–70' too quickly gathered dust on a library shelf (one

[57] Laslett, 'Foreword', p. xiv in J. H. Hexter, *Reappraisals in History* (London, 1961).

[58] John Cannon, *Aristocratic Century: The Peerage of Eighteenth-Century England* (Cambridge, 1984), p. 148. It seems safe to say that none of the Class of '68 would have written such words.

[59] It is remarkable how few found their way into print. For an example of what could be done, see John Cannon, 'The Parliamentary Representation of the City of Gloucester (1727–1790)', *Transactions of the Bristol and Gloucester Archaeological Society* 78 (1959), 137–52.

[60] Sir Lewis Namier and John Brooke (eds.), *The History of Parliament: The House of Commons 1754–1790* (3 vols., London, 1964).

must hope that a longer useful life is in store for Y. E. T. Another's thesis on 'The County Community and the Civil War in Everittshire, 1640–50').

The revisionism discussed in this book stemmed more from attention to ideology and action than to structure. As we have seen, 'Country' has been used to mean both localist introversion *and* a provincially generated campaign at the centre for national goals. It was this second meaning (in the works of such authors as Professors Dickinson and Speck) that early-Hanoverian revisionists scrutinised, arguing instead that a single identity failed to subsume its components, Whig and Tory, either tactically or doctrinally. It may indeed be that 'Country' in the first sense inhibited 'Country' in the second sense. But more important, suggested the early-Hanoverian revisionists, was the receptivity of local men to issues of principle, and on the part of Tory and opposition Whig a refusal to coalesce for profound and easily intelligible ideological reasons. What marked out the high-political revisionists was their insistence that the *issues* were not to be reconstructed on the teleological framework provided by the Old Guard, not a claim that localist introversion prevented national politics from being about issues of principle at all.

Could this position be integrated with the Provincialist one? The most recent studies suggest one way of doing so. Dr Morrill's perspective led in due course to a greater emphasis on (what had indeed always been visible under the Provincial microscope) *religious* conflicts. These, at least, could be documented within an institutional, financial and administrative framework at a local level. For the minority of activists on each side in 1642, 'religion was the crucial issue':

Quite simply, in most counties the active royalists are the defenders of episcopacy who saw in puritanism a fundamental challenge to all society and order, and the parliamentarians are those determined to introduce a godly reformation which might, for a few of them, leave room for bishops, but in most cases did not. What the puritan activists did agree on, however, was the need to go beyond a restoration of traditional pre-Laudian erastian Anglicanism to create a new, militant evangelical Church ... it was the men who felt most strongly about religion who began the war.[61]

It was the men who felt most strongly about religion, we might add, who were prepared to act in Monmouth's rebellion, in 1688, in the '15 and the '45; and the men at Westminster who built their political creed around an offensive doctrine of religious pluralism who destroyed the confessional

---

[61] Morrill, *Revolt of the Provinces*, pp. 47, 50; reiterated in John Morrill (ed.), *Reactions to the English Civil War 1642–1649* (London, 1982), pp. 15–17, 89–114; *idem*, 'The Religious Context of the English Civil War', *TRHS* 34 (1984), 155–78; *idem*, 'Sir William Brereton and England's Wars of Religion', *JBS* 24 no. 3 (1985), 311–32. I can accept Dr Morrill's analysis of the Civil War as a war of religion more happily if he does not require me to believe that it was the *last* war of religion.

State in 1828–32. Here, it seems, is a very different attitude to ideology – one much more reluctant to explain it in terms of anything else. It was this strategy for countering reductionism which was being exploited more fully by early-Hanoverian revisionists; but they did not owe it to a localist example. They owed it to a reconsideration of the social location of rebellion.

Historians of the 'county community' were sometimes humorously charged with having proved that the Civil War came to every county from without: with showing, in other words, that the Civil War never happened. Yet this satirical abridgement of a whole genre of scholarship does to an extent rebound on itself. County studies *have* succeeded in proving that there was no self-sufficient impetus to rebellion (let alone revolution) within the *English* counties. The English Civil War, we can then see, was the result of a 'domino effect' produced by successful rebellions in Scotland and Ireland.

Despite the merits of its anti-Whiggery, the Provincial school betrayed in an even more acute form the little-Englandism which has long treated 'English history' as a virtual synonym for the history of four nations – England, Wales, Ireland, Scotland. If the last three elements of the equation are suppressed, it might indeed seem both credible and inevitable that we should trace the breakdown of Stuart government in the 1640s to an internal English dynamic of constitutional evolution, of libertarian (and even democratic) pressure from below. But if these concerns would have taken a very different (and perhaps wholly unsuccessful) course without the Scottish and Irish insurrections, it is possible that historians will increasingly be led to detect a constitutional dynamic in the mutual relations of the four contrasting communities which have fought for power and primacy in these islands.

Just as the causes of the Industrial Revolution have proved so difficult to agree on because, as we now see, there was no 'Industrial Revolution' (historians have been chasing a shadow: a reified category), so one might suggest that historians have laboured misguidedly to discover causes sufficient to explain an *English* Revolution, an *English* Civil War. But the war that was actually fought was, in its origins, not English: it was a *Scottish* and *Irish* Civil War, which only later spilled over into the English shires.

There seem many strengths to the localist case, then, chiefly those points which have been taken up by early-Stuart parliamentary historians: the absence of some profound social schism, the failure of a complex local pattern to generate two parliamentary parties, the unimportance of pressure 'from without' for a campaign to seize the initiative from the Crown, but the concurrent failure of the Crown to raise adequate revenue in the localities. Granted these important insights, it may be that other elements in the Provincial case will be modified. In particular, revisionism in both periods resulted chiefly in a recasting of the inherited picture of national politics and national institutions. It is to this that we must now turn.

# 5

# THE MONARCHY AND PARLIAMENT

## THE HISTORIOGRAPHY

Professor Rabb helpfully summarised the early-Stuart high-political revisionist case under five propositions. First, Parliament before 1640 was weak *vis-à-vis* the King and indecisive in the conduct of its own business. Second, the House of Commons contained no organised and clearly defined 'opposition': consensus politics, not adversary politics, was the ideal; and to an extent this norm was maintained. Third, the grand issues occasionally raised in the Commons registered specific political interests: 'intrigues at Court, the war plans of the 1620s, plain economic interest, the pressure of local and county politics, the scramble for office'. Fourth, disputes in the Commons did not reflect a grab for power by the gentry, but the concerns of their patrons: 'the narrow factional ambitions of their superiors, the peers and the members of the Privy Council'. Fifth, there was no 'steady crescendo' of constitutional issues from 1604 to 1642: 'Developments were sporadic and uncertain, free from self-conscious or deliberate purpose'.[1] With the exception of the second, all these conclusions were discovered to apply in great measure to the early Hanoverian period also. Indeed, it was *because* the Parliaments of 1714–60 were discovered to have been polarised between the traditional parties of Whig and Tory that the applicability of the other points on Rabb's list was more striking.

These themes can, then, be traced in the historiography of both eras: they were related aspects of a common insight into the English past. Equally, for both eras, a negative case implied a positive one: the removal of a spurious model of English society encouraged historians to appreciate the great residual power of those institutions the major defeat of which was now to be redated to the years 1828–32: monarchy, aristocracy, Church. These were unfamiliar lessons. Even S. R. Gardiner had organised his story around the growing political power of 'the people' – first in the

[1] Theodore K. Rabb, 'Revisionism Revised: The Role of the Commons', *P&P* 92 (1981), 59.

ascendancy of the House of Commons over the House of Lords under the Tudor monarchy, then of the Commons over the Crown in the 1640s. Similarly, the Whig perspective depicted the triumph of Parliament over Crown in 1688, of Commons over Lords in *c.* 1714–60, and of 'the people' over an oligarchic Commons in the latter part of the century, beginning with Wilkesite disorders and culminating in the 1832 Reform Bill. Here again, the Old Guard used the same scenario for two centuries; here again, it can hardly be true of both, and its elastic qualities make one doubt whether it was true of either.[2] Both scenarios seriously understated the continuing power of sovereign and nobility in society at large, and of the Crown and the upper House in metropolitan politics; to create a counterweight, both personified a 'middle class' whose 'rise' made the events of the 1640s 'the bourgeois revolution' and, more excitingly still, made the later eighteenth century 'the day of the bourgeois radical'.

If 'the people' were so important, it had seemed natural to treat Parliament as their agent. The monarchy could thus be presented as the reciprocal of 'the people', the other weight in the scale: as 'the people' went up, the monarchy *must have* gone down. Granted that assumption, the power of the Crown in both centuries had been underestimated partly because academic historians had so overwhelmingly preferred to examine Parliament, and – even then – to focus on the Commons and to treat it as a self-contained, self-sufficient body. 'Parliamentary' history had to be expanded to mean the high-political history of Court and Ministry, Lords and Commons if their relative position was to be appraised. This result was achieved by early-Stuart revisionists tracing the dependence of Commons' business on external initiatives, and by early-Hanoverian revisionists exploring the voluminous records of contests for ascendancy among Whig ministers – contests which were played out only to a small extent on the floor of either House, but to a large degree in the shadow of the throne.

The Crown was seldom examined directly. It is a remarkable comment on the priorities of academic historians that, despite scores of books on Parliaments, parliamentary parties, ministries and the machinery of government both central and local, no serious long-term survey of the monarchy in the sixteenth, seventeenth or eighteenth centuries has been written since that of Sir William Anson (if indeed his constitutional study should be included in this context).[3] Despite the administrative revolution

---

[2] Except, perhaps, on the assumption of massive and draconian reaction in 1660. Yet the striking features of the Restoration settlement were the ease with which it was accomplished, and its wide popularity: see I. M. Green, *The Re-establishment of the Church of England, 1660–1663* (Oxford, 1978); Ronald Hutton, *The Restoration: A Political and Religious History of England and Wales, 1658–1667* (Oxford, 1985).

[3] Sir William Anson, *The Law and Custom of the Constitution. II. The Crown* (Oxford, 1892); see also Sir William Holdsworth, *A History of English Law*, vols. 9 and 10 (London, 1938).

of the early sixteenth century, however, more recent early-Stuart historians have remarked on the large extent to which government was still household government.[4] Even the expanding role of the bureaucracy outside the royal household, which had drained the latter of its administrative functions by the early eighteenth century, did not destroy the Court's role as the principal arena of intrigue and manoeuvre, the place where real power – royal favour and nomination to office – was fought for, won and lost.[5]

It was, indeed, an evidential problem which had contributed much to the underestimation of the monarchy's strength from the revolution to 1760. William III's role in business was consistently minimised by historians who did not read Dutch.[6] Similarly the role of George I and George II, even in English domestic matters, could be appreciated only through a working knowledge of German: it was largely hidden to those unable or unwilling to use the Hanoverian archives now so well exploited by Professor Hatton.[7]

By the early 1980s, however, developments in the scholarship of the Civil War were leading historians back to the question of the wider significance of the monarchy's role. The Tawney–Hill model of the 1640s as *the* English Revolution began to seem dubious for many reasons; and one body of evidence to the contrary was provided by the substantial, and increasing, power of the Crown after 1660. If the old assumptions were still valid that 'the great constitutional struggle of the seventeenth century' had witnessed 'the crucial turning-point for the constitution', the disqualification of the 1640s as a candidate for that role directed attention instead to the reign of William III: the monarchy must have been decisively weaker in the 1690s. If not 1642, then 1688 must have been the English Revolution.[8]

On the basis of those old assumptions, this new identification was persuasive. Yet a wider revisionism was under way which eventually challenged not only the Old Guard model but many of the Old Hat assumptions about constitutional evolution also.[9] In respect of the

---

4  Cf. Linda Levy Peck, *Northampton: Patronage and Policy at the Court of James I* (London, 1982), p. 215 and *passim*.

5  See Stephen Baxter, *The Development of the Treasury 1660–1702* (London, 1957); *idem, William III* (London, 1966); *idem,* 'The Age of Personal Monarchy in England', in Peter Gay (ed.), *Eighteenth Century Studies Presented to Arthur M. Wilson* (New York, 1972), 3–11; Edward Gregg, *Queen Anne* (London, 1980).

6  As is pointed out by Stephen Baxter, 'Recent Writings on William III', *JMH* 38 (1966), 256–66; a situation Professor Baxter did much to remedy.

7  Ragnhild Hatton, *George I Elector and King* (London, 1978).

8  As is argued by Angus McInnes, 'When Was the English Revolution?', *History* 67 (1982), 377–92. The revaluation of the events of 1688 owed much to J. R. Jones, *The Revolution of 1688 in England* (London, 1972), and J. R. Western, *Monarchy and Revolution: the English State in the 1680s* (London, 1972).

9  I fully accept Dr McInnes' arguments in 'When Was the English Revolution?' about the power of the Crown *c.* 1660–88; but his claim that there had 'undoubtedly' been a

monarchy as in respect of social structure, the revisionist answer to the question, 'when was the English Revolution?' was a disconcerting one: 'there was no revolution'.

## THE EIGHTEENTH CENTURY: WHAT WAS THE OUTCOME?

For most historians, it was from a closer attention to parliamentary matters that a revaluation of the power of the monarchy largely came. The emphasis in the two centuries was slightly different, however. If early-Hanoverian historians had been preoccupied with the warfare of party-politics, early-Stuart revisionists were the more careful students of parliamentary business. An important element in this re-examination of parliamentary business in 1604–29 was their questioning of what had always been assumed to be Parliament's ultimate deterrent: control of supply. The traditional account is familiar: the power of the purse was a principal weapon in Parliament's self-conscious struggle to frustrate Charles I's absolutist ambitions; in due course, in an era of warfare after 1689, it inevitably transferred political weight to the Commons and created the modern office of Prime Minister in the person of the First Lord of the Treasury, naturally sitting in the lower House.

Professor Russell first systematically challenged the validity of these assumptions for early-Stuart history. The same assumptions were not systematically questioned for the later period, except in so far as they bore on the relative political standing of the offices of Chancellor of the Exchequer and Prime Minister.[10] Yet, applying the same criteria, it is equally true of both 1604–29 and 1714–60 that Parliaments did not make redress of grievances a *condition* of the granting of taxation. Supply was not voted only after a list of measures had been extorted from an unwilling executive. These new insights into early-Stuart practice would have greatly reinforced Professor Thomas' discoveries about the realities which discredited Hanoverian rhetoric:

---

fundamental transformation 'by the middle years of the eighteenth century' is supported, as to mid-eighteenth-century practice, only by a reference to Sir Lewis Namier's Romanes Lecture 'Monarchy and the Party System', delivered in 1952 and now overtaken by other scholarship. Namier suggested a three-phase model of 'royal government', 'mixed government' and 'parliamentary government': though rightly sensing a transition between the second and third in the 1830s and 40s, he offered no guidance on the date of the supposed transition between the first and the second. Indeed Namier's evident ignorance of English politics before *c.* 1750 suggests that his simplistic three-phase model was based only on inherited or borrowed assumptions about the arbitrariness of early-Stuart 'absolutism'. It cannot now be accepted.

[10] J. C. D. Clark, *The Dynamics of Change: The Crisis of the 1750s and English Party Systems* (Cambridge, 1982), pp. 44–97. It seems unlikely, however, that any merely academic doubts will ever modify the popular desire to treat Walpole as the first 'modern' Prime Minister.

The traditional strategy of the House of Commons, a demand for the redress of grievances before the grant of money to the sovereign, had now been outmoded by constitutional and political developments. Opposition was never made to the formal principle of giving supply, except by hot-headed members [e.g. Jacobites] ... The elaborate procedure of raising money had been devised as a check upon the executive, and the parliamentary forms were strictly observed, even though they failed to ensure either any detailed scrutiny of the estimates or any exact appropriation of the money voted.[11]

Those disaffected toward the dynasty had good reason for viewing Whig constitutional rhetoric as a hollow sham. As far as most historians have been concerned, however, this absence of a systematic use by the Commons of its procedural levers against the Crown might mean one of two things. Either it was unnecessary, the Commons being already in a position of dominance; or it was irrelevant, no such bid for precedence being intended by the lower House. The traditional assumption was the first; revisionists increasingly rejected this view, and were driven to the realisation that the second was more appropriate both to the seventeenth and eighteenth centuries.

During the reigns of William III and Anne, successive Parliamentary Accounts Commissions did indeed demonstrate a considerable zeal in scrutinising public expenditure and a keen distrust of the executive. Yet this zeal was much more obviously fuelled by the party conflicts of Whig and Tory than by a conscious plan to expand the institutional role of the Commons. From 1702 the Commissions became exclusively associated with the Tories, and were naturally discontinued in 1714.

As a consequence, the routine supply procedures of the House of Commons exerted almost no pressure in the interests of accountability in the mid eighteenth century. Estimates of annual defence expenditure were given only perfunctory scrutiny, and accounts were not required. Pressure for inquiries was quickly stifled on the few occasions it emerged. The appropriation clauses, written into supply bills as a matter of course, were with equal regularity flouted. The submissiveness of the House of Commons to the demands made upon it went to the remarkable lengths of acquiescing, with increasing frequency, in Votes of Credit, which were blank cheques for large amounts granted to the government without estimate or appropriation.[12]

The 'emergency' expedient of Votes of Credit for unspecified sums, beginning in 1717 and quickly turned into a regular practice, was a characteristic Hanoverian device. So was the periodic presentation to the House of Commons of demands for the payment of debts on the Civil List.

[11] P. D. G. Thomas, *The House of Commons in the Eighteenth Century* (Oxford, 1971), pp. 65–88 at pp. 82, 85.
[12] Henry Roseveare, *The Treasury 1660–1870: The Foundations of Control* (London, 1973), pp. 56–61 at p. 59; *idem, The Treasury: The Evolution of a British Institution* (London, 1969), pp. 88–91. I owe these references to Professor Kenyon.

Both were regularly yielded to without the House demanding estimates or accounts. The specific appropriation of sums in Commons grants likewise declined into an empty formality, as Lord Mulgrave, one of the Lords of the Admiralty, candidly explained in 1778 (to Edmund Burke's synthetic indignation): 'the estimate was the usual mode of raising money, but never meant to state the purposes the money was to be applied to; that if it was a crime, it was one that had been often practised ever since the reign of James II'.[13] Some opposition attempts there were to probe the financial workings of the Hanoverian regime, but it is their gallant persistence and emptily rhetorical indignation rather than their success which is most evident.

The independence of the Crown had always varied to a considerable degree with the health of its finances. Just as James II was wafted by the breezes of commercial prosperity in the 1680s[14] (though shipwreck awaited him), so the position of George I and George II was not only a strong but a strengthening one. The 1698 Civil List Act eliminated most earlier sources of difficulty by transferring to Parliament responsibility for many areas of expenditure, leaving the King with certain Civil List revenues assumed to be sufficient for the purposes of government (among them ministerial salaries, the royal household, pensions and secret service, including political manipulation). But these had been, and continued to be, the most sensitive areas of expenditure, the areas most directly related to the King's ability to deal with and sway the Lords and Commons. Between 1698 and the 1780s this area of royal activity was to a large extent insulated from scrutiny by and accountability to the House of Commons.

Parliamentary provision for George I's Civil List was an improvement on Anne's; George II secured an even better deal, for Walpole bought his own political ascendancy by securing a generous Civil List which, moreover, allowed revenues surplus to the target figure of £800,000 p.a. to remain in the hands of the sovereign. George II thus left the monarchy in a strong and prosperous position, its income growing with the steadily increasing yield of the appropriated duties. Such a system, had it continued, would have produced a hugely affluent monarchy by the end of the century. It was George III who undid this system by idealistically accepting in 1760 a fixed (and, as it soon proved, inadequate) annual sum:[15] henceforth there was an inbuilt tendency to erode the position of the Crown, and to subject every office and pension to jealous parliamentary scrutiny, leading to Burke's Civil Establishment Act of 1782.

Although the Crown retained much power until 1832, the tide had now

---

[13] Quoted in Thomas, *The House of Commons*, p. 82; cf. p. 86.
[14] C. D. Chandaman, *The English Public Revenue 1660–88* (Oxford, 1975).
[15] E. A. Reitan, 'The Civil List in Eighteenth-Century British Politics: Parliamentary Supremacy versus the Independence of the Crown', *HJ* 9 (1966), 318–37.

turned against it: the reigns of the first two Georges seemed, in retrospect, a golden age. Where the Parliaments of William III *had* been willing to use the issue of the revenue as a check on monarchy (a willingness again evident on the part of the opposition from the 1770s), the Whig-dominated Parliaments of the first two Georges seem by contrast remarkably complacent in their attitude to an inescapably Whig dynasty.[16] The oppositions, of course, protested continually. In 1734 Samuel Sandys, MP, maintained: 'I believe it will be granted, that the prerogative, even within these last 30 or 40 years, has grown considerably. I believe every gentleman will admit, the power of the crown is now infinitely greater than it was for some years after the revolution.'[17] But such views accorded ill with the predictions of the 'Whig interpretation', and were usually dismissed by historians as the misrepresentations of an opposition as devoid of hope as of realism.

A case can at least be made out for their realism. Although William III encountered the hostility and suspicion of successive Parliaments, at least part of their desire to restrain his power derived from the equivocal allegiance of many men to a different monarch, not from their rejection of monarchy as such (though a few republicans did indeed sit in the Commons). And although the Revolution settlement contained some formal provisions to limit the Crown, these proved all too often to be paper safeguards. The 'Bill' of Rights of 1689 (1 Will. and Mar. s.2, c.2) was looked to as a landmark. It enshrined the principle that taxes might only be raised with parliamentary approval; but this was less than conclusive if parliamentary management grew ever more efficient, and if the national debt could be vastly expanded. Tories were repeatedly to complain that the country was bled white to pay for Dutch and Hanoverian wars, and after 1688 the combination of escalating taxation and spiralling debt yielded sums beyond the wildest dreams of Charles I or James II. The Bill of Rights prohibited 'the raising or keeping a standing army within the kingdom in time of peace unless it be with consent of Parliament': only a substantial and professionalised standing army, rubber-stamped by Whig parliamentary majorities, protected the Dutch and Hanoverian regimes against a Stuart restoration until the 1750s. It provided that 'Parliaments ought to be held frequently': the 1694 Triennial Act (echoing the Triennial

16 E. A. Reitan, 'From Revenue to Civil List, 1689–1702: The Revolution Settlement and the "Mixed and Balanced" Constitution', *HJ* 13 (1970), 571–88, and 'The Civil List, 1761–77: Problems of Finance and Administration', *BIHR* 47 (1974), 186–201. For a more teleological account, see Clayton Roberts, 'The Constitutional Significance of the Financial Settlement of 1690', *HJ* 20 (1977), 59–76. Such a position had just been seriously undermined by the arguments on the 'power of the purse' of Conrad Russell, 'Parliamentary History in Perspective 1604–1629', *History* 61 (1976).

17 Paul Langford, *The Excise Crisis: Society and Politics in the Age of Walpole* (Oxford, 1975), p. 18.

Act of 1641) was overset by the Septennial Act of 1716: George I even contemplated placing the Westminster Parliament on the same footing as its Dublin equivalent, which (until 1768) was dissolved only on the death of the sovereign. The most effective (perhaps the only really effective) provisions of the Bill of Rights were those which aimed to prevent Roman Catholics from occupying the throne.

Among the last attempts to restrain William was the Act of Settlement of 1701 (12 and 13 Will. III. c.2), which looked forward to the accession of another foreign sovereign. It provided that none of his ministers should be foreigners: this did not prevent George I from arriving with a team of Germans who enjoyed a *de facto* precedence until 1719.[18] It attempted to defend the traditional but declining institution of the Privy Council, where the King's advisers, signing its resolutions, could be held accountable for their conduct. It failed (this provision was repealed in 1706), and Cabinet Councils, doing business off-the-record and behind closed doors, were soon the norm. The Act of Settlement attempted to exclude placemen and pensioners from the House of Commons: these provisions were modified in 1706, 1708 and 1716, and became a dead letter. The House of Commons under the Georges was far more susceptible to manipulation than it had ever been under Charles I, or even Charles II and James II. The Act provided that the monarch should not leave the country without consent of Parliament: this too was repealed, in 1716, and Hanover remained the favourite residence of the first two Georges. It provided that, if a foreigner became King, 'this nation be not obliged to engage in any war for the defence of any dominions or territories which do not belong to the Crown of England without the consent of Parliament': this proved to be the most empty provision of all. Once again, the really effective provisions of the Act of Settlement were those which reinforced the Bill of Rights' defence of the Church of England against Rome.

The primary index to the power of the Crown to sway Parliament was not the monarchy's influence in the House of Commons, substantial though this remained, but its influence in the House of Lords. This indeed went virtually unchallenged either in theory or in practice: it was Court influence in the Lords which secured the rejection there of the Place Bills of 1712 and 1714, the unavailing culmination of a Country campaign.[19] That campaign's successes had proved largely empty: the provision that an MP accepting an office must submit to re-election failed to secure the defeat at the polls of crowds of greedy placemen, for (in the early eighteenth century as in the early seventeenth) electors realised too well the value of Court connections.

[18] Possibly the origin of the later myth of 'double cabinet'.
[19] G. S. Holmes, 'The Attack on "The Influence of the Crown" 1702–16', *BIHR* 39 (1966), 47–68, at 67–8.

Professor Holmes concluded: 'The Place campaigns of 1702–16, therefore, applied a brake to the "influence of the Crown" but did little more.' Two informal checks were more effective: triennial elections and the clash of party principles. 'It is ironical that the attacks on "influence" should have lost their impetus after 1716, at precisely the time when the first check disappeared and the second was already diminishing in force.'[20] If we no longer see such a diminution, Whig numerical preponderance after 1714 assumes even greater importance in our understanding of the power of the first two Hanoverian monarchs.

The thesis of the decline of the Crown used to be established, most simply, by reference to one of its prerogatives in particular. The royal veto was used less and less often after 1688, and for the last time in 1708. What Parliament demanded in 1714–60, it got; but this gives a partly misleading impression of its power. Increasingly effective pains were taken to ensure that it did not demand what the King was unwilling to agree to. There were no Petitions of Grievances under the early Hanoverians.[21] What distinguishes 1714–60 in this respect is not the weakness of the Crown but the efficiency of parliamentary management, and the dependence of this system of control on the clear distinctions engendered by a Whig v. Tory polarity. In a world of known and predictable *party* allegiances, dividing Parliament, the royal prerogative of veto *and* the Commons' right to refuse supply dwindled into distant abstractions. When it came to the point in 1783–4, after the old Whig v. Tory alignment was no more, it was clear that the Commons did not dare to use its ultimate deterrent: the destruction would be too general.[22]

We now see that if the Commons were often united against the Crown in 1604–29, it was more from weakness than from strength – from the hope that they could procure some assurance of regular sittings. Regular sittings did indeed result after 1689: but if the King needed Parliament for the revenues it henceforth provided, it might be added (in early-Stuart revisionist terms) that it was eminently worthwhile for monarchs to summon Parliaments which provided funds so lavishly. After 1689, and after 1714, both King *and* Parliament got their way, rather than one of the two at the expense of the other. A stronger State meant a stronger Parliament *and* a stronger monarchy. The weakness of the Crown in *c.* 1714–60 is an illusion caused mainly by the monarchs' inevitable dependence on the Whigs. A Whig ministry and a Whig monarchy were, to that degree, two aspects of the same entity. Historians employing Victorian

---

[20] *Ibid.*

[21] The analogy, perhaps, is Lords' and Commons' protests entered in the Journals; but these were the unavailing complaints of minorities, there for propaganda reasons only.

[22] John Cannon, *The Fox-North Coalition: Crisis of the Constitution, 1782–4* (Cambridge, 1969), pp. 190–205, 233–4.

assumptions observed a powerful ministry and inferred a weak monarchy: for this period at least, it is a *non sequitur*.

A Whig regime under the early Hanoverians also meant a Parliament with a decisive Whig majority in the Lords; the relatively low level of conflict in that House after 1714 reflects Whig strength rather than the hegemony of a bourgeoisie through its putative instrument, the House of Commons. A resolute upper House had no inhibitions about rejecting unwelcome Bills, and until the 1790s this function still aroused hardly any overt hostility to the role of the peerage in government. After 1760, the closing of the old rift between Tory and Whig only strengthened the House's resolve, and into the 1820s the Lords was perfectly willing to stonewall against repeated attempts by the Commons to pass contentious Bills (as, for example, on Catholic Emancipation). Sovereigns had little need to incur criticism by using a royal veto if the upper House was so willing to accept such a role.

In an era of general peace and of imperial disengagement after 1945, two subjects above all were quietly deleted from the agenda of most British historians and consigned to the attention of specialists: foreign policy and war. (They had, indeed, patriotic connotations which made them embarrassing in some quarters; they seemed obviously appropriate to narrative enquiries, which made them methodologically unfashionable.) Without these occupations, of course, it was by no means clear what kings and aristocrats *did*. Such elisions were welcome: the activities of the patrician elite were obviously anachronistic survivals after 1714 (or 1688, or 1642) in the new bourgeois world of possessive individualism. What could be more appropriate than to see the early Hanoverians as kings 'in toils'?

This, too, has changed. 'There was a period when scholars could write about eighteenth-century British politics as though Britain was not a monarchy', observed Dr Black: 'The closet had been stormed, kings were forced to accept the position and views of ministers who could control Parliament. Such a view is no longer tenable.'[23] Scholars now emphasised diplomacy and military affairs, above all, as two major aspects of governmental business in a century of endemic warfare. They were aspects which continued to be regulated by royal prerogative both in the choice of senior personnel and in daily decision-making. This was especially true of the first

---

[23] Jeremy Black, *British Foreign Policy in the Age of Walpole* (Edinburgh, 1985), p. 36; *idem*, 'George II Reconsidered', *Mitteilungen des Österreichischen Staatsarchivs* 35 (1982), 35–56; *idem*, 'An "Ignoramus" in European Affairs?', *BJECS* 6 (1983), 55–65; *idem* (ed.), *Britain in the Age of Walpole* (London, 1984), chapter 6, 'Foreign Policy in the Age of Walpole'. Dr Black demonstrates the limits of Walpole's competence in foreign affairs: it begins to seem that one reason for some historians' long-standing adulation of Sir Robert was that they knew rather little of the abilities and achievements of his fellow ministers and his sovereigns.

two Georges, whose Hanoverian involvement gave them an additional dimension of independent action.

In both spheres, moreover, the monarch's position was formally unchallenged: if the Commons' use of the 'power of the purse' was little more than an empty formality, and Parliament's ability to pre-determine the King's choice of ministers was fitful and haphazard before the 1830s, it was even more true that in respect of diplomacy and war there was no emergent body of theory, still less an active tradition, which sought to place either sphere under parliamentary scrutiny and control. In these respects as elsewhere, Parliament continued to act as a court: it censured incompetence and malversation, but it did not step forward to exercise the functions of those whom it might occasionally censure. Much depended on the relative zeal, industry and ability of senior figures: since these varied randomly, the balance between the King and his ministers would swing first one way, then the other. But even a greater (and, at the very end of the century, more lasting) role for the King's ministers *vis-à-vis* the King did not at once mean the assertion of parliamentary control: it meant the inheritance of the King's authority by his chosen servants.

In the perception of at least the Tory half of their subjects, both George I and George II had been trained in Germany in a school of autocratic princely rule beside which Charles II's (and even James II's) kingship paled into insignificance. The family remained autocratic rulers of Hanover into the nineteenth century.[24] Early Hanoverian princes were efficient administrators in this Teutonic mould (until the self-discipline of George III's sons was undermined by English indulgences), keeping a tight grip on the army[25] and on foreign policy which was justified by a detailed professional expertise in both fields.

None of the Hanoverians was born a democrat: their authoritarian tone was acceptable in England because they were (literally) born Protestants.

---

[24] Here again, dynastic and religious partisanship led one set of Englishmen to conflate 'absolute' and 'arbitrary' in the case of the Hanoverians, just as another set had conflated the two concepts in the case of the Stuarts. Yet Hanover was a State enjoying the rule of law, and imperial legal and political institutions – the Chamber at Wetzlar, the Aulic Council at Vienna, the Diet at Regensburg – qualified to some extent the freedom of action of German princes. (I am grateful to Dr Jeremy Black for advice on this point.) For an account of this, 'the most perplexed and complicated government, ancient or modern, that ever existed', see [John Campbell], *The Present State of Europe* (4th edn, London, 1753), pp. 212–35.

[25] Counter-factual analysis (*i.e.* guessing) is an art which should not absorb much of the historian's time, but it is important at least to reopen the options and hold the possibilities in one's mind: if Charles I had had a standing army comparable to the early Hanoverians', would he have lost his throne? Conversely, if George I's or George II's military resources had been similar to the early Stuarts', what would have been the result of the '15 or the '45? Against these possibilities we must set the fact that James II *did* have a sizeable standing army and that it failed to back him in 1688.

The association of Lutheranism with monarchical absolutism had been pointed out by the Commonwealthman Robert, Viscount Molesworth, in *An Account of Denmark*:

As long as the priests are entirely dependent upon the crown, and the people absolutely governed by the priests in matters of conscience as they are here [Denmark], the Prince may be as arbitrary as he pleases, without running any risque from his subjects: in due consideration of which benefit, the clergy are very much favoured here, and have full scope given them to be as bigotted as they please ... the Calvinist is hated by them as much as the Papist; and the reason they give is, because he is against absolute monarchy, and has a resisting principle ... It has been a general mistake among us, that the Popish religion is the only one, of all the Christian sects, proper to introduce and establish slavery in a nation, insomuch that Popery and slavery have been thought inseparable ... other religions, and particularly the Lutheran, have succeeded as effectually in this design as ever Popery did.[26]

After 1714 this insight was inconveniently taken up by Tories, who levelled such charges against an English Lutheran monarch, George I. Tory MP Sir John St Aubyn complained in a debate on Hanoverian troops in December 1742 that 'we lived under a Prince who being used to arbitrary power in his dominions abroad, was minded to establish it here'.[27] This rhetorical overstatement was not groundless: in England as in Lutheran Germany, Protestant Churches were enthusiastic preachers of obedience to legitimate (Protestant) monarchs. We should not forget that, in respect of their ideological structure, there were at least three equally viable forms of the ancien regime: Roman Catholic, non-Calvinist Protestant, Russian Orthodox.[28]

One seldom-examined practice throws the continuing power of the early-Hanoverian monarchy into sharp relief. George I and George II took every opportunity to visit their native Hanover (where, of course, they were at home). During their absence, Britain was administered by Regency Boards sitting in London. Far from the business of such Boards revealing the residual, figurehead status of the sovereign, they show the contrary: an anxious, scrupulous attention to royal initiatives which the monarch's

---

[26] [Robert, Viscount Molesworth], *An Account of Denmark, as it was in the Year 1692* (London, 1694), pp. 251–2, 258. (Ironically, Cambridge University Library's copy was the gift of George I.) Molesworth's condemnation was part of the Commonwealthmen's attempt in the 1690s to forestall a settlement of the Crown on the House of Hanover: a republic was still a preferred option for such men.

[27] Eveline Cruickshanks, 'The Political Management of Sir Robert Walpole, 1720–42', in Black (ed.), *Britain in the Age of Walpole*, pp. 23–43 at p. 30.

[28] It was the formidable force of Lutheran Church-and-State doctrine that the young Karl Marx revolted against, seeking first a theological critique of it in the circle of the Young Hegelians – Biblical scholars and critics like David Strauss and Bruno Bauer. A similar doctrine retained its force in England until the early 1830s.

personal absence (and contact with another set of politicians) both delayed and complicated.[29]

The Court, too, preserved its early-Stuart role as the prime arena of ministerial intrigue and manoeuvre into the reign of George I: Hanoverian government indeed added the refinement of social and political rivalry between the King's Court and the household of George, Prince of Wales, later George II.[30] The pattern survived with the Leicester House oppositions of Frederick Prince of Wales until his death in 1751, and in turn of his son George, Prince of Wales, in the 1750s. What made these family rows of national political importance was the continued central role of the Crown in politics and in the daily burden of administrative business, whether domestic, military or diplomatic,[31] a role which the virtually complete absence of written evidence by George II has for long disguised.[32]

In *this* sense, it could be argued that the English monarchy reached an apogee of power under the first two Georges. The situation which parliamentarians and extremists from Pym and Hampden to Algernon Sidney and the later Commonwealthmen had fought against actually came to pass. And what was the result? At least in the perception of the Whigs, it was an anticlimax. The heavens failed to drop on the heads of Englishmen as had been confidently predicted. A government somewhat more authoritarian proved widely acceptable so long as its power was used for certain purposes. What did stand out most clearly in retrospect was that the constitutional agonisings over monarchy had concerned not so much its power as an institution as the uses to which that power was put; in particular, it showed that the real issue all along had been religion.

In 1660, 1688 and 1714 the English monarchy was divested of some of its most problematic attributes. The result, unexpectedly, was to strengthen it in the exercise of those many powers and prerogatives which were no longer defined as a threat. Exactly the same happened in the American colonies after 1776: the early-eighteenth-century critique of the monarch was reflected in the newly defined position of the President. Paradoxically, Presidents soon wielded even more effective power than George III had done. In the United States, what was in effect an elective monarchy

---

[29] See State Papers Regencies, PRO, class SP 43.

[30] John Beattie, *The English Court in the Reign of George I* (Cambridge, 1967); Hatton, *George I Elector and King* .

[31] This emerges clearly from J. B. Owen, *The Rise of the Pelhams* (London, 1957), and 'George II Reconsidered' in Anne Whiteman *et al.* (eds.), *Statesmen, Scholars and Merchants* (Oxford, 1973), pp. 113–34, and is stressed in Stephen Baxter, 'The Conduct of the Seven Years' War' in Baxter (ed.), *Britain's Rise to Greatness, 1660–1763* (Berkeley, 1983). The evidence presented in Clark, *The Dynamics of Change*, fully bears out the political priority of the Crown.

[32] There is no scholarly biography of George II; because of the evidential problem it is not clear that one can be written.

enjoyed a lasting position of political dominance; in nineteenth-century England, an unreformed hereditary monarchy lost all but a tithe of the political power which even George IV and William IV had inherited.

This reinterpretation of the reigns of George I and George II cast its shadow both backwards in time, and forwards to the later eighteenth century. Did George III break constitutional conventions in the 1760s in respect of the role in government of parliamentary parties, or in the 1770s in respect of American liberties? This classic and long-running historical debate had resolved itself into two main schools of thought. One believed that George III deliberately acted to enhance the role of the sovereign after his accession and that he was justified in doing so, monarchical power having been usurped by an aristocratic faction under George II. The other school claimed that it was George III who distorted the constitution, since limited monarchy, party government and an executive steered by the cabinet and accountable in the Commons had been firmly established under the first two Georges if not under William III. Yet both these schools in fact rested on the shared assumption, never questioned, that the role of the monarchy *had* been reduced to 'modern' proportions in or by the early eighteenth century as a result of the constitutional initiatives first successful in the 1640s.

Was this assumption justified? There were in fact good grounds, on the basis of passages in the works of Sir Lewis Namier and Sir Richard Lodge, for believing the contrary. But these indications were long neglected, not least because of the modern aversion from diplomatic history. Several scholars, including Ian R. Christie and John Brooke, scrutinised the years after 1760 and remarked on the absence of evidence of a monarch deliberately perverting constitutional forms; but the acute shortage of research on the early Hanoverians denied scholars an accurate standard of comparison. J. B. Owen's characteristically perceptive essay 'George II Reconsidered' (1973) was the first to fracture this structure of assumptions: in the next two decades the weight of evidence slowly accumulated, until finally (and quite suddenly) the structure collapsed.[33]

If so, it might seem that Dunning's famous motion of 1780, that 'the influence of the Crown has increased, is increasing, and ought to be diminished' is evidence rather for the beginning of the erosion of the monarchy's position than for an attempt to create a new absolutism in 1760. George III's youthful ideals, inherited from the Leicester House oppositions to George II, indeed partly obscured the monarchy's surviving power, partly contributed in the longer term to undermine it. When those youthful ideals wore off, however, even George III could be seen as a

[33] The above draws on Ian R. Christie, 'George III and the Historians – Thirty Years On', *History* 71 (1986).

sovereign much closer to his grandfather's Teutonic model than his early rhetoric about 'glorying in the name of Britain' would indicate. Diplomatic and military realities continued to compel his close and independent involvement in German politics as Elector of Hanover, and not until the late 1780s did the direction of British foreign policy pass decisively to his ministers.[34]

Economical reform, an increasingly inadequate royal income, the expansion in volume and complexity of ministerial business, ill health: many things combined to diminish (though not to transform) the role of the monarchy in government from the last decades of George III's reign. Yet this role cannot be measured with a single, objective yardstick: royal power depended in part on the nature of the issues which entered the political arena, as in the 1780s when the *Fürstenbund* negotiations gave the King a renewed diplomatic importance. At home, the last decade of the old order similarly brought the Crown to the forefront in its involvement with the questions of the repeal of the Test and Corporation Acts, Catholic 'Emancipation' and parliamentary reform. As events cast the unlikely figure of George IV in the role of defender of the Protestant Constitution, the Whig opposition became even more paranoid in its identification of the Crown as the chief barrier to its success. As Lady Holland complained, 'This confounded division of the country into [pro-]Protestant and [pro-]Catholic makes the king as powerful as ever Henry VIII was. He is at present as anti-Catholic as his father, and has assured the Archbishop that they may depend upon him as Defender of the Church.'[35] It depended on one's perspective. But no perspective (except perhaps the somewhat hysterical one of Charles Bradlaugh and his like) yielded such a view of the monarchy after 1832.

Effective anti-monarchical initiatives in English politics must be postponed for many decades after 1688 and 1714: in this respect the legacy of the 1640s was vestigial. By the 1780s, however, the paranoid Rockinghamite myth of a royal conspiracy against English (and American) liberties had taken on a new and sinister undertone. The second generation of Rockinghamite Whigs, and especially the dubious figure of Charles James Fox, carried their discontent to the length of disaffection: an open scepticism of monarchical government, and a veiled rejection of the English monarchy itself.[36] This element remained in the opposition party of Grey and Holland, but it was implicit rather than overt: only in the

---

[34] T. C. W. Blanning, '"That Horrid Electorate" or "Ma Patrie Germanique"? George III, Hanover and the *Fürstenbund* of 1785', *HJ* 20 (1977), 311–44.

[35] Lady Holland to Lord John Russell, April 1827: Spencer Walpole, *The Life of Lord John Russell* (2 vols., London, 1889), vol. 1, pp. 135–6.

[36] See Ian R. Christie, *Stress and Stability in Late Eighteenth-Century Britain* (Oxford, 1984), pp. 39–45.

1830s did Whig success bring in its wake a fundamental restructuring of the monarchy of the ancien regime.

## THE SEVENTEENTH CENTURY: WHAT WERE THE ORIGINS?

If the eighteenth-century outcome was one of a relatively strong monarchy and executive, early-Hanoverian historians looked back to discover the earlier course of such developments in a new account of the early Stuarts. Two themes had been given prominence in recent reinterpretations of the Stuart monarchy: taxation, and the interpretation of constitutional documents.

In 1604–29 as in 1714–60, the revisionists suggested, the powerful parliamentary pressures to restrict taxation could best be traced to MPs' close dependence on their constituents, and especially on other gentlemen of similar standing in the county community, rather than to any desire to shackle the power of the Crown as such.[37] This should not imply that the issues of supply, grievances and Parliament's survival were unrelated in MPs' minds; the House of Commons was 'considered indispensable by all Englishmen', as Professor Rabb reminds us, partly because those issues *were* connected in popular estimation.[38] But we must resist the temptation to build this into an initiative-seizing perspective. It is this perspective which revisionism so helpfully dismantled, taking its cue from Professor Elton's suggestion in 1965.

That perspective had been too conveniently outlined by a constitutional document. In 1603 (as in 1689, 1714 and 1727) a foreigner ascended the English throne. According to the traditional account, the Commons' *Form of Apology and Satisfaction* of 1604 was a 'lecture to a foreign king on the constitutional customs of the realm which he had come to govern but which he so imperfectly understood'.[39] If that document indeed constituted a Whiggish statement of the conventions of limited monarchy, it would be understandable if those conventions had been defended in 1688 and definitively imposed on George I in 1714. It was appropriate, then, that this text should be put in its place: the address, not passed by the Commons and never presented to the King, represented the views of only some of those on the Committee that drafted it rather than a corporate view of the

[37] Russell, 'Parliamentary History in Perspective', pp. 7, 13 and *passim*.
[38] Rabb, 'The Role of the Commons', p. 63. It does not follow logically, as Professor Rabb implies, that the attempt to dispense with the Commons meant the collapse of the English government, which in turn produced the Civil War – in Harrington's famous scenario. Legislation was only one function of government and not, in the seventeenth century, a principal function.
[39] J. R. Tanner (1930), quoted by G. R. Elton, 'A High Road to Civil War?' (1965), in *Studies in Tudor and Stuart Politics and Government* (2 vols., Cambridge, 1974), vol. 2, p. 169.

House as a whole. The document argued against a feared erosion in the Commons' position rather than for a programme to expand its role. Though its ideas were familiar to parliamentarians before the Civil War, it was little known after the Restoration, and was 'effectively rediscovered' by Henry Hallam.[40] His *Constitutional History of England*, significantly published in 1827, expounds a position which was seemingly validated only by the collapse of monarchical power in the next few years.

The Old Hat account of the early Stuarts had located in their reigns an institutional conflict: 'a fundamental incompatibility had developed between the institution of Parliament and that of monarchy, and ... any resolution of that incompatibility would require the radical modification of one or the other'.[41] This came about, some believed, in the 1640s. Yet here again, other Old Hat or Old Guard accounts of the eighteenth century inconsistently located the shackling of absolute monarchy in the years following the Glorious Revolution. The debate on the significance of that event was therefore of the greatest importance. The scholarly deflation which Professor Elton applied to the *Apology* could profitably be applied to other famous documents, especially the Declaration of Rights of 1689; although an American scholar has engagingly sought to retain it within a libertarian tradition,[42] a contrary interpretation is to be preferred.

There was no such libertarian document in 1714, moreover; what legislation there was after the Hanoverian accession, like the Black Act, the Riot Act and the Septennial Act, seemed to point the other way. If 'the drafting of the *Apology* does not prove the existence in the House of an organised or systematic opposition to James I as early as 1604', as Elton argued, we now know, analogously, the ambiguities which surrounded George I's accession. Single-party government was not a foregone conclusion: many Tories still wished to accept office in a mixed ministry, as had

---

[40] Elton, 'High Road to Civil War?', pp. 169ff. for a discussion of the *Apology*; J. H. Hexter, 'Power Struggle, Parliament, and Liberty in Early Stuart England', *JMH* 50 (1978), 32–42, for an important reply. Professor Hexter nevertheless disowns 'the quite erroneous notion that, in the view of the Commons, the claim of privilege was a strategic move in a struggle for sovereignty in which the House was engaging against the King between 1604 and 1642. As Russell would rightly argue, there is not a trace of evidence that the authors of the *Apology* had anything of the sort in mind or that they perceived themselves as involved in such a struggle' (p. 36).

[41] Robert Zaller, *The Parliament of 1621: A Study in Constitutional Conflict* (Berkeley, 1971), p. 4.

[42] Lois G. Schwoerer, *The Declaration of Rights, 1689* (Baltimore, 1981). For contrary interpretations, cf. J. P. Kenyon, 'The Revolution of 1688: Resistance and Contract', in N. McKendrick (ed.), *Historical Perspectives* (London, 1974); Kenyon, *Revolution Principles: The Politics of Party, 1689–1720* (Cambridge, 1977); R. J. Frankle, 'The Formulation of the Declaration of Rights', *HJ* 17 (1974), 265–79; Howard Nenner, 'Constitutional Uncertainty and the Declaration of Rights', in B. Malament (ed.), *After the Reformation* (Manchester, 1980), pp. 291–308; John Miller, 'The Glorious Revolution: "Contract" and "Abdication" Reconsidered', *HJ* 25 (1982), 541–55.

been the norm. And of those Tories who were impelled towards Jacobitism it can be said with some confidence that it was not monarchy as such that they objected to. An 'opposition' was still a campaign, not an institution,[43] and the party composition of oppositions in 1714–60 was generally mixed; not until after 1832 were government and opposition both institutionalised in the two great parties of Liberal and Conservative. Ministries were identified to such a degree as the King's ministries under the early Hanoverians that opposition still carried the taint of dynastic disloyalty, as Tory affinities with Jacobites also demonstrated. Indeed the dynastic question emerged as a central preoccupation of revisionists: far from being a marginal, romantic irrelevance to an ideologically vacuous Whig oligarchy, Jacobitism was now revealed as one end of a dynastic ideological polarity which held many political institutions in its grip until the 1750s.[44] Dynastic issues were central to political theory because the monarchy was still central to government.

If the 'collapse' of early-Stuart government is deprived of the 'social stress' and 'Commons' initiative' components, it is driven back on the equally traditional explanation of military weakness and the incompetence of the monarchs. Even here, the beginnings of a defence of James I were evident[45] and attention shifted instead to short-term explanations of Charles I's decision to raise his standard at Nottingham in August 1642.[46] Those more sympathetic to the Old Hat constitutionalist argument seemed almost to be willing to salvage it by abandoning the notion of royal tyranny: Strafford's emphasis on power and punishment as the only sanction of royal government hardly seems to fit the record of its dealings with the English localities,[47] and the Provincialist thesis greatly qualified the easy Whig characterisation of monarchical 'absolutism' (except, perhaps, in Scotland and Ireland, which Provincial scholars were not forward in examining).

Despite its more archaic and ramshackle survivals, in many ways English government echoed developments on the continent. The early seventeenth century saw clearly the effect of the pressure of business on absolute monarchies in the emergence of chief ministers of the stamp of Richelieu in France, Olivares in Spain, Buckingham in England. Haphazard bureaucracies and the inefficiencies of representative institutions

---

[43] See John Carswell and L. A. Dralle (eds.), *The Political Journal of George Bubb Dodington* (Oxford, 1965), Introduction, p. xxii.
[44] J. C. D. Clark, 'A General Theory of Party, Opposition and Government, 1688–1832', *HJ* 23 (1980), 295–325.
[45] E.g. Kevin Sharpe, in Sharpe (ed.), *Faction and Parliament* (Oxford, 1978), pp. 36ff.
[46] E.g. Conrad Russell, 'Why Did Charles I Fight the Civil War?', *History Today* (June 1984), pp. 31–4.
[47] Derek Hirst, 'The Privy Council and Problems of Enforcement in the 1620s', *JBS* 18 no. 1 (1978), 64–5.

placed an immense burden on such men.[48] In this respect George Villiers, first Duke of Buckingham, and Robert Walpole, first Earl of Orford, have been implicitly contrasted by historians to illustrate the pre-determined thesis: the superior efficiency of parliamentary government, of the sound sense of a Norfolk squire, the apotheosis of Country solidity over the inefficiencies, the corruptions, the morally dubious power base of a Court favourite and of monarchical absolutism.

Our re-evaluation of early-Stuart and early-Hanoverian government demands, in turn, a reconsideration of the roles of the two men. Buckingham, under scholarly scrutiny, emerges as a far more effective and less sinister figure, struggling, like his two sovereigns, with the weakness and incompetence of the English State. Our new understanding of the problems of county government and taxation, military failure and parliamentary recalcitrance have redirected our attention away from one individual who could conveniently be saddled both with moral opprobrium and with an un-English ambition to block the advance of parliamentary government.[49] Such a reappraisal demands a reconsideration of Sir Robert Walpole also:[50] his fame as the sole architect of political stability, cabinet government and one-party rule is now in doubt, and the scale of his achievement is significantly diminished by our appreciation that the English State was far stronger in every respect than that with which Buckingham had to deal. But this diminution emphasises one point of similarity between the two men: Walpole too was totally dependent on the nomination and continued support of his sovereigns.

If, furthermore, we no longer see early-Stuart history in terms of the attempt by the monarchy to take over and use for its purposes a sturdily independent Common Law,[51] we can also be more cautious about imposing the same framework on James II's reign. The more cautious we are in both these areas, the less can we deduce from the absence of conflict between the Crown and the Law after 1714 that the monarchy was relegated to a figurehead role. The function of the law as a powerful support of the Hanoverian regime is a subject which has attracted an increasing number of (usually critical) historians. Yet however blank the face which justice presented to the common man, what the lawyers supported was not merely a regime, but a dynasty; not merely a dynasty but, necessarily, the Crown itself (it is no coincidence that the Hanoverian

---

[48] Cf. J. H. Elliott, *Richelieu and Olivares* (Cambridge, 1984).

[49] Roger Lockyer, *Buckingham: The Life and Political Career of George Villiers, First Duke of Buckingham 1592–1628* (London, 1981).

[50] A modern biography of Walpole is awaited from Dr Jeremy Black.

[51] W. D. Jones, *Politics and the Bench: The Judges and the Origins of the English Civil War* (London, 1971); W. R. Prest, *The Inns of Court Under Elizabeth I and the early Stuarts 1590–1640* (London, 1972); B. P. Levack, *The Civil Lawyers in England 1603–1641: A Political Study* (Oxford, 1973).

establishment was defended to the last by its most famous legal champion, Lord Eldon).

From the early seventeenth century, all currents seemed to be strengthening the executive, whether the superior efficiency of Privy Council and Star Chamber to ramshackle parliamentary institutions, the obvious advantages of standing armies over militias, or the growing emphasis on sovereignty in political thought and the declining popularity of the 'mixed monarchy' theories of Fortescue's day. If there was a growing self-awareness among parliamentarians in the early-Stuart period, it may have been largely a defensive one. Yet both Whig and Marxist historians had seen the seventeenth century as 'an ineluctable progression, either constitutional or social and economic': the monarchy of Charles II thus *had to be* weaker than that of Charles I.

Dr John Miller importantly challenged this picture for the period 1660–88:

At the Restoration, the Convention and Cavalier Parliament tried, in effect, to return to the constitutional balance which should have existed before the civil wars. The Convention agreed that the king should have a permanent revenue adequate to support the normal peacetime government. The Cavalier Parliament abandoned the executive role that Parliament had assumed from the end of 1641 and which had been resumed by the Convention, notably in paying off the New Model Army. From 1661 MPs showed that they no longer wanted the responsibility of governing the country, which was time-consuming and very hard work. They wanted the king to govern and provided him with the necessary revenue. Parliament could then revert to its traditional (and, for most, more congenial) role of criticizing and advising.[52]

If some events in 1667–8, 1673–4 and 1680–1 fit Macaulay's model of a Commons wresting the executive from the Crown, at other times the relations of Crown and Parliament were marked by 'exuberant harmony': 'the picture of an aggressive Parliament, steadily whittling away the King's power, is misleading'. Conflict was due more to Charles II's 'political failings' than to Parliament's aspirations; 'in the last analysis, the limitations on the monarchy were political rather than institutional'. No mechanism existed to force a king to rule responsibly or to prevent him from stretching his powers[53] (rebellion remained a necessary option until the 1830s).

---

[52] John Miller, 'The Potential for "Absolutism" in Late Stuart England', *History* 69 (1984), 187–207, at 201. The application of such arguments to the early-Stuart debate is made clear by Dr Miller's formidably destructive review of an Old Guard account of class conflict, Brian Manning's *The English People and the English Revolution, 1640–1649* (London, 1976) and restrained praise of John Morrill's *The Revolt of the Provinces* (London, 1976), in *THES* 28 May 1976, p. 16.

[53] John Miller, *James II: A Study in Kingship* (Hove, 1978), pp. 34–5, and 'Charles II and his Parliaments', *TRHS* 32 (1982), 1–23; McInnes, 'When Was the English Revolution?'; J. R. Jones (ed.), *The Restored Monarchy 1660–1688* (London, 1979).

## HOW, THEN, DO WE PICTURE THE MONARCHY?

If the Civil War was not the culmination of a long attempt to place limitations on the power of the Crown, it is less remarkable that so few signs of any attempt to insist on such limitations were evident in 1660. Was England an 'absolute monarchy' before 1688 – or after 1714? The equation of 'absolute' with 'Catholic' has been so automatic that historians have widely assumed from the deletion of the second after 1688 the absence of the first, and only recently has the concept of absolute monarchy itself been examined for the later-Stuart period. Yet Filmer, it has been suggested, was almost alone among royalist writers in treating 'absolute' and 'arbitrary' as synonymous.[54] Locke's alleged refutation of Filmer was therefore polemically clearly defined but practically unimportant: it left standing absolute monarchy in the sense in which it was not to be equated with arbitrary monarchy, and in this sense it was inherited by William III, Anne and the Georges. In *Taxation No Tyranny* (1775), Samuel Johnson set out a still-orthodox theory of political obligation which can only be understood as the lineal descendant of the doctrines of monarchical allegiance worked out under Charles II and James II.

A scholarly examination of the monarchy of the first two Georges in these terms has still to be written. Yet such a study is badly needed if we dispense with the traditional picture of the 1680s as a nightmare slide towards the precipice of absolutism, a fate from which England was providentially and permanently rescued by the Glorious Revolution. Such an examination must include a comparison between kingship under George I and George II and kingship under Charles II and James II. Thanks to the important work on the later Stuarts of Dr John Miller, this has begun to be possible. The differences between the powers of the monarch in Louis XIV's France and James II's England were more theoretical than real, he argued.[55] In most respects, Charles II and even James II made use of powers the monarchy already had (and, after 1688, kept): what made the latter's policy alienate such a large section of the nation were his plans for Roman Catholicism, not his attitude to the

---

[54] James Daly, 'The Idea of Absolute Monarchy in Seventeenth-Century England', *HJ* 21 (1978), 227–50 at 244–5; Professor Daly charges J. H. Plumb, *The Growth of Political Stability in England 1675–1725*, with 'simplifying everything' by 'using "absolute" and "arbitrary" quite interchangeably' (p. 248). This identification of 'absolute' with 'arbitrary' was a common one within a particular historiographical school: cf. Dickinson, *Liberty and Property*, pp. 13–14, 105. We should, of course, beware of assuming that there is only *one* model of 'absolutism' which can serve as a definition, and towards which other regimes were drawn: cf. J. P. Cooper, 'Differences between English and Continental Governments in the Early Seventeenth Century', in J. S. Bromley and E. H. Kossman (eds.), *Britain and the Netherlands* (London, 1960).

[55] Miller, 'The Potential for Absolutism'.

monarchy as an institution. If there was a potential for a more authoritarian, monarchical regime in the 1680s, argued Dr Miller, it was for an *Anglican* regime. It was this potential which Queen Anne and the early Hanoverians, not the other Stuarts, exploited.[56] Their attempt to bring such a regime into being aroused substantial (Tory-Jacobite) opposition but widespread (Whig) acquiescence; with Parliament's active co-operation, that attempt succeeded.

In 1660 the gentry – as Professor Underdown observed – reunited 'in defence of liberty and property, but this time against the sects, not the King'.[57] The rebellions of the 1640s delayed the rise of the English monarchy, but failed to stop it.[58]

Ironically, 1688 and 1714 had the same effect: in replacing a dynasty suspect on grounds of religion by dynasties which could be defined as the perfect embodiment of English liberties, the real power of the executive (and therefore of the Crown) steadily grew. The rebellion of 1688 was not a bid for a weak monarchy, but for a Protestant monarchy. Consequently, the legislative expressions of that attempt which followed had much to do with religion, but little to do with placing limitations on the monarch's prerogative in other spheres. Discounting the libertarian rhetoric which 1688–9 generated on the part of a small but vocal minority, it is possible to see that the effective powers of the Crown continued to grow.

Historians impressed by the increasing role of Parliament after 1688 had not considered that almost *all* institutions of government, from the Admiralty to the Treasury, from the Excise to the Ordnance, were similarly strengthening: the institution of monarchy, and the individual monarch (in so far as these can ever be distinguished in the realities of everyday politics) retained their centrality in the daily business of government from William III to George II and beyond. To this regime the only alternative was another dynastic one: in a near-confessional State, lacking a democratic ideology, parliamentary reform was a non-starter until the 1820s, and the amount of specifically anti-monarchical pressure was minimal until a late date. The central political issue until the 1750s was

[56] McInnes, 'When Was the English Revolution?', pp. 387–92, argues for a decisive reduction of the powers of the Crown under William III. Undoubtedly, his reign was a period of difficulty for the monarchy in some respects; but an attention to the letter of the Revolution 'settlement' exaggerates the degree to which the position of the sovereign was limited in practice. A perspective extending forward beyond 1702 would have revealed the resilience of royal power for many decades yet.

[57] David Underdown, *Pride's Purge: Politics in the Puritan Revolution* (Oxford, 1971), p. 353.

[58] For a survey of European absolutism in the sixteenth and early seventeenth centuries, which argues the similarities between the position of the English monarchy and those of France and Spain, see Perez Zagorin, *Rebels and Rulers, 1500–1660* (2 vols., Cambridge, 1982), vol. 1, pp. 87–121. This is, perhaps somewhat incongruously, combined with an Old Hat interpretation of the role of Parliament, reaching its culmination after 1689 in a settlement that 'made Parliament supreme': vol. 2, pp. 130–86.

expressed as a choice between dynasties, not as a choice between monarchy and other forms of government. Yet spontaneous Jacobite risings were exceptions in a polity (especially its English part) slowly but steadily growing collectively more peaceful, individually less violent, more efficiently under the rule of law: but for 1688 (one might speculate) the Stuart monarchy would have inherited this administrative stabilisation, and described it (as did its eighteenth-century French counterpart) as proof of the greater rationality of modern, monarchical absolutism.

What marks the early-Hanoverian period, the putative era of triumphant parliamentarianism *par excellence*, is the small extent to which the House of Commons entertained a self-image as the agent of a popular interest, and the general prevalence of ideals of unity and harmony expressed in the alleged tripartite balance of King, Lords and Commons. Contrary once more to Victorian expectations, the early-Hanoverian monarchy proves to have been strikingly formal in its insistence on most previous kingly dignities and prerogatives. Not until recently has the Court as a social and political institution attracted attention in this period, however, despite the pioneering work of Professor Beattie. The Court v. Country school of thought focussed on the 'Country' side of that analysis for an account of MPs' groupings in the Commons in the years 1714–60. In respect of the other half of the equation, many historians accepted with insufficient examination the implications of the early-Hanoverian 'oligarchy' model. Yet a closer look at the 'Court' has shown us the very large share of the Crown as such, and of monarchs as individuals, in the amalgam of Crown, ministers and bureaucrats which constituted the executive.

A more sophisticated attitude to political history has allowed us to break from Victorian assumptions about how that curious reification, 'the constitution', actually worked. A fully detailed examination of politics reveals how indeterminate constitutional conventions are: always developing, always the subject of argument, seldom easy to reconcile with the complexities of actual political situations. Indeed, on close examination 'the constitution' resolves itself into no more than a large number of men making claims about what the constitution is. So too Charles I, George III, and even latterly James II have been treated seriously by historians as legitimate contributors to an evolving constitution rather than as perverters of a fixed one. Revisionism must not be allowed to draw our picture of the constitution back into a timeless realm where evolution stands still; but many central features of the Victorian political world emerged at a very late date. Only at the end of the eighteenth century and in the early nineteenth – and especially after 1832 – did the slow but finally catastrophic drawing apart of Crown and executive produce the limited monarchy (and the limited religion) that some men had fought for in the 1640s.

Revisionism, then, had its effect on our understanding of both the inner workings and the relative balance of the institutions of government. Correcting the perspective in which early-Hanoverian as well as early-Stuart politics are usually seen will entail giving less prominence to the House of Commons, a little more prominence to the House of Lords, and a good deal more prominence to the Court and the monarch. It will also entail taking the Church of England seriously, and another area of revisionist attention was that of religion in its bearing on political ideology.

# 6

# POLITICAL IDEOLOGY

The reconstruction of the received account of parliamentary politics in the early-Stuart and early-Hanoverian periods can be illustrated also by its impact on the historiography of political and constitutional thought. To the Old Guard and Old Hat historians it seemed self-evident that seventeenth-century Englishmen fought each other over issues (religious or legal) but that their eighteenth-century descendants, weary of strife, and aware that these issues had been decided, lapsed into a state of ideological amnesia and conceptual vacuity, pursuing a complacent materialism in 'pudding time'. Both sides of this antithesis, it will be argued, have now collapsed: if early-Stuart scholars have revealed a world in which the grand libertarian issues were subordinate to their tactical location and overshadowed by theological dispute, early-Hanoverian historians have recovered a picture of a society that was profoundly divided over momentous ideological questions.

This was the final result: easy to describe, indeed; difficult and laborious to bring about. And there were many problems along the way. In the seventeenth century, the significance of arguments about parliamentary alignments for the history of political ideology was not initially obvious. The early-Stuart revisionist case, by solving one problem, made another more difficult to answer. 'If the Civil War came out of such a clear sky, if few wanted it and most of those who fought against the King did so for conservative reasons, why did things turn so *nasty*? Why was the King put on public trial and executed six-and-a-half years later? Why were monarchy, the House of Lords and the Church of England abolished?'[1] There was a similar problem for eighteenth-century scholars: if 1828–32 rather than 1688–9 was the more important divide between an old world and a new, where did that leave the Lockeian, secular, empiricist mental universe which so many historians had so resolutely ascribed to Hanoverian

[1] John Morrill (ed.), *Reactions to the English Civil War 1642–1649* (London, 1982), Introduction, p. 1

England? Why did things turn so nasty in 1715, 1745, 1776, 1798 and 1828–32? And if an ancien regime conceived in terms of social structure, ideology, religion and political motivation was strong enough to survive until the Reform Bill, must not many of its premises about human conduct and discourse have retained their force even for a much longer period?

## THE OLD GUARD RESTATEMENT: DID IT WORK?

The Old Guard offered little more than a restatement of their prepared answer. On the level of ideology, too, they believed that the three 'revolutions' of 1641, 1688 and 1776 could still be strung together on the old teleological framework.[2] Although Professor Stone partly accepted the demonstration by 'revisionist historians' of the limited and ambiguous nature of the Revolution Settlement after 1688,[3] he retained a reductionist methodology in arguing that 'theory continued to lag badly behind practice': men weakly failed to perceive that they were living in a new world of possessive individualism and, thanks to 'the limitless capacity for self-deception of the human mind', clung to the outdated superstition of divine right until about 1702. Tories, of course (whose capacity was presumably even greater), kept it going for another decade, but with the accession of George I 'divine right was finally dead, except in the minds of a tiny Jacobite minority'.[4] Professor Kenyon was castigated for daring to suggest that the ideas of Sir Robert Filmer continued to be important.

The 'Country' opposition to Walpole, maintained the Old Guard, was ideologically homogeneous: it was equipped with Whig-contractarian, not divine right, doctrine. Rationalism and scepticism meant the collapse of religious observance; Country doctrine led to a jealous watch on the executive for reasons of gentry self-interest. 'Rarely had men of property been better protected from interference by the central government in their

---

[2] Hence Stone's remark, 'The Results of the English Revolutions of the Seventeenth Century', in J. G. A. Pocock (ed.), *Three British Revolutions: 1641, 1688, 1776* (Princeton, 1981), p. 63: 'The cause of the Glorious Revolution is obvious enough ...'. History is only obvious if our theories prescribe our results in advance of research.

[3] Stone's paper, published only in 1980, had been delivered to a conference in 1976: he used J. P. Kenyon's preliminary paper in N. McKendrick (ed.), *Historical Perspectives* (London, 1974), and wrote before the appearance of Professor Kenyon's *Revolution Principles: the Politics of Party 1689–1720* (Cambridge, 1977). It is not clear that even the Old Guard could sustain their case in the light of Professor Kenyon's full results, except by relocating that case in the period after 1714. Regrettably, Professor Kenyon (*Revolution Principles* pp. 170–208) seemed to leave room for such a relocation. Other historians seek to extend Professor Kenyon's reinstatement of ideological conflicts in 1688–1714 to the period 1714–60 also.

[4] Stone, 'The Results of the English Revolutions', pp. 68–70.

lives, liberty and estates than in eighteenth-century England'.[5] Indeed, there was little other than property for political theory to be about: religion, according to Stone, was now a joke; the defeat of the '15 'put an end, once and for all, to the prolonged disputes about the succession which had been one of the most divisive issues since 1688'.[6]

The much-celebrated notion of political stability in early-Hanoverian England, classically formulated in the mid 1960s, rested initially on the notion (until then unchallenged) of a Lockeian ideological consensus. The alternative idea that political discourse was conducted rather within a generally prevalent neo-Harringtonian idiom,[7] underpinning a Court v. Country polarity, was a major advance: it explained, and identified, conflict and division where the Lockeian consensus had predicted non-party, or single-party, tranquillity. But, for the period after 1714 at least, some political historians soon succeeded in appropriating the neo-Harring-tonian thesis and using it to defend assumptions very similar to those which Locke had been used to defend. Conflicts were henceforth minor ones over the working of a largely agreed constitution, argued one school of his-torians, not major ones over basic issues of principle.[8] The supremacy of commercial, bourgeois, secularising values could still be maintained. It seemed natural to suppose that it was metropolitan, monarchical departures from this Whig consensus which, after the 1760s, provoked America's bid for independence, and a fuller realisation of Whig-individualist values, naturally demanded and inevitably achieved by the common man, which ed to English reforms in 1828–32.

The Old Guard history of the Stuart and Hanoverian periods was thus based on two linked assumptions which parliamentary historians in each field were the first to collide with and deny: that there was a revolution just waiting to happen in the 1640s (and, one might add, the 1680s, 1790s and 1810s), but no possibility of a revolution in the 1710s or 1740s: the '15 and the '45 were irrelevancies. The dismissal of Jacobitism was thus of peculiar polemical importance to Old Guard historians. Moreover, a certain account of the *direction* of social change had to be upheld.[9] There was

[5] *Ibid.*, pp. 71, 74.
[6] *Ibid.*, pp. 73–4, 87.
[7] It was principally devised, and introduced into the English debate from the late 1960s, by Professor J. G. A. Pocock, one of the scholars who stood outside the sociological categories employed in this book.
[8] E.g. H. T. Dickinson, *Liberty and Property: Political Ideology in Eighteenth Century England* (London, 1977), pp. 121–5.
[9] Cf.: 'it is generally held that there is little choice over the direction of change and that what is at stake is normally the pace of change': John Cannon, *Parliamentary Reform 1640–1832* (Cambridge, 1973), p. 260. The extensive implications of this dictum deserve careful consideration. For Professor Cannon's working-out of those implications, see pp. 158–60 below.

something profoundly wrong with Charles I's regime, they assumed; but, despite its corruption, the Whig ascendancy under the first two Georges was fundamentally sound: in 1714, Britannia set her face to the future. It was a bourgeois, commercial, contractarian and ultimately industrial–democratic future: divine-right doctrines were, by definition, an irrelevance to it, and could therefore be ignored.

Exactly when 'the future' arrived was curiously vague. Various estimates were available. Most of them, however, rested on a two-phase theory of the English past, whether in respect of the history of political thought or of the economy: an implied or explicit contrast between the 'world we have lost' and the world we now have. Some historians located this transition in the 1640s; others in the Glorious Revolution; others again in the Industrial Revolution. Some were frankly muddled about the date. All, however, wished partly to celebrate, partly to denigrate, 'the liberal bourgeois creed that emerged during this, the birth of bourgeois civilisation as we now know it'. One historian of political theory placed it confidently in the Hanoverian era:

Between 1760 and 1800 England was fundamentally transformed by the Industrial Revolution. All across England's 'green and pleasant land' were rising 'dark satanic mills'. These mills did more than mar the aesthetic landscape, they brought in their wake a new set of values and a new ideology – the values of the middle-class factory owners and managers, bourgeois values. Ultimately in the nineteenth century this ideology would triumph; the bourgeoisie would topple the aristocracy, and traditional society would give way to liberal capitalist society. In the late eighteenth century the battle lines were formed. Middle-class ideology was the challenger. It was radical and progressive; it called for changes to liberate and unshackle the individual still bound by traditional restrictions.[10]

Such assumptions relied on being largely self-evident: they could scarcely survive a detailed attempt to test them. The response of Old Guard historians to sophisticated political history was therefore dismissive in both periods. The publication of the 1628 debates, 'demonstrating a concerted and planned effort to establish [individual] liberties', announced Stone, 'effectively disposes of the revisionist view that there was no concerted opposition to the Crown before 1640'. 'The demands for individual liberty for *the men of property* lay behind the angry debates in 1628 over the Petition

---

[10] Isaac Kramnick, 'Children's Literature and Bourgeois Ideology: Observations on Culture and Industrial Capitalism in the Later Eighteenth Century', in Perez Zagorin (ed.), *Culture and Politics From Puritanism to the Enlightenment* (Berkeley, 1980), pp. 204–5. Cf. p. 208: '... Dissenters made up only 7 per cent of the population compared to over 90 per cent that were Anglicans. But it was this tiny 7 per cent that was at the heart of the industrial and bourgeois revolution that was transforming England', etc., etc. It is rough justice to single out one author to illustrate this position: scores of textbooks and monographs echoed these beliefs.

of Right.'[11] One school of historians of Hanoverian England equally took up this paranoid identification of mainstream Whig ideology with the material self-interest of 'men of property', based on Stone's confident knowledge that the developments in public credit and finance generally known as the Financial Revolution 'would certainly not have taken place if the Whigs had not won in 1688–89'.[12]

It was an interpretation which could be traced back many decades; but it received its most scholarly formulation relatively recently. Professor C. B. Macpherson, for example, had outlined a seven-point model of man in capitalist society. Political theories were powerful, he argued, to the extent that they recognised and incorporated these assumptions. They contained, however, 'one flaw': the failure, shared by Hobbes, 'to see that the market society generated a degree of class cohesion which made possible a viable political authority without a self-perpetuating soverign body'.[13] Macpherson's analysis brilliantly demonstrated the close relationship of liberal and Marxist premises about human motivation (as well as the more disreputable strategy by which Marxists have exploited gullible liberals); but it showed too that, in order to progress beyond that model, we must recognise in it not just *one* flaw but a whole series of flaws. The model of the atomised, acquisitive individual, dealing with others only through secularised market relations regulated by self-interest, is disastrously inadequate as an account of how real men behaved in real societies, as real historians ultimately discerned.

A seldom-defended assumption of several schools of historians of political thought was thus that the English utilitarian–contractarian tradition, stretching back through John Stuart Mill and James Mill to Bentham and Locke and perhaps beyond, simply provided a more or less accurate practical understanding of how men think and behave: systems of ideas (and political or social institutions) at odds with this tradition were

[11] Stone, 'The Results of the English Revolutions', pp. 34, 101; italics added. Whether Professor Stone's summary is correct may be judged by readers of R. C. Johnson *et al.* (eds.), *Commons Debates 1628* (New Haven, Conn., 1977–8).

[12] Stone, 'The Results of the English Revolutions', p. 42. One is sometimes tempted to envy historians whose ideologies confer on them this sort of privileged access to the past. There are, in fact, good grounds for thinking that the so-called Financial Revolution of the 1690s represented an extension of important innovations during later-Stuart 'absolute' rule: see Howard Tomlinson, 'Financial and Administrative Developments in England, 1660–88', in J. R. Jones (ed.), *The Restored Monarchy 1660–1688* (London, 1979), pp. 94–117.

[13] C. B. Macpherson, *The Political Theory of Possessive Individualism: Hobbes to Locke* (Oxford, 1962), pp. 263–5. The implications of these assumptions become clear at the end of the book, pp. 271–7. Modern liberal–democratic states cannot possibly survive, predicted the professor. Given an ordinary degree of rationality, the individual must now yield allegiance to the socialist world-state. The failure of this millennium to materialise since 1962 constitutes another test (if one were needed) of the 'liberal–democratic' model as an appropriate characterisation of western societies.

therefore *self-evidently* unrealistic and *obviously* imposed upon mankind by an act of tyranny which would eventually prove intolerable. Rebellion was presented as a natural, but insignificant, response – a mere trigger to the weightier business of revolution.

In the realm of social structure, this was countered by Dr Laslett's demonstration of the continuing force of those familial and patriarchal forms which provided the vocabulary for the political theory of Sir Robert Filmer and many of his contemporaries. In the field of party-political history, too, Sir Lewis Namier had been led to that author for an account of the most general premises of the late-eighteenth-century State: 'Correct perception of a psychological fact underlay Sir Robert Filmer's theory ... in eighteenth-century England, the King was still a real factor in Administration.'[14] In similar fashion, Professor Moore was led to a critique of James Mill in order to establish a more realistic framework for the reconstruction of early- and mid-nineteenth-century English politics.[15] Thirdly, in the realm of history of political thought, revisionists came to dispense with the idea that Locke (or even, in some presentations, Harrington) had swept the board clean of their opponents and engineered a homogeneous idiom of political discourse from which Burke was an isolated reaction, somehow 'irrational' in his rejection of self-evident positivist truth.

### RADICALISM: A COMMON THREAD?

In chronological terms, the Old Guard theory rested on an implied or explicit view of the great contrast between the world before and after 1688 (or 1642, or 1714); revisionist historians sought to test this implausible element in the argument. One route to an understanding of the relation between the two eras might be through an appreciation of the (presumably tightly coherent) visions of those who sought to bring about a transition from the first to the second by undermining the established order: a history, in other words, of what is presumed to be a single phenomenon, anachronistically labelled 'radicalism'. The problem is that the century 1660–1760 witnessed almost nothing to which the modern 'radical' has wished to accord that title. Revolution in our sense of the word, if it happened at all, was not planned.[16]

---

[14] Sir Lewis Namier, *England in the Age of the American Revolution* (2nd edn, London, 1961), pp. 26–9. I did not recall Namier's passage when I discussed Filmer's surviving influence in *English Society 1688–1832* (Cambridge, 1985). Writing in the late 1920s, Namier was unable wholly to free himself from the old assumption that in some sense Locke had refuted Filmer. His intuition is all the more remarkable.

[15] D. C. Moore, *The Politics of Deference* (Hassocks, 1976), pp. 420–47.

[16] There was, of course, a considerable potential for *rebellion*, initially republican, later Jacobite, finally Jacobin. In the early part of the century revisionist historians have so focussed on the Jacobite option that the republican challenge is, perhaps, in danger of

The Old Guard solution was a familiar one: radicalism was really there all the time, only one can't see it. It goes underground; but its causes and essence remain the same. The Levellers and Diggers of the 1640s came to the surface again, reincarnated as the English Jacobins of the 1790s (with, perhaps, a brief anticipation in the Wilkesite disturbances). Meanwhile, justified resentment must have simmered below the surface. A further problem then became easy to resolve: subversive agitation is clearly present in the 1790s and after *c.*1817, but the intervening period offered an awkward gap. Of course, the revolutionary tradition must have gone underground once more.[17]

The idea of an 'underground' radicalism is curiously reminiscent of that other standby of a certain cohort of historians, the 'underlying' cause. A social anthropologist might even detect echoes of much older ideas: dying and rising gods, or that folk hero, the king 'who is not dead, but sleepeth' (presumably in some underground place) and whose re-emergence will signal a radical regeneration of society. After 1660, in one such account, the sects were obliged

to combine political quietism with a kind of slumbering Radicalism ... which might, in any more hopeful context, break into fire once more ... one feels often that the dormant seeds of political Radicalism lie within [Dissent], ready to germinate whenever planted in a beneficent and hopeful social context ... Even in the darkest war years the democratic impulse can still be felt at work beneath the surface ... It was not until 1811 that the underground revealed itself again ...[18]

Such an argument was exceedingly useful for historians: it was wholly untestable.

It was, therefore, used in several areas to cover the shortcomings of Old Hat and Old Guard arguments. The 'constitutional demands' of the early-Stuart House of Commons were 'clearly innovatory and aggressive', believed Lawrence Stone; only one can't see them. 'The winning of the initiative by the House of Commons was a radical step achieved under the

being underestimated. But, as I argue elsewhere, the republican Commonwealthmen were very far from being social levellers: our own preoccupations with social engineering are not a sufficient account of rebellion in the 'old society'.

[17] Much damage was done to this part of the argument by J. R. Dinwiddy in his debate with J. L. Baxter and F. K. Donnelly, *P&P* 64 (1974), 113–35. The subsequent debate has been extensive, but see especially F. K. Donnelly, 'Ideology and Early English Working-Class History: Edward Thompson and His Critics', *Social History* 1 (1976), 219–38; John Dinwiddy, 'Luddism and Politics in the Northern Counties', *Social History* 4 (1979), 33–63. This argument was conducted in isolation from the seventeenth-century Old Guard's scenario of an underground radicalism between 1660 and the 1790s; but the idea of an 'underground' in the 1800s owes most of its force to the claims made for the wider thesis.

[18] E. P. Thompson, *The Making of the English Working Class* (1963; Harmondsworth, 1968), pp. 32, 39, 199, 529.

smokescreen of the conservative ideology of a return to the past.'[19] Mr
E. P. Thompson grappled with a similar problem: how do we explain
eighteenth-century social conflicts in class terms if contemporaries were as
yet innocent of the category of 'class'? His answer was the expected one:
class struggle was really there all the time, though we can't observe class in
its nineteenth-century form. We have class struggle without class.

There is very articulate resistance to the ruling ideas and institutions of society in
the seventeenth and nineteenth centuries: hence historians expect to analyse these
societies in some terms of social conflict. In the eighteenth century resistance is less
articulate ... One must therefore supply the articulation, in part by de-coding the
evidence of behaviour ... Again and again, when examining eighteenth-century
behaviour one finds it necessary to 'de-code' this behaviour and to disclose invisible
rules of action...[20]

To believe in these invisible phenomena was an act of faith, not of
scholarship. Indeed, of faith misplaced. Such arguments echo the scene in
*Brideshead Revisited* when the unspeakable Rex Mottram, determined to
marry Lady Julia Flyte, takes instruction in the Roman Catholic faith.
Father Mowbray has a difficult time:

Then again I asked him: 'Supposing the Pope looked up and saw a cloud and said
"It's going to rain", would that be bound to happen?' 'Oh, yes, Father.' 'But
supposing it didn't?' He thought a moment and said, 'I suppose it would be sort of
raining spiritually, only we were too sinful to see it.'

Some more recent historians are (and, of course, early-Hanoverian Whig
oligarchs were) too sinful to see an eighteenth-century 'radicalism', too.

The known invisibility of radical ideology was an effective reason for not
searching for it too hard. Yet even the politically respectable had a
powerful reason for not investigating 'radicalism' in the century 1660–
1760. If 'true radicalism' arose only in the late eighteenth century;[21] if,
thanks to Wilkes and the American colonists, 'the several strains of
eighteenth-century reformism' reached 'maturity' in the 1760s and 70s,[22]
their early-Hanoverian forms were presumably immature, and their
exponents therefore unworthy of serious study. To a remarkable extent,
they were *not* studied: the years 1714–60 especially were until recently the
darkest of dark ages in the historiography of English political thought.[23]

[19] Lawrence Stone, *The Causes of the English Revolution 1529–1642* (London, 1972), p. 93. The
allusion was to the classic Old Hat parliamentary study, Wallace Notestein's *The Winning
of the Initiative by the House of Commons* (London, 1924).

[20] E. P. Thompson, 'Eighteenth-century English Society: Class Struggle Without Class?',
*Social History* 3 (1978), 150, 154–5.

[21] Christopher Hill, *Reformation to Industrial Revolution* (1967; Harmondsworth, 1980), p. 214.

[22] John Brewer, 'English Radicalism in the Age of George III', in Pocock (ed.), *Three British
Revolutions*, p. 342. The teleology hardly needs to be stressed.

[23] This neglect gave a particular interest to Linda Colley's 'Eighteenth Century English
Radicalism before Wilkes', *TRHS* 31 (1981), 1–19. I could not, however, accept its

The notion that there is a single something called 'the radical tradition' which must be traced, in its adversity, between the English and American *revolutions*, continues to mislead, or to lead only into semantic debates about the application rather than the viability of the 'radical' label.[24] If that terminology only established itself tenuously in the 1820s and more substantially in the 1830s, the attempt to apply it to trace the continuity of 'radicalism' from the 1640s into the next century involves a deliberate act of anachronism, as an early-Stuart historian candidly admitted: 'Used with suitable qualification, anachronism is not only an appropriate tool but a necessary one, if historians are not to reject the cumulative insights of their culture and doom themselves to intellectual irrelevance.'[25] A revisionist must disagree: though we may temporarily use 'radicalism' as a shorthand term, the historian's task is to uncover the very different phenomena which have been obscured by the retrospective application of a blanket label – phenomena each with its appropriate, and seventeenth- or eighteenth-century, name.[26]

The question of methodology links with one of substance: as Professor Zaller noted, some revisionists prefer the title 'The Great Rebellion' for its historical authenticity: 'By a not surprising coincidence, these same historians tend toward the view that an exaggerated significance has been attached to the entire period. This is not untinged, in the writings of some, with the more or less explicit assumption that England would have been just as well off without the "rebellion", if not better.'[27] Political dissent was certainly there, he insisted, though 'muzzled' and therefore re-expressed,

argument in two main respects: (a) the category 'radicalism' is stretched to cover all forms of grass-roots political protest, which divests the term of usefully specific meaning and largely misses the role of ideology; (b) in order to trace such protest chiefly to Tories, the Dissenters are neglected as necessarily loyal to the Hanoverian regime before 1760: this conceals the close relation of subversive ideology with Dissent and, especially, with *heterodox* Dissent. I adopted a very different analysis in *English Society 1688–1832*, chapter 5, 'The Ideological Origins of English Radicalism, 1688–1800'.

[24] It is significant that even non-revisionist historians who use the words *radical* in the early eighteenth century, or *Tory* in the latter part of it, feel the need to enclose them within inverted commas.

[25] Robert Zaller, 'The Continuity of British Radicalism in the Seventeenth and Eighteenth Centuries', *Eighteenth Century Life* 6 (1981), 18. I was not aware of Professor Zaller's most interesting article when I wrote *English Society 1688–1832*; we have adopted very different approaches to a problem which we both recognise.

[26] I tried to begin this process in a schematic and preliminary way in *English Society 1688–1832*. The problems created by the deliberate and acknowledged imposition of an early-nineteenth-century category on much earlier practice are well exemplified by the otherwise admirable research of G. S. De Krey, 'Political Radicalism in London after the Glorious Revolution', *JMH* 55 (1983), 585–617. Dr De Krey defends this transposition in part by appeal to Zaller, 'The Continuity of British Radicalism'.

[27] It would be quite wrong to suggest that revisionists are all scholars with present-day conservative opinions. The ranks of the revisionists include figures of such diverse political opinions as Elton, Russell, Morrill and myself.

encoded, in religious terms: 'Our own secular orientation, and our tendency now to regard heaven as the province of the Right, make it difficult for us to recapture the potency of millennial language, and the extent to which aspirations for a just society were conflated with the vision of a new Jerusalem'. It was rather tiresome of Englishmen to talk so much about religion when they should have been addressing their 'major socio-political issue' – according to Professor Zaller, the 'profound ine-quity' of the distribution of property and 'the existence of a large unpropertied class', and even to go on talking about religion and divine right after 1688 when Professor Zaller knows that political discourse was 'profoundly desacralised, or if one prefers, demystified' by the second, and final, delegitimation of traditional monarchy.[28] Tiresome, too, no doubt, for revisionist historians to insist on listening to them.

Tiresome, but necessary. The task of linking historical interpretations of the seventeenth and eighteenth centuries is an important one; Professor Zaller is to be congratulated on a pioneering attempt. But its successful completion demands that it take as its end-point a model of eighteenth-century politics and ideology very different from that which we inherited from the 1960s. Professor Zaller wrote from the stance of an Old Hat political historian;[29] but his views harmonised with those of a certain school of Church historians, and their arguments too demand reconsider-ation. In the seventeenth and early eighteenth centuries, R. N. Stromberg had written, 'between religious radicalism and socio-political radicalism there is no necessary connexion'.[30] Revisionists now reversed this judge-ment. If the seventeenth century 'began in divine right monarchy and passed through a regicide republic to secular constitutionalism ... pro-ceeded from predestinarian orthodoxy through antinomian free grace to deism and scepticism' in the eighteenth,[31] then the scenario of a purposive and successful seventeenth-century 'radicalism' might stand; but it was this outcome which was called in question by early-Hanoverian historians.

There were, of course, two ways of testing it. One was an investigation of

---

28 Zaller, 'The Continuity of British Radicalism', pp. 18–19, 21–3. The historians mentioned are Elton and Russell: not, perhaps, bad company to find oneself aligned with. It would be interesting to know whom Zaller meant by 'our' and 'us'.

29 See Robert Zaller, *The Parliament of 1621: A Study in Constitutional Conflict* (Berkeley, 1971). It argued a role for Parliament (a strong corporate consciousness, an institutional continuity, a growing control of its own membership and forms of procedure, a self-image as the voice of the nation) for which there was 'no logical end ... but a total assumption of sovereignty, and this was exactly the position to which Parliament was led in the 1640s'.

30 Roland Stromberg, *Religious Liberalism in Eighteenth-Century England* (Oxford, 1954), p. 156. 'Liberalism' is, of course, a misnomer at any time before the 1820s.

31 Zaller, 'The Continuity of British Radicalism', p. 19. The emptiness of Professor Zaller's all-inclusive category is finally revealed at the end of his article (p. 35): 'Radicalism is not a doctrine but the belief that a just society can be achieved by human agency, and the demand that it be done.'

the rationale for the State in the late eighteenth and early nineteenth centuries, which revealed that 'secular constitutionalism' was only a part, and not a self-sufficient part, of the ideology of that social system which was shattered in 1828–32. The other was a deeper understanding of the nature of the radical critique which had brought that disaster about. Historians' assumptions about a great secularisation of politics and political argument in the 1640s, 1680s, 1710s or whatever period was chosen could be dramatically undermined by the discovery that into the 1820s the attack on the establishment was conducted primarily over religious issues and by those men who felt most strongly about them.

What, after all, was liberalism? Like all dominant belief systems, it had succeeded in having itself described retrospectively, in its own (later) terms; Englishmen (and still more, Americans) had never been greatly persuaded by the socialist redescription of it in economic terms. 'Liberal' was still widely taken as synonymous with 'nice', 'tolerant' or even 'centrist', assumptions which completely blocked even the perception that a problem of definition remained unsolved. Even into the 1980s, therefore, a study from the standpoint of political theory could trace the 'beginnings' of liberalism to the Renaissance and Reformation, discover its 'philosophical foundations' in seventeenth-century theorists, and identify the establishment of 'early bourgeois liberalism' in the 'English Revolution' of the 1640s. Liberalism and Whiggery were clearly the same thing; so, of course, thanks to 1688, the eighteenth century witnessed 'Whiggery triumphant'.[32]

Students of this and countless similar studies were never invited to consider the fact, long known to other sorts of historian, that the political concepts of *liberalism* and *radicalism* both came into existence at a particular time, neither earlier nor later, and for specific reasons. To attempt to write the history of *liberalism* before the 1820s is thus, in point of method, akin to attempting to write the history of the eighteenth-century motor car. There were, of course, forms of transport which performed many of the functions which the motor car later performed, the sedan chair among them. Yet to explain the sedan chair as if it were an early version of the motor car, and by implication to condemn it for failing so lamentably to evolve into the motor car, is to turn a modern error of scholarly method into a failure of men in a past society.

[32] Anthony Arblaster, *The Rise and Decline of Western Liberalism* (Oxford, 1984). Evidence for this schema proves chiefly to consist of secondary works by such authors as Harold Laski, R. H. Tawney, Christopher Hill, C. B. Macpherson, A. L. Morton, J. H. Plumb, George Rudé, E. P. Thompson, Douglas Hay, Karl Marx, etc., etc. Yet the modern academic genre of the study of political thought has not penetrated beyond this historical scenario. Even the most perceptive critic of Arblaster's book admitted: 'Most of this is familiar enough and, however much it might be qualified in detail, its broad outlines are scarcely open to serious dispute': John Dunn, 'Liberalism on the Run', *THES* 9 November 1984, p. 15.

To stretch explanatory categories so far that they lose their specific reference and become mere holdalls for our ahistorical assumptions about the eternal nature of human motivation is to condemn us merely to explore the inner landscape of the assumptions and to deny us any perception of a need to locate those assumptions in time. One result of the considerable academic isolation of the historians of different specialisms and periods has indeed been that the attempt to chart the genesis, chronology, teleological impulse and eventual transmutation of very many ideologies – what might be called their historical trajectories – has been a low priority of historians of political thought.[33]

Liberalism and radicalism have been the chief casualties (or, in practical terms, beneficiaries) of an academic unwillingness to attempt to understand the ancien regime in its own terms. For the Old Guard or Old Hat accounts to see British history in the seventeenth and eighteenth centuries as the triumph of liberalism was necessarily to devise an entity of which contemporaries were as yet innocent. Such a creation predictably embodied only the secular priorities of its authors. Placed in its correct historical setting of the 1820s, however, the polemical engagement of liberalism with orthodox political theology became plain. A member of the Oxford intelligentsia explained it in retrospect:

Now by Liberalism I mean false liberty of thought, or the exercise of thought upon matters, in which, from the constitution of the human mind, thought cannot be brought to any successful issue, and therefore is out of place. Among such matters are first principles of whatever kind; and of these the most sacred and momentous are especially to be reckoned the truths of Revelation. Liberalism then is the mistake of subjecting to human judgement those revealed doctrines which are in their nature beyond and independent of it, and of claiming to determine on intrinsic grounds the truth and value of propositions which rest for their reception simply on the external authority of the Divine Word.

Such insights were the achievement of 'the Toryism of Oxford and of the Church of England', believed Newman.[34] The formulation of a secular definition of liberalism by the practical role of the new Liberal party of the 1830s, and the destruction of the theological premises of the ancien regime, were profoundly related both chronologically and conceptually.

---

[33] E.g.: 'It cannot be said that political theorists have yet had much success in explaining the modern historical trajectories of representative democracy or of socialism': John Dunn, *The Politics of Socialism: An Essay in Political Theory* (Cambridge, 1984), p. 94. Perhaps a better understanding of some early-modern aims might shed more light on the failure of these dangerous projectiles to strike many of what we take to be their modern targets.

[34] J. H. Newman, *Apologia Pro Vita Sua* (ed. Martin J. Svaglic, Oxford, 1967), pp. 256, 258. Newman set out his understanding of the specific implications of liberalism in eighteen propositions: for which, see Appendix A below.

## WHAT HAS RELIGION TO DO WITH POLITICS?

A key component of the Old Guard vision had been its resolute insistence on minimising the sacred element in the self-image and rationale of past societies: what they claimed as the triumph of the secular opened the door to utilitarian, and so ultimately economic–reductionist, analysis. Hence the need to argue that 'By 1640 there was not much left of "the divinity that doth hedge a king"'. Of course, 'After the Restoration the clergy and the Tory gentry spoke incessantly of their devotion to the principles of Divine Right and Non-Resistance to a lawful king', but they could not be allowed to win: 'the very stridency of their professions betrays an inner insecurity'. In 1688 they 'abandoned all these notions with a suddenness which suggests that, beneath all the sound and fury, the concept of divinely inspired and ordained monarchy had been dealt an all but irreparable blow by the events of the first half of the century'.[35] Moreover, educated men had been taught 'to think for themselves: they could not easily accept the dictates of kings and bishops'. 'Competing religious ideologies shattered the unquestioning and habit-forming faith of the past.'[36] Orthodox theology and patrician social authority equals dogma produces bigotry demands unthinking acceptance or rational dissent: such was the pattern of prejudice which had hamstrung the scholarship of the Hanoverian era also.

So the notion of a bourgeois revolution had been seemingly salvaged, on the level of ideology. But this argument (like the denial of the importance of Jacobitism) relied on that most dangerous of historical strategies, the unresearched assertion of a negative. To a large extent the Old Guard model of post-1660 or post-1688 England rested only on ignorance of its Anglican, aristocratic, monarchical characteristics.[37] If such patterns were ignored, there seemed to be little else worth attending to, even before the Civil War:

Intellectual historians have often criticised the period for the 'poverty' of its ideology, for the mental blockage its thinkers and politicians displayed when, in an age of apparent constitutional conflict, they were not able to come up with

[35] Stone, *The Causes of the English Revolution*, pp. 90–1. The thesis of the secularisation of early-eighteenth century politics, so opening the way for the reconciliation of Tory and Whig elements in opposition to produce a united Country party equipped with a secular critique of the Walpolian regime, can be traced, for example, in W. A. Speck, *Stability and Strife: England 1714–1760* (London, 1977), pp. 6–7, 87–90, 103–4, 151, 165.

[36] Stone, *The Causes of the English Revolution*, pp. 96, 113; 'the legitimacy of authority depends upon its unquestioning, thoughtless acceptance', p. 100.

[37] E.g. 'there were no claims to the divine right of bishops or of tithes after 1660': Christopher Hill in Pocock (ed.), *Three British Revolutions*, p. 132. It should be unnecessary to say that many such claims continued to be made throughout the English ancien regime. In general terms, it might be suggested that within a Christian mental universe a right would almost necessarily be a divine right.

conflicting ideologies which made sense of their conflicting positions. The constant harping of contemporaries, whether members of the court or of the 'country', on 'unity', 'balance', and 'harmony' accorded ill with the presuppositions of a generation of historians nurtured on Whiggish ideas of a momentous conflict between prerogative and the ancient constitution. But if the notion of inexorable constitutional confrontation is defused, then the ideology begins to make sense.

Indeed, the 'legitimism and deference' of such protest as there was, and men's general acquiescence in direct and unambiguous royal orders suggest in both Charles I and most of his subjects a view of the moral weight of legitimate commands: attitudes, in other words, 'closely akin to passive obedience'.[38] In purely parliamentary terms, such views generated assumptions of unity, harmony and co-operation, not purposive struggle for primacy on the part of King, Lords or Commons.[39]

If, as Harrington famously remarked, 'The dissolution of this government caused the war, not the war the dissolution of this government', we might reasonably expect to find a mounting pressure of revolutionary, or at least anti-monarchical, ideology in England up to 1642. If such a model of social change were valid, then the same requirement would have to be made of the years before 1832. If neither can be found, then an explanation of the Civil War (or, we must add, of the Reform Bill) in terms of long-term social collapse is superfluous: 'simple short-term causes will suffice', even if those causes were as dramatic as defeat in war and the actions of an invading army.[40]

To put it in Stone's terminology, 'triggers' might be of far greater causal weight than 'preconditions' or 'precipitants': indeed, only once events have been triggered can we retrospectively classify previous events as preconditions and precipitants at all. To put it in our terminology: the more appropriate category is not revolution, but rebellion. This is equally true in the realm of political thought. Was a revolutionary ideology propagated in England before 1642? Partly the question seems to be a semantic one, but enough is now evident to say that the main thrust of seditious propaganda was not against monarchical government, the nobility, structures of economic ownership and control or a hierarchical social order as such, but against the Church of England and its episcopal organization.[41]

The political languages 'instinctively spoken' by early-seventeenth-century Englishmen were those of 'natural hierarchy, of ancient custom, of

[38] Derek Hirst, 'Court, Country and Politics before 1629', in Kevin Sharpe (ed.), *Faction and Parliament* (Oxford, 1978), pp. 124, 129–30; Hirst, 'The Privy Council and Problems of Enforcement in the 1620s', *JBS* 18 no. 1 (1978), 64–6.

[39] Sharpe, in *Faction and Parliament*, pp. 14–18; Robert Ashton, *The English Civil War: Conservatism and Revolution 1603–1649* (London, 1978), pp. 3–42, 98–126.

[40] Paul Christianson, 'The Causes of the English Revolution: A Reappraisal', *JBS* 15 no. 2 (1976), 47.

[41] Christianson, 'The Causes of the English Revolution'.

apocalyptic election and of prudent submission to providence'. In such a world,

republicanism in England was a language, not a programme. It is notorious that the historic constitution was not overthrown, nor the King executed, because men had conceived the desire to have a republic, in any of the various senses of that term; rather, the several doctrines which may be called republican – of which Harrington's classical republicanism was one – were articulated as men came to face the fact that the historic constitution had collapsed, and to formulate various moral, political and theoretical problems with which its collapse confronted them.

Rather, republicanism was relevant to Englishmen at that time not least in contributing to 'the quasi-millennial purpose of establishing a society whose godliness should be chiefly known by its repudiation of all forms of ecclesiastical authority'.[42]

The undervaluation of such ecclesiastical phenomena is a reflection of modern assumptions that religion is a small, specialised and insulated area of national life. Yet not even successful rebellion shattered this intellectual nexus in the seventeenth century: we are not entitled, on the available evidence, to associate a collapse of monarchical divine right with the events either of 1640–2 or of 1688–9 and 1714. Stone's case, like Plumb's, rested in part on the claim that 'Divine right had been transferred from Whitehall to Westminster'[43] and swiftly dissipated thereafter; but, here again, it is implausible that both can be right. Adopting a different set of categories, we might say that rebellion preceded revolution, not vice versa; and here too the priority of religious issues in the 1820s, and their tactical importance in producing parliamentary reform in 1828–32, should now warn us against seeing the democratic, semi-revolutionary outcome as the result of an ideologically structured campaign which had the 1832 Act as its appropriate or even inevitable goal. In the approach to 1832, as in the periods 1604–29 and 1714–60, parliamentary history and the study of political thought suffered from being pursued as largely separate disciplines, by different groups of historians.

If those who took up arms in 1642 were those who felt most strongly about religion, what were the religious issues? An important analogy with the Provincial case as initially formulated was provided by an account of the ecclesiastical disturbances of Charles I's reign as the result of a

[42] J. G. A. Pocock (ed.), *The Political Works of James Harrington* (Cambridge, 1977), Introduction, pp. 15, 42. I would stress this as a reason for the republication of Harrington's *Works* by freethinkers from John Toland (1700) onwards (see *Works*, pp. 77–99 for Harrington's 'polemic against clericalism' in the 1650s). 'There is a Socinian streak in Harrington, as there is in Hobbes', observes Pocock: 'neither saw much for the Son or the Spirit to do in a civil commonwealth which the Father had not done already' (p. 109; cf. p. 143).

[43] Christianson, 'The Causes of the English Revolution', p. 51; Stone, *The Causes of the English Revolution*, p. 90.

Court-sponsored Arminianism, championed by a small group of higher clergy, taken up by the King, and imposed on a recalcitrant and finally rebellious nation whose Calvinism was universal and deeply rooted.[44] This scenario was a welcome alternative to reductionist explanations of an initiative-seizing Puritanism, conceived as the economically purposeful ideology of a rising bourgeoisie. But while recognising the reality and force of the theological props to princely absolutism, it does not follow that Calvinist elements in the Church occupied a merely static and quietist position: it was they (and Roman Catholics) who were armed with a doctrine of the right of resistance, and it was resistance turning into rebellion which was at issue in Scotland and Ireland in the 1630s and 40s and at many points subsequently.[45]

Nor does it seem that Calvinist views on predestination provide the sole index to the nature of the *status quo* under James I: the Anglican religious heritage was diverse. Religious issues, too, existed within a wide strategic context, and the question of war with Spain and the defence of European Protestantism in the 1620s gave the rivalry of Calvinist and Arminian an application which they were to lack in the 1630s, until tactical political conflict again drew them to the forefront. 'From this perspective', concluded a more recent student, 'it is difficult to discern any doctrinal high road to civil war; and the "rise of Arminianism" looks like a Puritan alibi for repeated failure to impose rigid predestinarian doctrines on the Church of England.'[46]

Such enquiries were part of the wider attempt to disengage discussion of political ideology from that preoccupation with questions of property which was established as normative by such texts as R. H. Tawney's *Religion and the Rise of Capitalism* (1926) and C. B. Macpherson's *The Political Theory of Possessive Individualism: Hobbes to Locke* (1962). In both centuries, there were false starts. The reconstruction of political ideologies has been a field for some ingenious but speculative inventions. Professor Farnell's claim to have discovered a school of Livian republicans among parliamentarians from the end of Elizabeth's reign to the 1640s,[47] possessing an ideology justifying the leading role of the peerage, was among the

---

[44] Cf. especially Nicholas Tyacke, 'Puritanism, Arminianism and Counter-Revolution', in Conrad Russell (ed.), *The Origins of the English Civil War* (London, 1973), pp. 119–43. It was persecution of Calvinists in the 1630s which, in 'addition to creating widespread resentment of the episcopal hierarchy ... generated a Puritan militancy which in the early 1640s was to erupt in the shape of presbyterianism and congregationalism' (p. 139).

[45] Cf. J. F. McGregory and B. Reay (eds.), *Radical Religion in the English Revolution* (Oxford, 1984).

[46] Peter White, 'The Rise of Arminianism Reconsidered', *P&P* 101 (1983), 54.

[47] J. E. Farnell, 'The Social and Intellectual Basis of London's Role in the English Civil Wars', *JMH* 49 (1977), 641–60.

more fanciful offshoots of early-Stuart revisionism,[48] but was curiously akin to Professor Browning's attempt to construct an ideological battle in the early-Hanoverian period between Catonists and Ciceronians.[49] Ingenious, but wide of the mark. Both constructs were refreshing attempts to break from a too-familiar agenda of issues – 'liberty' under the early Stuarts, the oligarchic defence of property under the early Hanoverians – by recovering a quite different currency of debate. But in both periods this was more successfully done by a renewed attention to religion *as religion* rather than as a sublimation of something else.

Historians in the last decade thus found themselves drawn to challenge a major premiss of Whiggish historiography: the idea that English life and thought after 1688 were quickly secularised, swept by the waves of Lockeian empiricism and that scepticism and rationalism which were so often held to characterise 'the eighteenth century'. Text after text, for many decades, had taken this for granted. But was it true? Since historians were so sure of the answer, very few of them had sought to test the theological temperature of England's ancien regime. That amiable patriarch of ecclesiastical history, the Rev. Professor Norman Sykes, had really only apologised for the Georgian Church without challenging the interpretative framework, established by its enemies, within which it was still appraised. In respect of organisation, things were not quite as bad as they were painted, he argued; and eighteenth-century spirituality was characterised by a sane and pervasive Latitudinarianism which, to modern readers of Sykes, could not easily be distinguished from common human decency. The 'quiet pieties' of that age had been 'overlooked in much noisy denunciation of its infidelity'.[50] It was a weak apology. Latitudinarian meant lukewarm, inferred most subsequent historians.

This message was only reinforced, from a North American and Nonconformist viewpoint, in the works of a Dissenting minister, G. R. Cragg: 'simplicity and reason were establishing a virtual tyranny over men's minds' even in the late seventeenth century, and one result was a 'gradual decline toward mediocrity' in orthodox theological discussion. Consequently 'By the beginning of the eighteenth century we are already on the threshold of modern times', so that in England, as elsewhere, 'religious hostilities gave way to a growing awareness of class divisions'. The advance

---

[48] Devastatingly challenged in J. H. Hexter, 'Power Struggle, Parliament and Liberty in Early Stuart England', *JMH* 50 (1978), pp. 22–4, and Derek Hirst, 'Unanimity in the Commons, Aristocratic Intrigues, and the Origins of the English Civil War', *JMH* 50 (1978), 63–4.

[49] Reed Browning, *Political and Constitutional Ideas of the Court Whigs* (Baton Rouge, 1982); cf. the present author's remarks, *HJ* 27 (1984), 773–88.

[50] Norman Sykes, *Church and State in England in the XVIIIth Century* (Cambridge, 1934), p. 282.

of scepticism meant the triumph of Reason over Authority until the reaction of the Romantics at the end of the century.[51]

Such a perspective was given a continued currency by Professor Cragg's widely circulated writings, but it was not a new perspective. Just as the Victorians' models and categories of parliamentary parties had been carried back and anachronistically applied to the eighteenth century (and even, by Gardiner and others, to the seventeenth), so too the party alignments of Victorian churchmanship had been projected on to an earlier age. The Victorian conception of 'High Church' was one largely drawn from the Oxford Movement: applied to the world before 1832, few enough men could be found to fit it. Victorian and Edwardian historians inferred a pervasive, vacuous Latitudinarianism: with a few exceptions (J. H. Overton, J. Wickham Legg) their chosen categories prevented them from appreciating the profoundly conservative, theologically orthodox and devotionally viable nature of that pre-Tractarian High Churchmanship which was widely and deeply entrenched as the Georgian norm.

Professor Cragg's was the account of liturgical practice and theological argument which had prevailed, in effect, ever since the publication of Leslie Stephen's militantly agnostic *History of English Thought in the Eighteenth Century* (1876). Stephen, indeed, makes clear the role of this account within a particular form of social polemic, still current in the writings of the Old Guard as a hangover from 1930s atheism.[52] As an account of religion it had never been systematically challenged. Scattered studies existed which suggested (to those few who were aware of them) a vital and continuing role for the Church at parochial level, despite falling

---

[51] G. R. Cragg, *From Puritanism to the Age of Reason: A Study of Changes in Religious Thought within the Church of England 1660–1700* (Cambridge, 1950), pp. 9–11; *idem, The Church and the Age of Reason 1648–1789* (London, 1960), p. 19; *idem, Reason and Authority in the Eighteenth Century* (Cambridge, 1964). The second of these works formed volume 4 of *The Pelican History of the Church*: this imprint ensured that it has been the most widely circulated interpretation of its subject in the last quarter of a century. The extent to which the perspectives argued against in the present book are quintessentially Nonconformist and North American deserves consideration.

[52] The survival of this idiom is well exemplified by Christopher Hill, 'Irreligion in the "Puritan" Revolution', in McGregor and Reay (eds.), *Radical Religion in the English Revolution*, pp. 191–211. Hill treats 'anticlerical' and 'heterodox' as virtually equivalent to 'secular', which obscures more than it explains: 'Though the motives of the sectaries were religious, the objective content of their demands was secularist', etc., etc. Some men undoubtedly adopted genuinely materialist–secularist views: Hill has not shown them to be more than a small minority. Only a different quantification could validate his argument that 'Neither the causes nor the outcome of the Revolution were primarily religious' (pp. 196, 209). Hill's model of revolution entails that 'When the lid is taken off, what bubbles out must have been there all the time' (p. 210): like the theory of 'underground radicalism', this thesis is in principle impossible to verify. As stated, it is at least a *non sequitur*.

numbers of communicants.[53] The results of such works were sometimes noticed in passing, as exceptions to and deviations from a somnolent norm; but it has now occurred to scholars that these results, organised and given focus, point to a quite different norm.[54]

These older attitudes, drawn from an inadequate understanding of developments in theology, had explicitly meshed with the Namierite undervaluation of parliamentary parties. Roland Stromberg, writing in 1954, believed that 'It was notoriously difficult to tell a Whig from a Tory' in the period 1688–1750. 'By 1720 the question of the succession was placed beyond dispute; Jacobitism had died save as a romantic pose ... the old High Church dogma of divine right had become an anachronism.'[55] The early-Hanoverian revisionists' reinstatement of parliamentary parties thus inevitably led to a questioning of the assumption of secularisation in the field of political ideology, still current into the 1980s in the vision of some historians of previous generations.

Upsetting the assumption of the secularisation of the establishment had its effect in turn on our understanding of the nature of, and motivations for, those who attacked the establishment. That the secularised concept of 'radicalism' did not emerge until the 1820s and 30s reminds us that the

[53] One might recall a handful of works over many decades: T. T. Carter (ed.), *Undercurrents of Church Life in the Eighteenth Century* (London, 1899); J. Wickham Legg, *English Church Life from the Restoration to the Tractarian Movement* (London, 1914); D. McClatchey, *Oxfordshire Clergy 1777–1869* (Oxford, 1960); C. J. Stranks, *Anglican Devotion: Studies in the Spiritual Life of the Church of England between the Reformation and the Oxford Movement* (London, 1961); Horton Davies, *Worship and Theology in England 1690–1850: From Watts and Wesley to Maurice* (Princeton, 1961); Arthur Warne, *Church and Society in Eighteenth-Century Devon* (Newton Abbot, 1969); James Downey, *The Eighteenth Century Pulpit: A Study of the Sermons of Butler, Berkeley, Sterne, Whitefield and Wesley* (Oxford, 1969); Eamon Duffy, 'Primitive Christianity Revived: Religious Renewal in Augustan England', *SCH* 14 (1978), 287–300; Tina Isaacs, 'The Anglican Hierarchy and the Reformation of Manners 1688–1738', *JEH* 33 (1982), 391–411. Such works did not find their way on to the agenda as far as most historians of the period were concerned.

[54] John Redwood, *Reason, Ridicule and Religion: The Age of Enlightenment in England 1660–1750* (London, 1976); F. C. Mather, 'Georgian Churchmanship Reconsidered: Some Variations in Anglican Public Worship 1714–1830', *JEH* 36 (1985), 255–83; Salim Rashid, 'Christianity and the Growth of Liberal Economics', *Journal of Religious History* 12 (1983), 221–32. Professor Mather is engaged on a study of late-eighteenth-century High Churchmanship centreing on Bishop Samuel Horsley. See also D. R. Hirschberg, 'The Government and Church Patronage in England, 1660–1760', *JBS* 20 no. 1 (1980), 109–38; Françoise Deconinck-Brossard, *Vie Politique, Sociale et Religieuse en Grande-Bretagne d'après les Sermons Prêchés ou Publiés dans le Nord de l'Angleterre 1738–1760* (2 vols., Paris, 1984); and the many writings on Methodism of Dr John Walsh.

[55] Stromberg, *Religious Liberalism in Eighteenth-Century England*, chapter 9, 'The Secularisation of Politics'. This view of theology harmonised with a 'social change' theory: early-Hanoverian England was ruled by 'a conservative oligarchy' of 'the new bourgeois potentates' who stifled moves towards democracy, etc., etc. (pp. 122–3). Cf. Christopher Hill, *Some Intellectual Consequences of the English Revolution* (London, 1980), p. 87: 'With the eighteenth-century enlightenment we are in the world of secular bourgeois thought', etc. etc.

conceptual framework of disaffection continued for many decades to be provided by theology.[56] Even the paradigmatic status of 1789 as the defining instance of a new, wholly secular model of revolution is now in doubt.[57] The social-structural interpretations of the French and English revolutions, as we have seen in chapter 3, were nineteenth-century inventions. In the 1790s, even observers fully aware of the importance of events in Paris could analyse them in terms which seem more appropriate to our revived understanding of England's 'Puritan Revolution'. Burke described the French revolution as quite different from those 'which have been brought about in Europe, upon principles merely political. *It is a Revolution of doctrine and theoretic dogma.* It has a much greater resemblance to those changes which have been made upon religious grounds, in which a spirit of proselytism makes an essential part.' So immense were its implications that Burke could only liken the French Revolution to the Reformation.[58]

### WHY DOES JACOBITISM MATTER?

The Old Guard, then, still applied similar assumptions in both centuries. Lawrence Stone's model of social and constitutional change equally entailed a secularising view of political ideology: 'no sensible man could take [James I's divine right] claims too seriously', he believed.[59] The framework of assumptions which surrounds parliamentary history is profoundly altered, however, if we take such ideologies seriously in either period. It has become possible to do this in the seventeenth century thanks to the work of scholars including Daly, Greenleaf, Laslett, Pocock, and Schochet; now, stemming from research into parliamentary politics, the debate over Jacobitism in the period 1714–60[60] seems likely to be the route to a more extensive reconstruction of eighteenth-century ideologies also.

Historians had long written, with incurious complacency, about a Lockeian consensus which had been swiftly established after 1688 and which ensured that eighteenth-century England was devoid of funda-

[56] As I argued in *English Society 1688–1832* (1985). Dr John Gascoigne was independently working on the same question, and came to similar conclusions in 'Anglican Latitudinarianism and Political Radicalism in the late Eighteenth Century', *History* 71 (1986), 22–38. I was not persuaded that 'Latitudinarian' was a usefully specific category, however, and had sought to discover its theological roots. The social location of Unitarians is further explored in John Seed, 'Gentleman Dissenters: The Social and Political Meanings of Rational Dissent in the 1770s and 1780s', *HJ* 28 (1985), 299–325.

[57] Cf. François Furet, *Interpreting the French Revolution* (Cambridge, 1981).

[58] *Thoughts on French Affairs* (1791), in *The Works of the Right Honourable Edmund Burke* (12 vols., London, 1887), vol. 4, pp. 318–19.

[59] Stone, *The Causes of the English Revolution*, p. 94; quoted Christianson, 'The Causes of the English Revolution', p. 53.

[60] Cf. the works discussed in Appendix B below.

mental ideological conflict. Namier's model of parliamentary alignments harmonised with these assumptions about ideology, and provided further reasons for not testing them. Among historians of political theory, the re-examination of Locke himself in this respect effectively began (and, as far as his subsequent significance in the century after his death was concerned, almost ended) with research published by John Dunn in 1969.[61] Mr Dunn portrayed a Locke whose *Two Treatises of Government* were first ignored, then misunderstood (Englishmen failing to perceive their profoundly subversive implications), then relegated to the harmless role of platitudinous defences of the existing order.

This dethronement of Locke represented a considerable gain in understanding, yet seemed to offer little help in understanding the nature or explaining the cause of those bitter practical conflicts which scholars in the 1960s were recovering, especially in the period 1689–1714. To provide one explanation of a theoretical impetus behind these conflicts was, in particular, the achievement of Professor J. G. A. Pocock. He took up Professor Caroline Robbins' account of the continuing influence of a set of Englishmen imbued with a classical republican ideal (men such as James Harrington, Andrew Marvell, John Milton, Algernon Sidney)[62] and modified it in the light of two criticisms:

Because she identifies the ideas she studies with a chain of intellectual groups arising to the left of Whig statesmen and constantly criticising them in the name of their own official ideals, she does not take account of the role in the history of these ideas of men like Bolingbroke, and so does not see that they can often better be understood in a Court–Country context than in a Tory–Whig or a Whig official–Whig intellectual one. Secondly ... she does not do all that might have been done to study their assumptions or consider them as a commentary on English politics which entailed certain intellectual consequences for those who adopted it. Something can be done, I believe, to remedy these deficiencies, if we go back to the fountainhead – that is, if we go back to Harrington, who is in a special sense the central figure among the 'classical republicans' of 'the Whig canon', and trace from his time the descent of certain ideas, the uses that were made of them, and the changes which they consequently underwent.[63]

---

[61] Principally John Dunn, *The Political Thought of John Locke: An Historical Account of the Argument of the 'Two Treatises of Government'* (Cambridge, 1969), and 'The Politics of Locke in England and America in the Eighteenth Century', in J. W. Yolton (ed.), *John Locke: Problems and Perspectives* (Cambridge, 1969). Political historians were slow to draw the moral from Mr Dunn's work for the period after 1714. Cf. also Martyn P. Thompson, 'The Reception of Locke's Two Treatises of Government 1690–1705', *Political Studies* 24 (1976), 184–91.

[62] Caroline Robbins, *The Eighteenth-Century Commonwealthman* (Cambridge, Mass., 1959).

[63] J. G. A. Pocock, 'Machiavelli, Harrington and English Political Ideologies in the Eighteenth Century' (1965), reprinted in *Politics, Language and Time* (London, 1972), pp. 104–47, at pp. 107–8; cf. 'Civic Humanism and its Role in Anglo-American Thought' (1967), *ibid.*, pp. 80–103.

Professor Pocock went on to trace this mode of political discourse in a succession of authors, and in such political conjunctures as the American Revolution.[64] This represented a major advance on assumptions about a 'consensus' which left little conceptual room for ideological conflict. Yet the conflicts which the neo-Harringtonian thesis chiefly explained were ones initially defined as particularly appropriate to a Court v. Country alignment of forces, and Pocock made explicit the close links of his thesis with the political model of J. H. Plumb's *The Growth of Political Stability in England* (1967), Geoffrey Holmes, W. A. Speck and others.[65]

Other historians of political thought had also taken their cue from parliamentary historians who had asserted the extinction of the Tory party in *c*.1714–16 and looked to a polarity of Court v. Country to provide an alternative framework for analysing Westminster alignments. A Country ideology, appropriate to those alignments, had been reconstructed in the secular terms which seemed natural once Whig and Tory issues had allegedly faded: Court corruption, placemen, bribery, the danger of standing armies. Such matters were indeed prominent ones in political discussion, and the ideas of a Country party and a Country ideology appeared to confirm each other. The most effective challenge to these linked and seemingly supportive notions came from a parliamentary historian, Dr David Hayton. If the Court v. Country alignment was not an axis cutting at right angles across the Whig v. Tory axis (see below, pp. 136–44), then we can see the Commonwealth theorists of *c*.1690–1730 – John Toland, Walter Moyle, Robert Molesworth, John Trenchard, Thomas Gordon and others – as a small group of Whig extremists seeking (often unsuccesfully) to devise an ideological platform for a 'Country' opposition the great majority of whose adherents now prove to have been unambiguously Tory.[66]

Appropriately, the most successful planks in that platform were ones which had long been familiar to Tories and which did not depend on conscious or unconscious borrowing from Edmund Ludlow, James Harrington or Algernon Sidney: suspicion of Court corruption; hostility to

---

[64] For Harrington's influence, see especially Pocock, *The Machiavellian Moment* (Princeton, 1975), pp. 401–505; *idem* (ed.), *The Political Works of James Harrington*, pp.128–52; *idem*, *Virtue, Commerce and History* (Cambridge, 1985).

[65] J. G. A. Pocock, '*The Machiavellian Moment* Revisited: A Study in History and Ideology', *JMH* 53 (1981), 49–72, at 50, 62.

[66] I add this interpretation to the argument of David Hayton, 'The "Country" Interest and the Party System, 1689–c.1720', in Clyve Jones (ed.), *Party and Management in Parliament, 1660–1784* (Leicester, 1984), pp. 37–85. Parliamentary history thus offered a more effective route to a revision than, for example, J. R. Goodale, 'J. G. A. Pocock's Neo-Harringtonians: A Reconsideration', *History of Political Thought* 1 (1980), 237–59, or J. C. Davis, 'Pocock's Harrington: Grace, Nature and Art in the Classical Republicanism of James Harrington', *HJ* 24 (1981), 683–97.

standing armies, high taxation and the burden of national debt: a belief
that landowners were the natural rulers of the State.[67] To claim that there
was a single, coherent body of doctrine which might be labelled 'Country'
was in itself a political gambit; but despite common ground on issues such
as standing armies, the profound and lasting ideological antipathies
between Tories and opposition Whigs over religious and dynastic issues,
even exacerbated after 1714, were to prevent them from cementing an
effective union either ideologically or tactically.

Professor Pocock had taken care to dissociate his account of Harrington's thought during Harrington's lifetime from the social-change interpretations premised upon that author by such historians as C. B. Macpherson and H. R. Trevor-Roper.[68] Nevertheless, the reinterpretation of
neo-Harringtonianism, as scholars moved the Court v. Country axis
much closer to the Whig v. Tory one, had its consequences for the credibility of claims, from R. H. Tawney through Christopher Hill to John
Cannon (see below, pp. 158–60), that a necessary pattern of social and
political change was to be found conveniently epitomised in Harrington's
writings.

This questioning of the thesis of a Lockeian consensus or of an ideological polarity explaining a Court v. Country conflict directed historians'
attention instead to the great body of monarchical, legitimist theory by
reference to which both Stuart and Hanoverian zealots expressed their
claims. It is in relation to *this* set of ideas that the position of many of the
members of the Long Parliament or the Convention Parliament of 1689
was violently subversive: though not social revolutionaries, they were
rebels, and it is the devastating impact on the established order of aims
which had nothing in common with later economic–redistributionist ones
which has now to be recaptured. Modern interests lie overwhelmingly in
the phenomenon of revolution; modern man is so used to rebellion, and so

---

[67] While accepting Dr Hayton's able account of parliamentary alignments, I am more
cautious of believing that the Commonwealthmen's writings were generally received with
enthusiasm by Tories on many other issues than these (p. 56). The Commonwealthmen's
theological heterodoxy and anticlericalism, and the wide social and political consequences
of those things, were anathema to Anglican Tories.

[68] Pocock, *Politics, Language and Time* (London, 1972), pp. 108–11: 'the only image of the
English political economy which Harrington need have had in order to express his theory
of power is one which showed it as consisting of households or families, themselves
polarized into masters and servants'. Nevertheless, Professor Pocock then argued for a
posthumous reformulation of Harrington's ideas in the 1690s by a group of men whom he
termed 'neo-Harringtonians', and this reformulation made those ideas much more useful
for historians of another persuasion: 'Harringtonian doctrine had to be partly transformed
before it could be used in the way Trevor-Roper says it was used at its inception, and before
it could mean at least one of the things it ought to mean before Harrington can occupy his
proper place in a neo-Marxist scenario' (p. 115); cf. *The Political Works of James Harrington*,
pp. 56ff.

quick to condone it, that historians have difficulty in attaching due significance to it in past contexts.[69]

If the model of conflict between long-meditated positions of royalist–absolutist (Court) and parliamentarian–libertarian (Country) is discarded (and also the related model of conflict between feudal and bourgeois), then we can see how (with the exception of the 'freethinkers' and republicans on the extreme wing of the Whigs) 'the leaders and spokesmen of all shades of opinion really held fundamentally identical views'.[70]

They were not, indeed, constitutional–libertarian–democratic views. Equally, if the familiar model of 1688 (or 1714) is dropped which depicts Lockeians sweeping aside Filmerians, we can see that most Whigs and most Tories after the Glorious Revolution shared a similar ideology: not Lockeian and contractarian, but (in different and antagonistic senses) monarchical and Christian.[71] It used to be thought that it was principally opposition Whigs who led the campaign against the Walpolian regime. In that case, what was at stake seemed the official betrayal of a libertarian Whig creed for oligarchic lucre. Once we appreciate that it was in fact Tories who chiefly sustained that opposition, then we can begin to see in their stance some wider commitments than just supporting either the country squires or the lesser merchants or other middling urban interests in large constituencies.[72]

Historians, argued early-Stuart revisionists, had wished to see polarities where ideas of consensus dominated in order to build a Whig teleology into their accounts of constitutional change: another model was needed to explain the undoubted conflict. Historians, argued early-Hanoverian revisionists, had imposed a picture of a Walpolian consensus on a bitterly polarised society for the same reason: to avoid considering the implications of the long survival of the supposedly anachronistic, backward-looking, Tory/Jacobite alternative to modernising Whig rule. Moreover, Whiggish historians then tried to have it both ways: shifting their perspective to *c*.1760–1832, the inherited 'oligarchy' was made to stand for the corruptions of the old order which 'the rise of true radicalism' (Hill) eventually broke down.

The concentration of scholarship on 1689–1714 and 1760–84 by contrast with the great scarcity of work on the last two decades of George II's reign

---

[69] Used seriously, the word can still be emotive. I note that my transatlantic colleagues are quite content with the 'American Revolution' (which it may or may not have been) but are peculiarly annoyed if I write of the 'American Rebellion' (which it certainly was). One might think it no longer mattered.

[70] Elton, 'The Unexplained Revolution' (1970), in *Studies*, vol. 2, p. 183.

[71] I have set out this argument at length in *English Society 1688–1832*, chapters 2 and 3.

[72] But see the valuable work on the social location of metropolitan Toryism of Nicholas Rogers, Appendix B below.

produced, by very weight of emphasis, a 'large measure of agreement' about 'the near-stultification of the mid-century'.[73] Yet, as we can now see, the years 1740–60 were marked by the most bitter tactical and theoretical conflicts over religion, war, the dynasty and the possession of power within the Whig party which had no reflection in a rising number of contests at general elections (that figure, indeed, is a most unreliable index to the level of popular political involvement or to the extent of a regime-sanctioning consensus).

As Professor Rogers observed, the idea of the early-Hanoverian oligarchy, allegedly blanketing opposition in early-eighteenth-century society, had distracted attention from the actual widespread disaffection to the Whig regime.[74] It did not help, however, that historians like Professor Rogers, valuably exploring low-political phenomena, should wish to dismiss 'the study of political strife after 1725' as 'still largely a matter of factional in-fighting and aristocratic feuds' as politics was transformed into 'a system of spoils, interest and preferment'.[75] More sympathetic explorations of early-Hanoverian parliamentary *tactics* led scholars who pursued them into a quite different and unfamiliar ideological framework, and the emerging history of those reigns necessarily came to concern itself as much with ideologies as with the structure of parliamentary groupings. This could be expressed in another way, too: as a revision of the largely static model of eighteenth-century England bequeathed by that peculiarly Victorian academic genre, 'constitutional history'.

### PARLIAMENTARY ALIGNMENTS AND POLITICAL THEORY: THE REBIRTH OF CONSTITUTIONAL HISTORY?

The pattern of parliamentary alignments had been a theme which historians of political thought had not seen as central to their account. Historians explaining the 'Country' ideology of 1714–60 as a neo-Harringtonian nexus of ideas had noticed that it was articulated both by opposition Whigs and by Tories; but, as Professor Pocock explained, 'the ideology is much the same whoever expresses it'.[76] And it is indeed true that there were elements in the opposition's critique of ministerial Whigs which were common ground between the two components of opposition. Revisionist

---

[73] Nicholas Rogers, 'The Urban Opposition to the Whig Oligarchy, 1720–60', in M. and J. Jacob (eds.), *The Origins of Anglo-American Radicalism* (London, 1984), p. 132. Professor Rogers did much to rescue the period from this stultification.

[74] *Ibid.* The prevailing consensus has perhaps been responsible for an undervaluation of Dr Rogers' work on Toryism, though he and I adopt different positions on the question of the relative importance of Jacobitism in the opposition to the early Hanoverian regime.

[75] *Ibid.*, pp. 132–3.

[76] J. G. A. Pocock, '1776: the Revolution against Parliament', in *Three British Revolutions*, p. 287, n. 12.

historians, however, increasingly attended to those elements of the Tory and opposition Whig cases which were not only not held in common, but completely antithetical. To the present author, it seemed that these antithetical elements both outweighed the elements held in common, and provided the definition of that which was distinctive in the two identities. In this sense, conflict was more fundamental than it had been usual to depict it.

It is true that parliamentary historians, seeking a tactical explanation of conflict, must not explain too much: the Civil War *was* in some sense an ideological clash. Ideals of harmony and unity may have delayed that schism; they did not avert it. But, as Professor Hirst reminds us, the divisions took place largely within a shared body of ideas. There were indeed long-standing differences over the constitution, though 'this is not to say that these views can be easily identified with "government" and "opposition"'. Nor does Professor Hirst maintain 'that constitutionalist fears became the stuff of politics'.[77] The qualifications are important ones: an ideological conflict, if not constitutionalist, is more obviously theological in its intellectual structure.

This way of structuring conflict had important implications for the way in which the constitutional issues of the Civil War were to be explained. If large areas of men's *secular* political beliefs *were* held in common, despite the divisions of the Civil War, we can carry this insight forwards past 1688, thanks to the work of Professors Greenleaf, Kenyon, Schochet, Straka and others.[78] Revisionists sought to carry it further, into the years 1714–60: the uncharted heartland of the 'Whig interpretation'. Moreover, if this traditional picture of the secularisation of Walpolian politics is challenged, we are drawn on to reconsider the familiar account of Wilkesite rioters and 1790s English Jacobins in the familiar economic–reductionist terms of the social strains engendered by urbanisation and industrialisation: the survival of 'traditional ideals of social order' was the unfashionable conclusion of one late-eighteenth-century Provincial study.[79] Even when large-scale rioting convulsed many counties of southern and eastern England after the Napoleonic wars, culminating in 1830, the historians of those events failed

---

[77] Derek Hirst, 'Revisionism Revised: The Place of Principle', *P&P* 92 (1981), 81–3, 87, 89.

[78] W. H. Greenleaf, *Order, Empiricism and Politics: Two Traditions of English Political Thought 1500–1700* (London, 1964); G. M. Straka, *Anglican Reaction to the Revolution of 1688* (Madison, Wisconsin, 1962); *idem*, 'The Final Phase of Divine Right Theory in England, 1688–1702', *EHR* 77 (1962), 638–58; *idem*, 'Sixteen Eighty Eight as the Year One: Eighteenth-Century Attitudes Towards the Glorious Revolution', in Louis T. Milic (ed.), *The Modernity of the Eighteenth Century* (Cleveland, Ohio, 1971); G. J. Schochet, 'Patriarchalism, Politics and Mass Attitudes in Stuart England', *HJ* 12 (1969), 413–41; *idem*, *Patriarchalism in Political Thought* (Oxford, 1975); for Professor Kenyon's work, see above, p. 93.

[79] John Money, *Experience and Identity: Birmingham and the West Midlands 1760–1800* (Manchester, 1977).

to find 'many signs of a new political or social ideology. On the contrary, there is evidence that the labourers still accepted the ancient symbols of ancient ideals of stable hierarchy.'[80] Historians of political thought in the Hanoverian era might have discovered much from such Provincial studies – even, at times, those of the Old Guard.

These early-nineteenth-century survivals seemed remote from early-Stuart scholars, however. They often deferred to a quite incompatible model of English society and ideology in the succeeding century, seemingly unaware of the barrier it placed across the path of early-Stuart revisionism. A number of strategies seemed promising as ways of integrating these two schools of thought. Revisionists sought to explore new ways of elucidating the bearing of ideological conflicts on political conflicts – ways which broke decisively with those favoured by the Old Guard or the Class of '68. One mode (though this was not evident to its opponents, who saw it as desiccating history) was the high-political study of the House of Commons. Its first task, at which it was all too successful, was to show what politics was not about. It led parliamentary historians, as in Sedgwick's 1715–54 volumes of the *History of Parliament*, to a realisation of the quite different issues which *were* at stake. Approaching political thought through an agenda written by parliamentary historians meant attending to what might be called the social history of ideas – a study of what the intelligentsia as a whole announced to the nation, and how far the nation absorbed the message, rather than a textual or even a cosmetically contextual analysis of the main writings of those highly unusual figures who run in the relay race of political thought as it is still widely taught: Hobbes handing on the baton to Locke, and so on to Hume, Bentham and Mill.

An older way of dealing with very similar problems is traditional constitutional history, once associated at Cambridge with the name of J. R. Tanner and at Oxford with the name of Sir David Lindsay Keir, and now proposed as a suitable genre for revival by J. H. Hexter.[81] I confess in retrospect that the Lindsay Keir tradition was one of which I disapproved so strongly that it hindered my critique of it in the Introduction to *The Dynamics of Change*. It may well be, however, that new life can be breathed

---

80 · E. J. Hobsbawm and George Rudé, *Captain Swing* (Harmondsworth, 1973; first pub. 1969), p. xxiv. The authors did not explore ideological questions directly, however, largely it seems because of their ritualised desire to denigrate the local role of the Church. Their theme was an Old Guard economic one: 'What happened was ... that a rural society which was in some senses traditional, hierarchical, paternalist, and in many respects resistant to the full logic of the market, was transformed ... into one in which the cash-nexus prevailed ... The worker was simultaneously proletarianised ... the full triumph of rural capitalism', etc., etc. (pp. xxi–xxv).

81 J. H. Hexter, 'The Early Stuarts and Parliament: Old Hat and the *Nouvelle Vague*', *Parliamentary History* 1 (1982), 207–8.

into this long-abandoned tradition: works such as Gary Wills' *Inventing America: Jefferson's Declaration of Independence* (1978) and Lois Schwoerer's *The Declaration of Rights, 1689* (1981) show what can be done with a document. An approach from that other neglected area, the history of law, might be equally fruitful – classically in J. G. A. Pocock's study *The Ancient Constitution and the Feudal Law* (1957), and more recently in works such as Colin Tite's *Impeachment and Parliamentary Judicature in Early Stuart England* (1974), Howard Nenner's *By Colour of Law: Legal Culture and Constitutional Politics in England 1660–1689* (1977), L. A. Knafla's *Law and Politics in Jacobean England* (1977), S. D. White's *Sir Edward Coke and the 'Grievances of the Commonwealth', 1621–1628* (1979), and some important articles. It may be that we shall see a revival of constitutional and legal history considered as an aspect of the history of ideas, with those fine (but woefully Whiggish) scholars Sir William Holdsworth and Sir William Anson as its S. R. Gardiner and Sir Charles Firth; with Margaret Judson's *The Crisis of the Constitution* (1949) and Corinne C. Weston's *English Constitutional Theory and the House of Lords, 1556–1832* (1965) as the neglected pioneers. Listing these titles suggests, indeed, that the revival is well under way already.[82]

It was a revival largely confined to the seventeenth century, however. The survival of greater quantities of evidence meant that Hanoverian scholars were usually able to reconstruct the complexities of politics in considerably more detail than their early-Stuart colleagues. Recent Hanoverian historians thus tended to avoid constitutional history as an unnecessary abridgement of something which, on the contrary, deserved to be reconstructed in full. It was this detailed, technical scholarship in early-Hanoverian politics which launched the revisionist movement in that period, and it is this which we shall now examine.

[82] For the Stuart period, it produced a significant landmark in Corinne Comstock Weston and Janelle Renfrow Greenberg, *Subjects and Sovereigns: The Grand Controversy over Legal Sovereignty in Stuart England* (Cambridge, 1981). Since I dissent from the main thesis of this work, I wish to record my admiration for the scholarship with which its authors have supported it. For appreciative but critical reviews, cf. Gerald Aylmer in *EHR* 97 (1982), 371–4; T. C. Barnard in *History* 67 (1982), 328–9; Mark Goldie in *HJ* 26(1983), 1029–30. Once again, I would suggest that Old Hat historians of Stuart England have assumed (1) an eighteenth-century outcome which never materialised, a 'community-centred view of government' achieved in 1689 at the expense of a rival nexus of divine right and patriarchalism; as well as (2) an early-Stuart political polarity which the work of Conrad Russell and others has now made untenable.

# 7

# PARTY STRUCTURE AND THE HOUSE OF COMMONS

In respect of both periods, the controversy over Parliament was partly about the teleological significance of arguments rehearsed on the floor of each House, partly about the tactical groupings in the Lords and Commons to which such ideological alignments could be related. Did the material self-interest of the nation, reflected at Westminster, produce a Court v. Country pattern, or was it other commitments (ideological, religious) which were reflected in the parties of the Civil War or the early Hanoverian era? These questions were linked to the third aspect of the debate: the question of the electorate and its behaviour at the polls.

## THE ROAD TO 1640: THE SIGNIFICANCE OF ISSUES

We know that certain arguments were advanced in the Parliaments of 1604–29 about parliamentary privilege and the civil and religious liberty of the subject. Were these issues, thus discussed, (a) a necessary and sufficient cause of the outbreak of the Civil War (Gardiner); (b) a necessary but not a sufficient cause (Hexter, Hirst, Rabb); or (c) neither a necessary nor a sufficient cause (Russell, Fletcher and the other revisionists)? The revisionist debate was conducted around and between these three alternatives. The main reply of (b) to (c) was that the Commons' substantive debates were more purposive, consistent and highly charged than has been admitted; 'that 1628 was further along the ideological road to 1640 than Russell or the new revisionists are prepared to allow'.[1] What revisionists refused to accept was the very idea of an 'ideological road'. They focussed discussion of this rhetoric on the necessary vehicle of any movement along such a road, the institution of Parliament itself. Professor Russell noticed that

---

[1] Derek Hirst, 'Parliament, Law and War in the 1620s', *HJ* 23 (1980), 460–1. Hirst denied that anyone adopted position (a), 'not even the most unregenerate Whig or Marxist': 'Revisionism Revised: The Place of Principle', *P&P* 92 (1981), 97.

there is very little evidence to suggest that, before November 1640, many members wanted Parliaments to do more than they had. In particular, there is no sign during the 1620s of any change in the idea that Parliaments were occasional and short-term assemblies. Without a change in this point, Parliaments could not enjoy much more status than they already had. Charles I's continental wars offered the prospect of very frequent Parliaments, but the reaction of members was not to cry out for annual Parliaments: it was to cry out against annual subsidies.[2]

Professor Kenyon wrote:

I agree with Stone that the spectacular exploits of the Long Parliament as an executive body from 1642 to 1653 ought to have raised the status and affected the attitude of all subsequent Parliaments, but there is absolutely no evidence that they did, and the striking thing about the Parliament of 1661–78 is that it behaved in exactly the same way as the Parliaments of 1625–29.[3]

Perhaps this made the point too strongly: there were some new developments in the Cavalier Parliament, though more to do with ways of controlling it than with ways of its controlling government.

The failure of Parliaments after 1660 to behave as if they had entered a promised land mapped out by early-Stuart Old Hat historians was a valid insight, however. Hanoverian revisionists provided important corroboration. Even when Parliaments merged into Parliament after 1688 – when hitherto-occasional assemblies now met annually and retained an institutional continuity from session to session – this did not at once transform them into democratic-participatory bodies. Even English demands in and after the 1770s for 'no taxation without representation' were chiefly protests against taxation and Court corruption rather than attempts to use the Commons in an instrumental role as a democratic agent. Parliament's well-known concern for its privileges in the eighteenth century reflected a strong and perhaps strengthening desire to maintain its independence from both Crown *and* electorate. The 'ideological road' did not lead to the destination the early-Stuart Old Hat historians assumed it led to.

Nevertheless, there was clearly much debate in both centuries about civil liberties and the rule of law. What divided scholars was mainly the nature of the explanatory framework on which these controversies should be arranged. Professor Hirst valuably emphasised the extent to which the great constitutional debates of 1628 were not only a reaction to wartime stresses but expressed fears, voiced from the earliest years of James I's

---

[2] Conrad Russell, 'The Nature of a Parliament in Early Stuart England', in Howard Tomlinson (ed.), *Before the English Civil War* (London, 1983), pp. 141–2.

[3] J. P. Kenyon, 'The Great Rebellion and its Results', *TLS* 6 March 1981, p. 261. Professor Kenyon's choice of 'Rebellion' rather than 'Revolution' reflects the arguments advanced in his *The Stuart Constitution 1603–1688* (Cambridge, 1966, 1985). In that book 'The Revolution' meant 1688, not 1642; and the title 'the Glorious Revolution' is a merely conventional one for the later episode. A lucid survey of the whole century in revisionist terms is J. P. Kenyon, *Stuart England* (Harmondsworth, 1978).

reign, which united MPs with constituents in strong and eventually
mounting concern at the course of events at Westminster;[4] but there is
much that we still need to know before we could read this in a teleological
sense. Why, granted that the issues had been rehearsed so early, was the
breakdown in government so long in coming? Does this argue for an
inevitable process, or even for a process at all? Did polarisation lead to war,
or war to polarisation? Did parliamentary victory mean the birth of
modern freedom?[5]

If it did, it would surely be possible to trace this theme through the
eighteenth century. Yet here not only the revisionists were sceptical.
Hanoverian England praised and claimed a particular and individual
social code; but it was one which modern students, expecting to find
'modern' freedoms, find alien and shocking. Appropriately so, replied the
revisionists: England before 1832 was different from us both in degree and
also, more importantly, in kind. This was true of institutions as well as of
values. If we can at least say what 1688 was *not* about, it was *not* a conflict
between the institutions of monarchy and Parliament, let alone between
King and Commons. Equally, there was no such clash of opposites in 1714.
It is therefore hardly surprising that 1688 and 1714 did little to advance the
House of Commons to the role described for it by Bagehot and Dicey: its
position, though not static, was not central. In the early-Hanoverian as in
the early-Stuart period, 'Parliament' and 'government' were not synonymous;[6] monarchy, not democracy, generated society's dominant ideology.
An early-Stuart scenario which conflicted with this outcome would not be
tenable.

Even those Hanoverian historians who sympathise with the attempt to
qualify some of the more extreme early-Stuart revisionist arguments will be
deterred by the residual teleology embedded in the Old Hat judgement
that 'What Englishmen were groping toward in the period before 1640 was
a means to express political dissent within a legitimate framework', and
that this was achieved in 1689.[7] That this was the intention or the result of

---

4  Hirst, 'Revisionism Revised: The Place of Principle'.
5  J. H. Hexter, 'The Birth of Modern Freedom', *TLS* 21 Jan. 1983, pp. 51–4.
6  The world before 1760 (and even, in some respects, 1832) could most profitably be
   re-examined in the light of the arguments in Russell, 'The Nature of a Parliament in Early
   Stuart England'. There are important differences between Parliaments in the two eras; it is
   time to look also at the similarities. Such a re-examination, for the period 1714–60
   especially, would be a necessary preliminary to a fully rounded picture of the early-
   Hanoverian State on the lines of Penry Williams, *The Tudor Regime* (Oxford, 1979).
7  Robert Zaller, 'The Concept of Opposition in Early Stuart England', *Albion* 12 (1980), 232.
   Why is political dissent legitimate? Sir Lewis Namier summarised one eighteenth-century
   orthodoxy: 'The proper attitude for right-minded Members was one of considered support
   to the Government in the due performance of its task. What other grounds could there be for
   a "formed opposition" than disloyalty to the established order (e.g. Jacobitism) or a selfish,
   factious conspiracy of politicians to force their way into offices higher than they could obtain

the Glorious Revolution was not the perception of English Jacobites or, later, of the English Jacobins, and they had the soundest reasons for believing that much-vaunted English liberties represented only the self-praising conventions of a world made safe for conservative Whigs. Here, as elsewhere, a view of eighteenth-century history represents a decisive test of the arguments of seventeenth-century historians, and it is a test in which the early-Stuart revisionists generally score highly.

How was this teleological picture of Parliaments purposefully pursuing constitutional liberties undone? One important method was a much closer study of parliamentary business and procedure. G. R. Elton's accusation of 1970 has since been heeded by early-Stuart historians but remains valid for most of the parliamentary history of the Hanoverian era: we had neglected to study a not-insignificant element of Parliament's role – the legislation it passed.[8] 'The period of parliamentary history likely to profit most is the early seventeenth century, which badly needs liberating from the bonds of doctrine: it would really be nice to know what actually happened in the Parliaments of James I and Charles I instead of continuing to think in terms of "constitutional conflicts".'[9] The pioneering work of Sheila Lambert and others has had a profound effect on seventeenth-century studies but little in the succeeding century (where, perhaps, it is more needed). Yet in both centuries an examination of procedure reveals a Commons concerned only to a small degree with itself in an instrumental role as a democratic agent. 'Everyone up to 1770 thought, as Charles James Fox [and, one might add, many others] continued to do long after, that the House of Commons was a check not only on Monarchy but also on Democracy.'[10]

The assumption that early-Stuart Parliaments were hyperactive and purposeful in Notestein's 'winning of the initiative' has been steadily qualified by this detailed examination of parliamentary business. Against the rhetoric about privilege and liberty should be set the more mundane, but inescapably weighty, record of what Parliaments actually *did*. Secondly, in respect of Parliament's sense of its own independence and

---

by loyal co-operation with their Sovereign and his Ministers?': *The Structure of Politics at the Accession of George III* (2nd edn, London, 1957), p. 212. This orthodoxy prevailed as long as the pre-Reform Bill non-party pattern: cf. Peter Fraser, 'Party Voting in the House of Commons, 1812–1827', *EHR* 98 (1983), 763–84.

[8] This stricture applies particularly to *The Dynamics of Change*, whose author should have known better.

[9] G. R. Elton, 'Studying the History of Parliament', *British Studies Monitor* 2 (1971), 10; cf. subsequent exchanges with J. H. Hexter, *ibid.* 3 (1972), 4–22.

[10] J. Steven Watson, 'Parliamentary Procedure as a Key to the Understanding of Eighteenth Century Politics', *The Burke Newsletter* 3 (1962), 126; cf. also Sheila Lambert, *Bills and Acts: Legislative Procedure in Eighteenth Century England* (Cambridge, 1971); P. D. G. Thomas, *The House of Commons in the Eighteenth Century* (Oxford, 1971).

destiny, the continued role of the Courts of Chancery and Star Chamber in disputed returns to the early-Stuart Commons does not bear out the rhetoric of Commons' independence to which the 1604 Buckinghamshire dispute classically gave rise. 'The House of Commons does not seem, on this issue, to have been overwhelmingly concerned with the preservation of every one of its privileges and immunities, and the amassing of more by whatever means', observed Professor Hirst; 'the famed aggressiveness of the Commons is not apparent', even on the eve of the Civil War.[11]

Instead of picturing the early-Stuart Parliament as an increasingly powerful institution, standing forward to win initiatives, revisionists reverted to a view of an institution in decline, meeting less and less often, passing fewer bills. But this was not least the result of Parliament's delay and inefficiency in conducting its own business. 'Since nearly all Stuart government was local government, Parliament, as a body, played little part in the governance of England', noted Dr Sharpe.[12] Much of this continued to be true in the early eighteenth century. Regular sittings did not of themselves expand the role of the Commons in government, and although its role was greater it was still not a dynamically expanding one.

Similarly, a scholarly investigation of the peculiarly difficult subject of Commons' procedure does not bear out the sort of purposive evolution towards institutional 'maturity' which an earlier school posited. Indeed, the Commons was strikingly reluctant to codify its privileges and procedures for fear that such a precise account of them would lead to a restriction of their scope.[13] Equally, in the eighteenth century, the Commons' jealous regard for its privileges usually expressed a defensive desire to maintain the influence it had by preserving its independence, not a forward-looking urge to increase its power by shackling the King, still less to do so by emphasising its representative role. One party there was which belatedly entertained such ideas, the Whigs of Grey and Holland: but their day did not come until 1830–4.

Professor Elton's argument that the Commons' *Apology* of 1604 is not to be read as a polemically Whiggish statement of the Parliament-dictated bounds of limited monarchy has already been noted. Similarly, the famous Commons' petition of 3 December 1621 had been treated by most historians as a constitutional landmark, an attempt by the House to seize an initiative and encroach on the authority of the Crown by debating and

---

[11] Derek Hirst, 'Elections and the Privileges of the House of Commons in the Early Seventeenth Century: Confrontation or Compromise?', *HJ* 18 (1975), 859–60.

[12] In Kevin Sharpe (ed.), *Faction and Parliament* (Oxford, 1978), pp. 18–37.

[13] Sheila Lambert, 'Procedure in the House of Commons in the Early Stuart Period', *EHR* 95 (1980), 753–81, at 781. For the removal of Notestein's teleological model of the Parliaments of Queen Elizabeth's reign, see G. R. Elton, 'Parliament in the Sixteenth Century: Functions and Fortunes', *HJ* 22 (1979), 255–78.

petitioning on the hitherto reserved subject of foreign policy; but Professor Russell's close analysis of the debate now shows it to have been nothing of the sort. Instead, it marks either the incompetence of James I's parliamentary management, or possibly a deliberate distraction from Parliament's desire for foreign military intervention. In either case, the debate 'shows a House of Commons in which Court–Country and Government–Opposition divisions, in terms of which debates have normally been analysed, were entirely inoperative'.[14]

For early-Stuart Parliaments the problem was not so much the achievement of dominance but their own survival. This depended not least on foreign military intervention: the Scots in 1640, the Dutch in 1688.[15] If so, the fact that Dutch intervention was directly aimed at displacing James II, not strengthening Parliament, sheds much light on the diffidence shown by the Commons in their failure to assume control of early-Hanoverian government. Far from seizing the initiative for the Commons, early-eighteenth-century Whigs (who comprised the majority of MPs) were more concerned that the chief agent of all initiatives in government, the Crown, should not be seized by the Stuart dynasty. The reinstatement of Jacobitism as a profoundly important issue was a major achievement of recent scholarship in the early-Hanoverian field. Here indeed was an issue of principle: but it was one which could not be fitted into a teleological framework. That is to say: the road to 1640 actually led on to 1715 and 1745.

This claim did not go unchallenged, however. By the late 1980s, the early-Hanoverian debate seemed to present three options. (a) The Old Guard/Old Hat model: there was no (or no significant) Tory party after c.1714–16, and Jacobitism was consequently trivial and without practical parliamentary impact (Plumb, Holmes, Speck, Dickinson); (b) a compromise, but one which proved to have been constructed on Old Guard assumptions: a Tory party existed under the first two Georges and for some unspecified period thereafter, but had very little to do with Jacobitism (Rogers, B. W. Hill, Colley); (c) the revisionists: the Tory party survived until the 1750s, and its survival had much to do with Jacobitism both as a tactical option and as an ideology (Cruickshanks, Fritz, Erskine-Hill, Clark, McLynn, Black, Szechi, Monod). Chronologically, the progression was from (a) to (c); (b) represented a useful but temporary resting place on

[14] Conrad Russell, 'The Foreign Policy Debate in the House of Commons in 1621', *HJ* 20 (1977), 289–309, modified by Russell, *Parliaments and English Politics 1621–1629* (Oxford, 1979) pp. 129–35.

[15] Koenigsberger, quoted in Conrad Russell, 'Parliamentary History in Perspective, 1604–1629', *History* 61 (1976), 2. Should we add the threat of civil war in Ireland in 1828–9 to this list, as a tactical explanation of the Reform Bill? Cf. Clark, *English Society 1688–1832* chapter 6, 'The End of the Ancien Regime, 1800–1832'.

the way to a more profound rethinking of the issues involved, and a more adequate attention to the full range of the evidence.

Why did most early-Hanoverian Tories stand by their party rather than pursue a ministerial career by joining the ranks of the Walpolian, Pelhamite Old Corps – as a few did, and as more did in 1760? Why, granted their long sojourn in opposition, did Tories not fuse – tactically and organisationally – with opposition Whigs? It was the remarkable evidence of the Tories' *tactical* involvement with the intermittent Jacobite option which at last made comprehensible their conduct as a party, and which made incomplete any attempt to write their history without this element, whether it was in the foreground or the background of the Tory vision.[16]

Except for a small number, even the Whig majority in both Houses under the first two Georges was not anti-monarchical: it was pro-Hanoverian. This loyalty, made compulsory by the Stuart threat, meant that there was very little scope for an active, jealous House of Commons to expand its function at the monarchy's expense, and a striking feature of the 1715–54 volumes of the *History of Parliament* is how few symptoms there are of the advance of the lower House.[17] If it is the case (as the present author has argued) that the key to the disintegration of the traditional party polarity is to be sought in the tactical conflicts and ideological transformations of the 1750s, then the instability which followed the accession of George III can be seen as the result of parliamentary weaknesses, not of an attempt by the monarchy to burst the constitutional bonds legitimately imposed on it by a succession of strong, and strengthening, Parliaments. The dismantling of the myth that either of the first two Georges was a 'king in toils' entails a view of parliamentary history much closer to (though not of course identical with) that given by revisionists for the 1620s.

Moreover, the perspective of almost all scholars had been restricted in a way that had largely gone unremarked. The road to 1640 was not being

---

16 See the works discussed in J. C. D. Clark, 'The Politics of the Excluded: Tories, Jacobites and Whig Patriots, 1715–1760', *Parliamentary History* 2 (1983), 209–22.

17 Those volumes, though published in 1970, inherited Romney Sedgwick's interpretation of Walpole as the first modern Prime Minister, based on much older assumptions about the power of the House of Commons and the weakness of the House of Lords under the first two Georges. *The House of Commons 1715–1754* (2 vols., London, 1970), though containing much fine scholarship, did nothing explicitly to question those assumptions. This was hardly surprising: the editor of that work was Romney Sedgwick himself. Indeed his section of the Introduction repeats not only the argument but much of the wording of his earlier statement of his view: [Romney Sedgwick], 'Sir Robert Walpole 1676–1745: The Minister for the House of Commons', *TLS* 24 March 1945, pp. 133–4. The interpretation, then, had been devised before any of the research for the History of Parliament had been carried out. The vintage of Sedgwick's view of politics can be better understood from his article 'The Inner Cabinet from 1739 to 1741', *EHR* 34 (1919), 290–302. Subsequent work on Tudor and early-Stuart Parliaments demands a reassessment of the early Hanoverian House of Commons also.

followed in the metropolis alone. Historians preoccupied with the alleged strength and success of the Westminster Parliament might usefully draw comparisons with the very different track records of the Parliaments of Edinburgh and Dublin. The assumption that there is in representative institutions some inherent tendency to seize governmental initiatives or expand civil liberties looks much weaker in the light of the experience of those two bodies.[18] This is true both from our perspective, and in the perceptions of contemporaries. If eighteenth-century Englishmen were the heirs to the constitutional achievements of early-Stuart Parliaments, it is paradoxical that Hanoverian parliamentarians displayed a great insensitivity to the possibility of representative institutions playing the sort of initiative-seizing role which Old Hat historians had traditionally scripted. It is true that the assemblies of Dublin and Edinburgh played no such role; but the paradox is heightened by the fact that other assemblies within the British empire manifestly did.[19] For in the half century to 1776, in colony after colony on the North American continent, the lower Houses set about eroding the power of the Governor and the authority of the metropolis in ways which fit the Whig model uncannily.[20]

Despite the repeated warnings of colonial Governors, successive British ministries seem almost blind to what was going on: not so much unaware of the facts as incapable of formulating a predictive theory of constitutional developments on the basis of them. Eighteenth-century English Whigs indeed inherited from the seventeenth century an unspecific rhetoric about the superior morality of parliamentary institutions, but they had little technical, concrete understanding of how such ideals were supposed to have been, or currently might be, translated into practice: the rhetoric therefore acted as a barrier, rather than aid, to understanding. As far as most Englishmen were concerned, the Stamp Act crisis came out of a clear blue sky. This was not as negligent as it might appear, however: American representative assemblies did not take on their purposive role in response to a democratic imperative. The franchise for elections to colonial Assemblies was already broad (and turnouts often low). It was a drive to

[18] It is a curious feature of English (and even American) historians' preoccupations with Parliament that the three Parliaments of Westminster, Dublin and Edinburgh have almost never been studied on a comparative basis.

[19] See Leonard W. Labaree, *Royal Government in America: A Study of the British Colonial System before 1783* (New Haven, Conn., 1930); Jack P. Greene, *The Quest for Power: The Lower Houses of Assembly in the Southern Royal Colonies, 1689–1776* (Chapel Hill, 1963); James A. Henretta, *'Salutary Neglect': Colonial Administration under the Duke of Newcastle* (Princeton, 1972); Robert W. Tucker and David C. Hendrickson, *The Fall of the First British Empire* (Baltimore, 1982), pp. 146–86.

[20] It is significant that Professor Pole's American colonial research led him to adopt a 'winning of the initiative' perspective on seventeenth-century British parliamentary institutions, citing Notestein: J. R. Pole, *Political Representation in England and the Origins of the American Republic* (London, 1966).

independence which turned those institutions into initiative-seizing bodies, and this imperative was one which Englishmen (having no analogy at home) failed to recognise for what it was.

Changes took place, of course. The early-Stuart Provincials had not uncovered a model valid for all periods. It was apparent to the early-Hanoverian revisionists that the centre altered its relation to the localities as time went by. After 1660, and especially after 1688, Parliament assumed a more permanent role as a national arena at the same time as growing political business transcended localist federalism and welded the State into much more of a unity (including, in 1707, the Scottish union which early-Stuart localist and other pressures at Westminster had successfully resisted). At the same time, Parliament took on much more of that self-preoccupation, that introversion, that resistant life-of-its-own that develops in all enclosed or corporate bodies from public schools and Oxbridge colleges to regiments and Inns of Court. In this process, the national government may actually have become *less* responsive to 'issues' or to localist pressures. By the 1750s, a detailed study of the workings of Court, Ministry and Commons revealed very little attention to that street agitation (doubtless as perennial a feature of English life as men's appetite for violence) which the Class of '68 in particular had sought to enlist in the old scenario of political change.[21]

This was a pattern which was confirmed by a string of other high-political studies of the following two centuries. They recorded a self-absorbed ruling elite, a self-sufficient political culture: modified, indeed, by the consequences of 1828–32 and by the rise of a popular press in the 1850s, but not profoundly altered until the impact of the mass media since *c.*1945. As with these later studies, to make this point for the eighteenth century was held by some reviewers to be peculiarly sinful: one was failing to do justice to the common man (let alone to the radical demagogue). Historians who wished to celebrate the activities of mobs and to credit them with the purposes entailed by the Whig teleology did not wish to be told that eighteenth-century conceptualisations failed to define the issue of the role of the populace in these terms. No debate developed: the Class of '68 regarded the revisionists as having set up their enquiries in such a way as deliberately to ignore politicians' responsiveness to a popular dimension and its assumed libertarianism. Revisionists claimed that theirs was the result one found if the politics of the period were studied closely, without Victorian assumptions. There was a certain lack of amity between these two schools of thought, and little of the profitable discussions that graced the early-Stuart period.

[21] J. C. D. Clark, *The Dynamics of Change: The Crisis of the 1750s and English Party Systems* (Cambridge, 1982).

Yet a comparison of the political experience of the two centuries warns us against treating England after 1688 as the era of triumphant parliament-arianism, if by that we understand a cherishing of representative institu-tions and an extension of their democratic function. Certainly, the West-minster Parliament became stronger. But this was importantly offset by its use of its power to suppress the Parliaments of Edinburgh (in 1707) and Dublin (in 1801). In England itself, the early Hanoverians' anti-libertarian preferences equally produced the suppression of a major representative institution – the Church of England's Parliament, the Convocations of Canterbury and York, in 1717.

This was merely a working-out of earlier developments, however. The Stuarts' suspicion of representative assemblies meant that, when in 1664 Archbishop Sheldon arranged with Clarendon to give up the clergy's separate right to tax themselves, Convocations became more of a burden than a benefit to the executive, and were not allowed to sit to do business until 1689. This was all too easy to bring about: Convocations, assembling simultaneously with Parliaments and sometimes claiming equal and independent powers, could be prorogued by royal prerogative; even if assembled, they could be reduced to inactivity, to a formal existence only, by withholding the royal licence to transact business. Thus the experience of one real Convocation in 1689 was enough to persuade William III to defer a second experiment until 1701. Convocations assembled yearly with Parliament from 1701 to 1717 with the exception of the years of Whig dominance 1708–10; but the political furore triggered by Benjamin Hoadly, Bishop of Bangor, in 1717 was enough to induce the Whig establishment to prorogue Convocation and to withhold its licence to do business thereafter.[22] So effective indeed was this suppression that Convo-cation was even erased from the pages of the history of representative government.

Less important in itself, though no less symptomatic of the nature of Hanoverian government, was the suppression of the Parliament of Tinners, that ancient representative body which played a central role in the regulation of Cornwall's major industry with implications for the county's politics as a whole. With 44 seats at Westminster and a violent industrial proletariat famous for its military achievements in the Civil War, its noisy loyalty during the Restoration and its suspected Jacobitism thereafter, Cornwall briefly assumed a disproportionate place in metropo-litan calculations. Like the Convocation of the Church of England, the Parliament of Tinners was prevented from meeting in the reigns of

[22] There was an exception in 1741, when Whig High Churchmen secured the concession of a real Convocation. But the old divisions immediately reasserted themselves, and the experiment was swiftly terminated.

William III and George I. Not until 1750 was a Convocation of the
Stannaries revived, this time as an episode in the electioneering of
Frederick, Prince of Wales: even then, the re-emergence of old divisions
disrupted business, and the Parliament of 1752, now carefully managed by
the ministry, was the last.[23] The early Hanoverian Whigs (as, later, the
men who passed the Reform Act of 1832) could pose as the champions of
English liberties only by defining those liberties in a new way.

This deletion of a teleology built around representative–democratic
'issues' entailed a quite different, and much lesser, significance for parliamentary conflicts. In a pre-democratic age neither the press nor Parliament itself filled the constructive role each was later to define for itself: the
contribution of both was often negative. It was not debate but the
experience of war in the 1640s, 50s and 90s which taught masses of
ordinary Englishmen in the shires the costs of modern government and the
inescapable need for provincial men to shoulder that burden despite their
talk of the priority of local needs, local poverty, and the immorality of
national exactions for grand purposes.

Parliaments on the pattern of 1604–29 had proved themselves wholly
unable to sustain a viable State apparatus. Their incompetence and
obstruction registered, among other things, a localist unwillingness to pay.
Successive monarchs therefore sought to minimise the role of Parliaments.
The result was a backlash, when external circumstances made it possible,
in 1640–2 and again in 1688. Though they toppled individual kings, these
petulant outbursts did nothing to modify the hard realities of war and
diplomacy. After 1688, Parliament on the model of 1604–29 was not
abolished: it was drastically reformed, modernised and subordinated to the
executive. Granted the show of power, it was assimilated to the State
machine. Parliament was tamed.

The famous 'winning of the initiative' by the early-Stuart House of
Commons[24] has been postponed by Dr Cromwell to the half-century after
*c.*1780, when the erosion of ministerial patronage powers[25] allowed back-

[23] I am indebted for this account to the only modern study of the subject, Eveline
Cruickshanks, 'The Convocation of the Stannaries of Cornwall: The Parliament of Tinners
1703–1752', *Parliaments, Estates and Representation* 6 (1986).

[24] Wallace Notestein, *The Winning of the Initiative by the House of Commons* (London, 1924)
advanced, as one reason for that development between the reign of Elizabeth I and the
Long Parliament, the withdrawal of the Privy Council from its role in arranging and
steering Commons' business, and the assumption of that role by MPs, 'a group of leaders,
who had no official connexion with the government . . .'. It should be added that Professor
Notestein was more cautious than some of his followers in seeing a teleological process at
work: 'These men without purpose or intent but to do the next that came to hand, created a
new leadership' (p. 4).

[25] Archibald S. Foord, 'The Waning of "The Influence of the Crown"', *EHR* 62 (1947),
484–507, suggests that this erosion began to concern ministers only after 1818. The

bench MPs to become increasingly wayward and develop tactics for disrupting ministerial business. It was a modest victory, however: the volume of government legislation continued inexorably to increase, and the disruptive abilities of backbenchers found little expression in constructive institutional innovations which would have given the Commons a more positive role. Moreover, an 'initiative' so weak and so lacking in self-conscious purpose was easily lost: from the 1830s onwards successive ministries, by a variety of procedural means, and irrespective of the strength or weakness of parties, steadily tightened their grip on the allocation of parliamentary time.

From the 1820s, radical MPs such as Joseph Hume pursued a campaign for greater financial accountability; yet even when this campaign achieved a formal success in the Exchequer and Audit Departments Act of 1866, the accelerating growth in the scale of public expenditure and the complexity of public business placed effective control as far beyond the grasp of the ordinary MP as it had been in previous centuries. If it was evident even in the 1960s that the nineteenth century saw a 'losing of the initiative by the House of Commons',[26] early-Stuart and early-Hanoverian scholarship now allows us to appreciate, *pace* Professor Notestein, that the Commons had never had much initiative to lose. In the 1860s, a writer on the constitution described existing practice in terms which could almost serve for the 1760s or 1660s:

So long as Parliament continues its confidence in ministers, it ought to be willing to leave the exercise of the prerogative in their hands, unfettered by restrictions in regard to its exercise, and should refrain from interference therewith, unless under circumstances of imperious necessity. The general responsibility of ministers for the wisdom, policy, and legality of the measures of government should be sufficient guarantee, in all ordinary cases, for the faithful discharge of the high functions entrusted to them.[27]

This was the ideal; the reality, as the *Quarterly Review* pointed out in 1901, was that Commons' procedure was still 'stereotyped as a machine of protest'; its 'organization as a machine of governing democracy has yet to be accomplished'.[28]

---

restriction of monetary rewards was partly offset by the unrestricted growth in the grant of honours. The impact of Burke's 'Economical Reform' campaign should not be overstated.

[26] Valerie Cromwell, 'The Losing of the Initiative by the House of Commons, 1780–1914', *TRHS* 18 (1968), 1–23.

[27] Alpheus Todd, *Parliamentary Government in England: Its Origin, Development and Practical Operation* (2 vols., London, 1867–9), vol. 1, p. 256: quoted Cromwell, 'The Losing of the Initiative', p. 23.

[28] Quoted in Peter Fraser, 'The Growth of Ministerial Control in the Nineteenth-Century House of Commons', *EHR* 75 (1960), 444–63, at 462. Professor Fraser illustrates the emptiness and final curtailment of the ancient claim of 'grievances before supply'.

PARTY ALIGNMENTS: THE SIGNIFICANCE OF STRUCTURE

*Was there an opposition?*

In its second aspect, the elucidation of parliamentary groupings, the early-Stuart revisionist movement may be said to have begun in 1951 with Brian Wormald's insight, in respect of Clarendon's career, that the clear-cut royalist and parliamentarian options so evident in retrospect did not emerge until shortly before fighting began in 1642. This explosive idea lay embedded within the received orthodoxy for two decades, but finally destroyed it. The links with more recent revisionism were, in effect, acknowledged by Mr Wormald in the Preface to the 1976 edition of *Clarendon*: from the original insight had flowed a whole host of consequences, demolishing the old scenario of seventeenth-century England as an epic conflict between King and Parliament, resolved in 1688–9 by the destruction of divine right monarchy. The effective absolutism of the King was actually strengthened by the fiction of the King-in-Parliament within the Clarendonian constitution as implemented after 1660. Consequently, 1688–9 'did not resolve the issue of sovereignty in favour of the representative principle', nor did it liquidate the monarchy. 'William III was no puppet. The mixture was as before'.[29]

The implication of all this, as Wormald saw, was the invalidity of the title 'The English Revolution' for the events of 1640–60. The further consequence, for Hanoverian historians, was the re-examination of the orthodoxies which had been premised on the Old Hat and Old Guard accounts of the Stuarts. Before such extensive general conclusions could be demonstrated, however, much detailed research had to be done into the daily course of politics. Recent close examination of the business of early-Stuart Parliaments has been largely devoted to demonstrating that they do *not* adumbrate the party alignments which followed the outbreak of the Civil War. Recent scholarship on early-Hanoverian Parliaments has similarly argued that the alignments of 1714–60 do not anticipate the Namierite pattern of the 1760s, but the argument is in the other direction: the pattern under the first two Georges was overshadowed by a Whig–Tory polarity. But it expressed a conflict within a nexus of ideas (if Jacobitism is taken seriously) which was the reverse of 'forward looking' in the tradi-

---

[29] B. H. G. Wormald, *Clarendon: Politics, History and Religion* (Cambridge, 1951; 3rd edn, Chicago, 1976), Preface, *passim*. Wormald's name should be considered with that of his colleague Butterfield. To what extent both early-Stuart and early-Hanoverian revisionism can be traced to the ideas of these two men is an interesting question.

tional sense. Consequently the denial of party formation in *c.*1603–40 and the assertion of party survival in *c.*1714–60 had the same effect, of countering an Old Guard model.

Just as the parliamentary history of 1660–88 failed to demonstrate the institutional effects of a triumph of *the* opposition in 1604–29, so also the reign of George III failed to record the effects of any opposition triumph in 1714–60. Indeed, to the extent that Tories under the first two Georges entertained the Jacobite option, their opposition proved futile: the ancient parties of Whig and Tory disintegrated in the 1750s, and the famous ministerial instability of the 1760s is evidence of the institutional failure of Parliament to generate a coherent, credible alternative to the Whig Old Corps. It was the monarchy, not successful parliamentary oppositions, which continued to institute and sustain stable ministries in the period 1760–1832. It was a world which owed little to Victorian notions of the 'adversary system' as a long-evolved guarantor of English liberties.

S. R. Gardiner, argued Professor Kishlansky, 'held to two static notions of political participation: that the system by which politics operated was an oppositional one and that those who composed the contending camps did so on the basis of a single, consistent set of principles – an ideology'.[30] Subsequent scholarship, argued Kishlansky, had substituted other groups for Gardiner's without breaking with his assumption that parliamentary politics was already adversary politics. Blair Worden's suggestion that 'we can no longer think of the war and peace parties as parties in the modern sense'[31] raised more insistently for the early-Stuart revisionist the questions with which Hanoverian historians had grappled since Namier: what form did parties take, in respect of organisation, behaviour and ideology, if those forms over time differed profoundly from their late-nineteenth-century paradigm? How far could parties subsist, or play a constructive role, if opposition itself were illegitimate?

To ask such questions of the early seventeenth century was to go to the root of the matter, and to confront a long-standing historiographical problem. An assumption drawn from a later period and anachronistically imposed on early-Stuart Parliaments, argued Professor Kishlansky, was the adversary system: two 'sides' defined over against each other as government and opposition. Such an alignment, he argued, cannot be

[30] Mark Kishlansky, 'The Emergence of Adversary Politics in the Long Parliament', *JMH* 49 (1977), 617, argues that adversary politics developed during the Civil War, not before its outbreak. Perez Zagorin, 'Did Strafford Change Sides?', *EHR* 101 (1986), 149–63, restates the Court v. Country thesis.

[31] Blair Worden, *The Rump Parliament* (Cambridge, 1974), p. 6

found before 1646.[32] Professor Hexter's counter-suggestion[33] of some
continuity of personnel and issues in 'the opposition' from 1604 to the
1620s hardly seems to meet the case: sometimes to give the Crown
uncongenial counsel is far from having an allegiance to a personified body,
'the opposition'. 'I recently revised a book called *The Century of Revolution*,
wrote Christopher Hill, 'and one change I found necessary to make was to
delete the word 'the' in the phrase 'the opposition' whenever it occurred'.[34]

Happy the historian who can adapt his old orthodoxy to new research by
so easy a step. The revisionist case went somewhat deeper than this,
however. The absence of an organised and lasting parliamentary unit 'in
opposition' is associated with the absence of a reified opposition standpoint
created by the purposeful championing of great constitutional issues. The
absence of an opposition confirms the invalidity of a Whig teleology concerned with the ambition of Parliament, or at least of one major element
within it, to dominate the government. Professor Rabb sought to salvage the
word: 'Cannot the term "opposition" be descriptive without necessarily
implying a resounding Whig view of English history?' Conflict between
princes and representative institutions was endemic in seventeenth-century
Europe: 'they have to be seen, therefore, as sustained and deliberate conflicts' articulated by 'opposition' groups, 'whether organised and systematic
or not'.[35] Here indeed is the point: the difference between MPs *opposing* the
Crown on specific issues and being members of *an opposition*, organised or not,
with or without the name, is more than a difference of degree: it is a difference
of kind, and lies at the heart of this debate. To show that momentous issues
*were* at stake, that debate was sometimes heated, that some MPs expressed
profound misgivings (or made portentous and emptily rhetorical remarks)
about the encroachment of the prerogatives of the Crown on the liberties of
the subject – all this cannot add up to *an opposition* and revolution, if there was
one, cannot have been the result of an *opposition* campaign.

It is important in this context that the phrase 'His Majesty's Opposition'
was coined, and then in jest, only in 1826. Its foremost student, in seeking

32  Kishlansky, 'The Emergence of Adversary Politics in the Long Parliament'. That the
    debates of the army in Putney church during the autumn of 1647 do not reveal two
    pre-existing parties is argued by Mark Kishlansky, 'Consensus Politics and the Structure
    of Debate at Putney' in M. and J. Jacob (eds.), *The Origins of Anglo-American Radicalism*
    (London, 1984), pp. 70–84.
33  J. H. Hexter, 'Power Struggle, Parliament, and Liberty in Early Stuart England', *JMH* 50
    (1978), 24–30.
34  Christopher Hill, 'Parliament and People in Seventeenth-Century England', *P&P* 92
    (1981), 104. For the survival of a teleological picture of opposition parties forming in both
    Houses from 1621 around 'long-range ideological issues', seeking to challenge the Crown,
    see J. S. Flemion, 'The Nature of Opposition in the House of Lords in the Early
    Seventeenth Century: a Reevaluation', *Albion* 8 (1976), 17–34.
35  Theodore K. Rabb, 'Revisionism Revised: The Role of the Commons', *P&P* 92 (1981),
    66–72.

implausibly to trace its emergence from the beginning of the Hanoverian era, was led to define it in terms appropriate only to the nineteenth century, significantly adding: 'He who conceives of the institution in these terms belongs to that school of Western thought generically classified as liberal.'[36] Although the term 'the Opposition' was current from the 1730s, Professor Foord's evidence could be argued to show not the steady evolution of a convention of legitimate opposition as the basis for an alternative ministry waiting in the wings, but the long absence of such a convention, from an MP's complaint in Anne's reign –

If a gentleman stands up to complain of grievances, although this House meets in order to redress them, he is represented as a person that obstructs Her Majesty's business; if he finds fault with the Ministry, he is said to reflect upon the Queen; if he speaks against the continuance of war to prevent the beggary of the nation ... then he is to be no object of Her Majesty's favour and encouragement[37]

– through the opposition's open disaffection (perhaps treason) during the American rebellion, to a backbencher's reaction in 1830 to the idea of replacing the ministry with its opponents: 'Sir, I would as soon choose for a new coachman the man who shied stones best at my old one'.[38] In practice as well as in theory, not until after 1832 did the alternation of two great parties in power terminate the pattern which dated from *c.*1714–16 and confer on oppositions anything more than a negative, anomalous and usually futile role in government.

The danger, here as elsewhere, is to infer from the currency of a word or phrase at a particular moment that it was then invested with its later meaning. Moreover, too much personification can lead us back to Trevelyan's 'great issues' approach, in which orators or institutions (but especially oppositions) represent causes:

If one asks whom the Civil War in England was between, the answer that least drastically distorts the evidence is 'King and Parliament'. If one goes further and

---

[36] Archibald S. Foord, *His Majesty's Opposition 1714–1830* (Oxford, 1964), p. 3 (an eulogy of liberalism which reads strangely today). Professor Foord, a Yale historian, acknowledged the help of his colleague Wallace Notestein in the composition of this book. Foord's view echoed the Old Hat model exactly: 'peaceful change' could not 'become the norm before agreement on fundamentals made resort to revolution unnecessary ... In 1714 Britain finally settled her dynastic problem ... In 1717 the prorogation of Convocation ... signalised the disappearance of fierce theological controversy from political life ... the clerical disputes which had produced revolutionary cleavages in British society were silenced. Henceforward political parties were not to be based upon religious cleavages ... Hanoverian rule rightly engendered not suspicion but trust, an element indispensable to peaceful constitutional development'; the years 1714–1830 'constitute the germinating period of the modern institution' of opposition (pp. 8–11). His evidence actually demonstrated those years to be an era of sterility: germination came suddenly, in the 1830s.

[37] W. C. Townsend, *History of the House of Commons* (2 vols., London, 1843), vol. 1, p. 309.

[38] Walter Bagehot, *The English Constitution and Other Political Essays* (New York, 1911), p. 396; Foord, *Opposition*, pp. 6–7.

asks, 'Why did the war break out between King and Parliament?' an evasive but useful answer would be, 'Troubles had been brewing between them for a long while.' It is useful because it pushes us toward the next question, 'What was the long trouble between King and Parliament about?'[39]

In the wake of – to name only one book – Cooke and Vincent's *The Governing Passion* (1974), we can no longer write political history like this.

Attempts to rehabilitate the concept of an 'opposition' in the early-Stuart period, notably Professor Zaller's careful and illuminating study,[40] focussed on *issues*, their coherence and continuity, rather than on *action*, especially voting behaviour in the Commons. It may indeed be agreed, as Professor Zaller maintains, that the Commons *eventually* polarised itself into a 'side' over issues; and that these issues had long previously been discussed. But did the discussion produce the polarity? Was the Civil War, in the Old Hat formulation, 'about' English liberties, one 'side' (the opposition) being for them, the other against? If not, how do the tactical alignments express the purposes of the participants? It was these questions which Old Hat restatements did not really answer. Yet many scholars would agree that the obvious route to an elucidation of the teleological force of issues lay through a renewed attention to parliamentary history, and it was this which gave added point to the unfolding debate over the nature of parliamentary parties – those institutionalised engines, as the Victorians thought, of political change.

## Court and Country or Whig and Tory?

The emerging problem for a teleological account of early-Stuart parties was that, as on other matters, historians of Hanoverian England were successfully labouring to detach it in interpretation from the conventions and perspectives which arose after 1832. An historian of early-Hanoverian high politics notices, like his early-Stuart colleagues, that only a small part of what mattered (and that seldom the most important part) took place in either House. In a political world like that of the early eighteenth century in which only about a third of seats at each general election were contested; in which the turnout of even gentry voters at some county elections might be under 20 per cent; and in which only the rarest and most momentous Commons' divisions attracted the attendance of as many as 300 out of 558 Members, it cannot be the case that the lower House was widely regarded as the legislative agent of English commoners: we must find other conceptual frameworks than Bagehot's to explain the undoubted fact that Parliaments were a focus of Englishmen's (and, to a lesser extent,

[39] Hexter, 'Power Struggle, Parliament, and Liberty', p. 29.
[40] Robert Zaller, 'The Concept of Opposition in Early Stuart England', *Albion* 12 (1980), 211–34.

Irishmen's and Scotsmen's) affection, ambition and jealous regard long before the arrival of mass participatory democracy. If, indeed, it ever really arrived at all.[41]

The early-Hanoverian Old Guard solved this problem (to their own satisfaction, at least) by speaking of participatory democracy frustrated by the ascendancy of the Court. At this point, their interpretation significantly diverged from the Old Hat account of the early-Stuart achievement of liberty. The early-Hanoverian Old Guard wished to minimise the survival of Whig and Tory identities and conflict and to redescribe such phenomena under the labels of Court and Country. They did so in order to place a particular interpretation on the priority of particular historical *issues*: to minimise the importance of religion and dynastic loyalties, and to cast political motivations within an economic–reductionist framework as the individualistic pursuit of material self-interest (electoral deference to gentry leadership could then be redescribed as oligarchic repression). Court and Country could be depicted as rooted in the inevitable economic rivalry of centre (bureaucracy, high finance, trade) and periphery (agrarian, backward-looking, anachronistic, 'falling' lesser gentry squeezed by the land tax).

The Court v. Country analysis, for the early-Stuart period, had meant two rather different things. The analysis broke down, therefore, because of developments in two seemingly related, but actually alternative, chains of argument. By 'Country', some historians of the seventeenth century had meant introverted Provincialism – the value-nexus of the 'county community', self-righteously virtuous and defined over against the moral and political vices of the Court. It was this sense of 'Country' as the basis for an analysis of Westminster politics which was undermined by the localist critiques of the 'county community' of scholars such as Professor Clive Holmes, explored in chapter 4, pp. 58–61.

Secondly, by 'Country' other historians had meant something rather different: not *introverted* Provincialism, but a coherent, articulate, provincially based campaign at Westminster to redress local grievances. With this position in particular was associated a view of material self-interest pulling the two entities apart, social strains producing political friction and breakdown in the 1640s. Scrutiny of this second position was begun by Professor Elton in 1970.[42] It is fair to say that the early-Hanoverian Old Guard were far more reductionist in this respect than Professor Zagorin:

---

[41] Clark, *English Society 1688–1832* chapter 1; cf. John Vincent, *Pollbooks: How Victorians Voted* (Cambridge, 1967); D. C. Moore, *The Politics of Deference: A Study of the Mid-Nineteenth Century English Political System* (Hassocks, 1976).

[42] See G. R. Elton's remarks on Perez Zagorin's *The Court and the Country: the Beginning of the English Revolution* (London, 1969): 'The Unexplained Revolution' (1970), in *Studies*, vol. 2.

and this perhaps explains the latter's difficulty in outlining a category of 'Country' sufficiently sharp to bear the weight he sought to place on it. Men of similar social and economic strata can be found in both camps, and if religion was the great exception to this generalisation, its polarising effects were neglected for the history of the first two Georges also. A picture of society naturally divided in two by material self-interest has more to do with the antagonism of North v. South in England since the 1960s than with the alignments of any previous age. Indeed, it is striking that while the early-Hanoverian scholars who champion the Court v. Country analysis mostly hail from the North or from the Celtic fringe, the Whig v. Tory theorists were usually born, or have pursued their careers, in the English heartlands: that England whose northernmost latitude is exactly defined by Magdalene College, Cambridge, and whose westernmost longitude is precisely fixed by Christ Church, Oxford.

As an analysis of alignments at Westminster, the Court v. Country framework was equally called in doubt in the early-Hanoverian period by Professor Elton's objection that 'a great deal of the political conflict occurred among the Court factions ... the members of the governing clique were usually more troubled by one another than by any regular opposition from the alleged "Country"'.[43] In both periods, 'Country' was chiefly an historiographical device to balance 'Court': 'Country' could not ultimately be depicted as a coherent party. For Pulteney, Carteret and Bolingbroke in the 1740s as for Coke and Wentworth in the 1620s, a 'Country' stance was dictated by their exclusion from office, a situation which they hoped manoeuvre could reverse, not by their typologically representing a pattern of forces in society at large. 'What we are really faced with is politics', concluded Professor Elton, and political realities dissolved the vast person-ifications of both periods alike. Detailed political studies were consequen-tly unwelcome to the Old Guard in both areas.

High-political revisionism, here as elsewhere, rested on an explicit negation of the Old Guard's economic–reductionist case. Russell main-tained that two clear-cut parties did not exist in Parliaments before 1640 because 'where there is not a divided society, there is not the fuel to sustain a division into two parties'.[44] For the 1640s also, high-political revisionism rejected ideas of social revolution as a prior cause: 'the ultimate split was quite clearly a split within the governing class'. Equally, the idea of Court v. Country had failed: 'Most of those involved' in the events unfolded in Anthony Fletcher's *The Outbreak of the English Civil War* 'did not think of themselves as belonging exclusively to either entity'. Mr Fletcher was

43  Elton, 'The Unexplained Revolution', p. 185.
44  Russell, 'Parliamentary History in Perspective, 1604–1629', *History* 61 (1976), 20.

brought back to the wider ideological issues: 'There is a real sense in which the English Civil War was a war of religion.'[45]

Professor Hirst, too, argued for a rephrasing of the simple polarity. The existence of 'Country' in the sense of aggressive localism, in so far as it did exist, was provoked by royal centralisation. Yet, at the centre, parliamentary rhetoric gives a false impression of purposive and ideologically identified parties; organised localist obstruction of early-Stuart legislation is markedly absent; parliamentary conflicts in 1604–29 do not reveal the existence of two 'sides', two coherent groups of peers or commoners, whether of Court or Country.[46] In respect of the careers of individuals, too, a simple ascription of loyalties on a two-party model will not fit. Many of the conflicts can be explained by individual reactions to the distortions of the system and of conventional expectations produced by the exceptional and widely resented dominance of Buckingham (the analogy with Walpole was made in the latter's own day), and by James I's and especially Charles I's increasing departure from the Elizabethan practice of a mixed Privy Council in favour of a homogeneous group of advisers[47] – in early-eighteenth-century terms, single-party government. Similarly, the careers of those parliamentarians enlisted by Professor Zagorin in the Country seem hardly to bear out an indelible ideological loyalty: most are better described as 'intelligent and frustrated courtiers'.[48] Equally, in the localities the need for access to power at the centre prevented the emergence of a monolithic bloc in opposition to the royal administration.[49]

The early-Stuart period witnessed a new phenomenon: 'the ambitious politician who made the life of government so difficult that it seemed best to solve the problem by giving him office' – Sir John Eliot, William Noy, Sir Edwin Sandys, Sir Thomas Wentworth[50] – not committed members of a Country interest, but natural 'ins' alienated only by their exclusion from power and influence. Similarly, once we dispense with the notion that early-eighteenth-century Tories were natural backbenchers (some were, but then so were most Whigs) we can appreciate that both elements of the opposition, Tory and opposition Whig, genuinely sought office and fought for it with all the arts of electioneering and manoeuvre.

Early-Stuart historians validly retrieved a meaning for 'Country' as a nexus of ideas, attitudes and dispositions – the moral superiority of rustic

---

[45] Anthony Fletcher, *The Outbreak of the English Civil War* (London, 1981), pp. 407–8, 417–18.
[46] Derek Hirst, 'Court, Country, and Politics before 1629' in Sharpe (ed.), *Faction and Parliament*, pp. 105–37.
[47] *Ibid.*, pp. 105–12.
[48] *Ibid.*, pp. 114–15.
[49] *Ibid.*, pp. 118–23.
[50] G. R. Elton, 'Tudor Government: The Points of Contact. I. Parliament', *TRHS* 24 (1974), 200.

values over Court corruption. Much more was entailed, however, by reifying this nexus and projecting it on to the parliamentary stage, treating Country as an organised unit committed to implementing such attitudes as a programme. This was the 'great leap' to which John Morrill objected in Lawrence Stone's work.[51] The 'pure' Country as localist introversion and as value system certainly existed, maintained Morrill, but it had difficulty in co-operating with those metropolitan politicians who said they represented it (but who, like Francis Russell, 4th Earl of Bedford, pursued policies little different, except in religious matters, from the Court's). Historians of what they saw as an early-Hanoverian Country party could profitably have used this analysis. They should also have been warned by available studies of pollbooks that the gentry were divided on many issues; co-operative gentry could always be found to by-pass the recalcitrant, and, as in the 1680s, the executive might even go beyond the ranks of landed patricians in its search for local agents. A divided county gentry, especially after 1688, looks much less like a Country party or even a Country interest the more it is studied at local level.

The eighteenth-century restructurings of the Commissions of the Peace, however, show the continued scope for executive use of a landed elite. In a conflict between centre and periphery, the centre held most of the Court cards. The administrative and political relationship of central and local elites was a reciprocal one, as Professor Hirst rightly insisted; 'their relationship is so integral that if they can be identified as opposed entities then government has reached a stage of major crisis, and even breakdown'.[52] And it was a breakdown traced not to administrative problems *tout court*, but to these only when the Court seriously began to undo the religious settlement. In the 1680s, equally, Stuart management of merely secular affairs was surprisingly successful until religion was allowed to intrude. It was a lesson which George I and George II learned well: if the Hanoverian Whigs sought to stifle one sort of controversy above all, it was politico-theological controversy, and for so long as dynastic–religious issues did not explode, the Crown had no difficulty in 1714–60 in ruling through local elites, even divided elites.

Since it was now clear that the 'Country' did not identify itself in the years before the Civil War, it became more difficult to visualise a clearly defined opposition. If a parliamentary 'Country' alignment can be listed in 1640, it must be remembered that it was split in 1642 by the final need to take sides: in half the English counties, one Member chose the King, one Parliament; peers formerly associated with the Court were similarly

[51] John Morrill, *The Revolt of the Provinces* (London, 1976), p. 17.
[52] Hirst, 'Court, Country, and Politics before 1629', p. 123.

divided.[53] In the early Hanoverian period too, historians were forced to attend to the *divisions* within the Country bloc, which the threat of a Stuart restoration kept alive: Tory and opposition Whig were in many ways opposites, not natural allies. Not only did they fail to cement an effective tactical liaison, but their temporarily united front shattered under the stresses of the 1740s.

The 'myth' that even the Long Parliament 'was united against the King from the first' was effectively challenged by Sheila Lambert: it, like all previous Parliaments, 'had come to do business as usual', not to seize sovereignty from the Crown. Moreover, a study of the Lords' and Commons' *Journals* suggests that it was 'the role of the peers, not the Commons, that was crucial';[54] and a London-oriented peerage seems a less obvious candidate for a Country role than the gentry, reluctantly brought to Westminster from their rural pursuits. Conrad Russell, too, suggested that that Parliament was not called by the King with the intention of making inevitable concessions, but that he was persuaded of the need to do so only a month after it had met. If even the King did not perceive a nexus of grievances resolving itself into a 'Country' position, the historian might be more cautious in supplying a category which contemporaries had failed to devise. And if even the Civil War cannot be explained in terms of a Court v. Country polarity, in which above all it ought to be visible, the revisionist should be equally cautious of describing the more muted social stresses of 'pudding time', *c.*1714–60, in similar terms.[55]

The survival of far greater numbers of division lists after *c.*1689 offered the possibility of testing the rival theses with more certainty for the later period. It was the scholarly analysis of these lists which called in doubt the Old Guard's reductionist assumption that Court and Country were in some sense the underlying and permanent phenomena, and that Whig and Tory were a temporary superstructure which, for a time, masked a locally and economically rooted reality. One such analysis by a member of the History of Parliament team suggested that, for the period 1689–*c.*1720 at least, the division between Court and Country coincided quite closely with the division between Whig and Tory: far from being fundamentally different polarities, the similarities between the two classifications were more important.

Moreover, in this later period as before 1642, Court and Country existed mainly as attitudes, stances, clusters of ideas. Although a Court interest was clearly defined, no such precision attached to the adherents of the Country. Dr David Hayton, discussing the reigns of William III and

[53] Morrill, *Revolt of the Provinces*, p. 18.
[54] Sheila Lambert, 'The Opening of the Long Parliament', *HJ* 27 (1984), 265–87, at 285.
[55] Conrad Russell, 'Why Did Charles I Call the Long Parliament?', *History* 69 (1984), 375–83.

Anne, drew an explicit analogy with the work of Professors Derek Hirst and Conrad Russell. In both periods, 'Country' MPs prove to have a close involvement with the world of Court patronage and commercial, financial, legal or bureaucratic profit. Sir Lewis Namier's bucolic model of the independent country gentleman was revealed as an ideal type rather than a widespread species: in the seventeenth century as in the eighteenth, rural isolation and Provincial introversion were broken down by the City associations and political contacts of many gentry, especially those affluent enough to seek parliamentary seats. In both centuries, too, Court contacts were exceedingly important to Country politicians seeking to defend and strengthen their local positions, and Court or Country alignment might often be an unedifying consequence of whether a man was 'in' or 'out': 'nearly all the principal figures among the Country Whigs had feet of clay', concluded Dr Hayton: 'Far from being disinterested patriots, they appear as peevish or ambitious opportunists.'[56]

Similar arguments can be extended forward to the 1750s. Much of the force of the claim that in 1714 'the structure of politics changed from a division along Whig–Tory lines to one along the lines of Court and Country' had derived from the assumption that, even in 1689–1714, the Court v. Country polarity had been a powerful, underlying and radically different one which naturally reasserted itself at a time of political stability.[57] The removal of that assumption further weakened the force of the Court v. Country analysis for the years 1714–60. It had for many years been reinforced by a fortuitous coincidence: a retrojection of the Namierite model of the 1760s, and the seventeenth-century Old Guard's need to find an oligarchic–bourgeois end-point to their argument. Now, parliamentary historians pushed forward the applicability of Namier's account to its proper habitat, the first decade of George III's reign: the fragility of the Old Guard account of the first two Georges was thereby thrown into sharp relief.

A defence was nevertheless bravely attempted by Professor Speck.[58] Although he was now obliged to concede what the research of the History

[56] David Hayton, 'The "Country" Interest and the Party System, 1689–c.1720', in Clyve Jones (ed.), *Party and Management in Parliament, 1660–1784* (Leicester, 1984), pp. 37–85, citing Derek Hirst, 'Court, Country and Politics before 1629', in Sharpe (ed.), *Faction and Parliament*, and Conrad Russell, *Parliaments and English Politics 1621–1629*. For a defence of the Court v. Country thesis, see D. A. Rubini, 'Party and the Augustan Constitution, 1694–1716: Politics and the Power of the Executive', *Albion* 10 (1978), 193–208.

[57] Hayton, 'The "Country" Interest and the Party System', p. 40, citing H. T. Dickinson, *Liberty and Property: Political Ideology in Eighteenth Century England* (London, 1977), pp. 91, 102, 123, and W. A. Speck, *Stability and Strife: England 1714–1760* (London, 1977), p. 7.

[58] W. A. Speck, 'Whigs and Tories Dim their Glories: English Political Parties under the First Two Georges', in John Cannon (ed.), *The Whig Ascendancy: Colloquies on Hanoverian England* (London, 1981), pp. 51–70.

of Parliament team had uncovered – that oppositions were composite bodies made up of a large and consistent group of Tories in uneasy alliance with fluctuating groups of Whig 'outs' – he sought to deny that those Tories were 'ideologically distinct from opposition Whigs'.[59]

This denial had a number of components. Professor Speck suggested that the Commons' division lists which found their way into print in the years 1714–42 'do not reflect the survival of issues which polarized the political world into Whig and Tory parties in Anne's reign. On the contrary, they record the eclipse of those issues and their replacement by questions which created tensions between Court and Country.'[60] Yet, if anti-ministerial strength could only be maximised on issues which seemed to avoid the old issues of greatest sensitivity (religion and the dynasty prominent among them), then opposition leaders chose their ground wisely. To Professor Speck's published lists, however, must be added one on a classic issue, the Bill to repeal the Occasional Conformity and Schism Acts in January 1719. Whig ministries thereafter tried hard but not always successfully to evade parliamentary conflicts on Church matters, as the indecently hasty Pelhamite retreat on the Jewish Naturalisation Act in 1753 abundantly illustrated. Despite Whig schisms, moreover, the parliamentary lists of the early eighteenth century continued to distinguish the two party identities of those MPs hostile to the ministry.[61] If Court and Country are to be seen as reflecting a quite different polarity and agenda from Whig and Tory, then the prominence of Court v. Country issues clearly failed to destroy the tactical groupings of Whig and Tory: yet this assumption itself is now called in question by Dr Hayton's analysis.

It would at least be a *non sequitur* to argue that the absence of published division lists on the old issues proved those issues' demise: sufficient conflict on such matters can be amply documented from other sources throughout the 1720s, 30s and 40s. Professor Speck, on the contrary, wished to argue from evidence other than from that provided by division lists that those issues swiftly faded: Jacobitism became the commitment of a tiny minority of extremists; the politics of other men were progressively secularised. Consequently, underlying causes could have their effect: 'To some extent the transition from the rage of party to the struggle between Court and Country was due, not merely to the passing of the old issues

---

[59] *Ibid.*, p. 59.

[60] *Ibid.*, p. 60. Speck cites the published lists on: the Septennial Bill, 1716, the Peerage Bill, 1719; the Civil List, 1729; Hessian troops, 1730; the army estimates, 1732; the Excise Bill, 1733; a Bill to repeal the Septennial Act, 1734; the Convention of Pardo, 1739; a place Bill, 1740; the election of a chairman of the Committee of Privileges, 1741; Hanoverian troops, 1742.

[61] A list by Newcastle's parliamentary manager Thomas Hay, Viscount Dupplin, of the Commons returned at the general election of 1754 divides MPs into 'for', 'against Whigs', 'against Tories' and 'doubtful': British Library Add. MSS 33034, ff. 173–81.

which had divided Tory from Whig, but also to changes in society which created a conflict of interests cutting across the old party lines.' Such causes were both underlying and ante-dating: 'Court and Country were much older divisions than Whig and Tory, dating back at least to the 1620s ...'[62]

It seemed, then, that the Court v. Country analysis was not established by the evidence of division lists: it was illustrated by an interpretation of that evidence. The real warrant for that analytical framework was the moral righteousness of the critique of the Walpolian oligarchy offered by the Commonwealth ideologists from Trenchard and Gordon back to Sidney and Harrington.[63]

### From what time do modern parties date?

The Old Hat school, from Feiling and Trevelyan (and beyond) had seen the origin of the eighteenth-century parties of Whig and Tory in what they had defined as the long-growing, libertarian–constitutionalist opposition to the early Stuarts.[64] The early-Stuart revisionist demolition of this scenario thus linked appropriately with a growing understanding of the uniqueness and importance of the Exclusion Crisis of 1678–81 – not only as the occasion of Locke's *Two Treatises*,[65] but as the genesis of those Whig and Tory parties which took on a more coherent and lasting form in the 1690s.[66]

A different dating, of course, meant different issues and a different dynamic to the story of party: politico–theological issues revolving around the dynasty and receiving their most sophisticated treatment in the long-ignored writings of the Nonjurors were a world away from the Old Hat conception of civil liberties and limited monarchy as the achievement of the 1640s or 1688, and offered little support for a teleological picture of

[62] Speck, 'Whigs and Tories Dim their Glories', pp. 57–9, 63–7.

[63] Cf.: 'Morally the worst period of all for England in transition seems to have been the opening decades of the eighteenth century': Christopher Hill, *Some Intellectual Consequences of the English Revolution* (London, 1980), p. 84.

[64] Keith Feiling, in *A History of the Tory Party 1640–1714* (Oxford, 1924), despite fancifully tracing Whig and Tory to the Reformation, correctly denied the continuity between parties in 1660–1714 and those of the nineteenth century (though he wrongly thought the Tories 'vanished' in 1714); G. M. Trevelyan, in *The Two Party System in English Political History* (Oxford, 1926), disastrously asserted such a continuity, and this view was confusedly adopted in Feiling's subsequent *The Second Tory Party 1714–1832* (London, 1938). Precisely what the liberals thought was often rather muddled, except in so far as (like Trevelyan) they unthinkingly absorbed Marxist ideas.

[65] The dating was established by Peter Laslett's edition of John Locke, *Two Treatises of Government* (Cambridge, 1960).

[66] J. R. Jones, *The First Whigs: The Politics of the Exclusion Crisis 1678–1683* (London, 1961); Robert Willman, 'The Origin of "Whig" and "Tory" in English Political Language', *HJ* 17 (1974), 247–64; Henry Horwitz, *Parliament, Policy and Politics in the Reign of William III* (Manchester, 1977).

1760–1832 as the culmination of a grand historical process whose dynamic was correctly exploited by radicals' championing of parliamentary reform. Early-Hanoverian revisionism, indeed, uncovered a party pattern which disintegrated in the 1750s. It was now clear that (*pace* Trevelyan) the English experience had not been of a single party system, sometimes in good repair, sometimes working badly, always looking forward to a Victorian heyday. If the political practices of each age were assessed in their own terms, it could validly be argued that England had experienced a series of party systems, each expressing a unique combination of conventions, each equally valid for its own time.

At local level, too, it was not the Civil War but the Exclusion Crisis and the Glorious Revolution which fundamentally altered the issues and alignments. In most local communities until 1688 the basic pattern had been that of an Anglican gentry majority, often with a considerable degree of corporate solidarity, but challenged by the competing claims of smaller groups of Puritans and Roman Catholics on either flank. Moreover, the Anglican 'county community' was often profoundly uneasy at the policies of central government, which seemingly threatened to turn either minority into a majority or, at least, to hand them local power. In 1688, what was most remarkable about the county gentry was their unanimity in rejecting James II.

After 1688 this pattern changed profoundly. A *modus vivendi* was worked out with both minorities. Although not wholly placid, a formula combining toleration of worship with substantial exclusion from political participation remained a workable one into the reign of George III. The Anglican gentry majority was henceforth entrenched in a dominant position both locally and nationally; the numerical strength of the two minorities steadily shrank. But there was one important difference. From the 1690s to the 1750s the Anglican majority was split down the middle between the two great parties of Whig and Tory.

This split had much to do with religion, as before, but now it was about how the Anglican hegemony was to be understood and defined. What was the Church of England? High Church and Low Church parties (to use the terminology of Anne's reign) offered fundamentally different interpretations of a common – but ambiguous – Anglican inheritance. And, equally importantly, the split had to do with the dynasty. Who was the rightful king? Did Anglican political theology permit the succession to be altered? If it did, was the Church *ipso facto* merely a department of State? If not, could the Church defend itself against the claims of a Papist monarch?

With little essential change, these agonising choices and insoluble riddles structured the political thinking of Britain from 1688 to the 1750s. The gentry elite, in the counties and at Westminster, was divided by clear marks of identity. Party allegiances passed from father to son. Local rivalries were subsumed within wider national antagonisms: Whig and Tory were burned into the elite's political consciousness in a way that was to prove almost indelible. How this polarity was superseded at local level has scarcely yet been investigated by historians.[67] Their attention was initially focussed on Westminster, where the break-up of the old party system was eventually traced to the 1750s.

If the Whig v. Tory polarity was to be firmly located in the decades from the 1690s to the 1750s, with a premonition in the Exclusion Crisis of 1678–81, where did that leave the traditional Old Hat account of the breakdown of 1642 as the culmination of conflict between a political elite which had for decades been divided into two (or more) clearly antagonistic parties? Scholarship since Brian Wormald's *Clarendon* had already profoundly modified this picture by showing how *late* to emerge was the distinction between Royalist and Roundhead.

This insight had to be reconciled with the new understanding of the importance of religious conflicts. As Anthony Fletcher summarised it,

It is right to look to the early years of Charles I's reign for the beginning of that 'mutual commerce of fear' which we have to understand if we are to explain why political deadlock ended in war. By 1628 Charles and Laud had destroyed the religious unity of England, which many gentry saw as the foundation of monarchy, liberty and law. The eventual outcome of the division created by the promotion of Arminianism in the 1620s was the division Pym created in 1641 by his attempt to use Parliament as an instrument to ward off popish conspiracy. In this sense religious issues provided the fundamental cause of the civil war. But any such assertion carries the danger of over-simplifying the events of 1641 and 1642. It is the many-sidedness of the political process of these years that needs to be stressed at the outset.[68]

Were 'parties', thus generated, a lasting phenomenon? Were the alignments of the 1640s essentially the same as the alignments of the 1690s? On the question of party structure, early-Stuart revisionists might have profited from a longer perspective. Professor Kishlansky suggested that 'Parties, in the modern sense, did appear in the Revolution [of the 1640s], but the inconsistent use of the term made it seem that they had existed from the beginning of the war or, from Clarendon's account, even earlier.'[69] While the correction of pre-1640 misstatements is valuable, the early-Hanoverian revisionist would add that there is no *one* modern sense of party: the phenomena of parties have continued to develop, fragment,

[67] For an initial enquiry see Philip Jenkins, *The Making of a Ruling Class: The Glamorgan Gentry 1640–1790* (Cambridge, 1983), pp. 172–84. Dr Jenkins somewhat underestimated the potential for a Stuart restoration in the 1740s, however.

[68] Fletcher, *The Outbreak of the English Civil War* , pp. xxix–xxx.

[69] Kishlansky, 'The Emergence of Adversary Politics', pp. 626–7.

collapse and redevelop in many forms over many centuries, and we are not justified in elevating one model rather than others as a norm.

Other early-Stuart historians thought that Namier's analysis applied more properly to the Hanoverian period, since eighteenth-century England was a society untroubled by divisions over 'compelling issues of principle, in which therefore the motive force of personal ambition could freely operate within the network of interest-groups and connections'. Nevertheless, scholars such as Professor Underdown came to see much value in applying Namier's analysis of parliamentary groupings to the Long Parliament: the small minority of professional politicians; the Court and Treasury group of office-holders, basically loyal to the King's government as such; the independent country gentlemen, preoccupied with local issues, seeking to defend the values of the county communities at the centre. Underdown added another category: 'the clients of great noblemen'. 'All four categories can be observed in the Long Parliament', he noted, 'and it is through their interaction that the party system, in its limited and often confusing way, operated.' Consequently, 'Parties, it is clear, were at best vague, ephemeral and transitory, loose associations of individuals or groups who might temporarily co-operate on some of the major issues of the day, but might equally well be divided quite differently on others.'[70]

This was a valuable corrective to the 'two-party system' of Presbyterian and Independent posited by Gardiner. Professor Underdown's insight was an important stage along the revisionist road which led from Hexter's *The Reign of King Pym* and Wormald's *Clarendon* to Russell and the other authors of the last decade. If early-Stuart high-political history was indeed influenced by Namier, this was not illegitimate: revisionist writing in the eighteenth century took the form not of a repudiation of Namier, but of an elucidation of the exact chronological period to which his analysis applied.[71] It was the 1760s and early 1770s, not the century as a whole, which witnessed the absence of an overriding polarity giving order to parliamentary alignments; and in this sense the politics of 1603–42 legitimately drew on Namierite insights on the relation between centre and locality. In this sense, too, the Old Guard and Old Hat historians reacted

---

[70] David Underdown, *Pride's Purge: Politics in the Puritan Revolution* (Oxford, 1971), pp. 2–3, 47.

[71] Namier, as a careful student of the Newcastle Papers, seems to have realised that transitions were occurring in the 1750s which transformed the Whig v. Tory alignment of the early eighteenth century into the multi-factional pattern which characterised the 1760s: cf. the references cited in J. C. D. Clark, 'The Decline of Party, 1740–1760', *EHR* 93 (1978), 499–527, at 502. A possible charge against Namier is that despite this youthful insight he did not afterwards object when his pupils and colleagues suggested that a Namierite analysis in terms of factions applied to much larger areas of the eighteenth century than that which it was devised to fit.

in both periods against a phenomenon which they described (strictly inaccurately, but not without some point) as a recrudescence of Namierism.

Some early-Stuart revisionists were evidently over-enthusiastic in their
resort to Namierite weapons, however: they place a reliance on them which
early-Hanoverian revisionists had already learned not to place. Professor
Christianson, writing in 1976, believed that the old orthodoxy about an
initiative-seizing Commons was to be countered by a proper appreciation
of the power of the aristocracy in the period up to 1642; and that this in turn
would lead to analyses of Westminster politics in terms of patron and client
rather than forward-looking parties. 'Historians can turn to the promising
task of charting the networks of patronage, kinship and friendship which
dominated the politics of court and country and of analysing the conceptualisations of proper paternalistic order which these groups aimed to
establish or uphold – including office for themselves'.[72]

Some of this had been anticipated. Professor Snow's study of patronage
and politics focussed on the third Earl of Essex revealed much about the
origins of parliamentary conflict in the strife of peers, and about the continued priority of the House of Lords even after 1640.[73] The two 'sides' in
the Civil War were King and Parliament, not King and Commons. The
challenge which this view posed both to the traditional Whig historiography of the Long Parliament, and to the argument of Lawrence Stone's *The
Crisis of the Aristocracy 1558–1641* (1965), was correctly perceived at the
time.[74] An affluent and powerful peerage hardly squared with assumptions
about the Commons' seizing of the initiative, and doing so for 'constitutional', meaning commoner–libertarian, issues of principle. 'Detailed
studies of the patronage of the seventeenth-century peerage are badly
needed', concluded Professor Farnell in 1972. 'And those working on the
House of Commons should be fully awake to the realities of peerage influence in that House at elections, in day-to-day political manoeuvre, and in
relationship to the bedevilled subject of party alignment. Only then may
the political dynamics of the Long Parliament and other Stuart parliaments be fully understood.'[75]

His programmatic remarks came to fruition (or, as some would argue,
were displayed in their most extreme form) five years later in the same
journal.[76] To the eighteenth-century historian, such work had a familiar

---

[72] Paul Christianson, 'The Causes of the English Revolution: A Reappraisal', *JBS* 15 no. 2 (1976), 60–7 and sources cited; cf. Sharpe in *Faction and Parliament*, pp. 31–2.

[73] Vernon F. Snow, *Essex the Rebel: The Life of Robert Devereux, the Third Earl of Essex 1591–1646* (Lincoln, Nebraska, 1970).

[74] James E. Farnell, 'The Aristocracy and Leadership of Parliament in the English Civil Wars', *JMH* 44 (1972), 79–86.

[75] *Ibid.*, p. 86.

[76] Cf. the articles by J. K. Gruenfelder, P. Christianson, C. Roberts, M. Kishlansky and J. E. Farnell, *JMH* 49 (1977), 557–660.

ring: in this direction the process of revisionism had already proceeded further in the later period. Indeed, such Namierite *techniques* had already doubled back in terms of *results*, and revealed a most unexpected political environment in the 1715–54 volumes of the *History of Parliament*: both the parliamentary arena and constituency politics were still dominated by the traditional great parties of Whig and Tory, dating in their essentials from the 1690s if not from the Exclusion Crisis of 1679–81. Nevertheless, for the earlier period, there initially seemed to be much to be gained from investigations of such carefully defined subjects as, for example, John Pym's dependence on the Earl of Bedford.[77]

Similarly, Professor Hirst sought to dissolve the clear and mutually exclusive categories of Court and Country (which supported assumptions of adversary politics) by analogy with later practice: Court v. Country was too simple a picture, he argued; Hanoverian scholars had progressed beyond it.

Historians of the early eighteenth century tend to describe political alignments almost in terms of boxing the compass: and when feuds like that of Wentworth and Savile cut across apparent political assumptions, with both sides making approaches to Buckingham and both sides appealing to anti-court prejudice in the country, it does not seem that navigation of some areas of the early seventeenth-century terrain was much more straightforward.[78]

The reference was to Robert Walcott's Namierite model of the Commons in 1689–1714:

It is possible ... to read the roster of party groups as though we were boxing the compass: courtiers, Court Tories, Churchill Tories, Harley Tories, Rochester Tories, Nottingham Tories, October Club Tories, Country Tories, Country Members, Country Whigs, Junto Whigs, Walpole–Townshend Whigs, Court Whigs, and so back to courtiers ... we venture to say that the description of party organization under William and Anne which Trevelyan suggested in his Romanes lecture on the two-party system is less applicable to our period than the detailed picture of eighteenth-century politics which emerges from Professor Namier's volumes on the Age of Newcastle.[79]

Although Professor Hirst's point was a correct one, it could have been much more strongly made by reference to the more recent scholarship of the eighteenth century. Professor Walcott's attempt to read back a factionalised model to the period 1688–1714 had been received with private scepticism by Namier himself,[80] and virtually every historian to work on

[77] Conrad Russell (ed.), *The Origins of the English Civil War* (London, 1973), pp. 109–14.
[78] Hirst, 'Court, Country, and Politics before 1629', pp. 136–7.
[79] Robert Walcott, 'English Party Politics (1688–1714)', in *Essays in Modern English History in Honour of Wilbur Cortez Abbott* (Cambridge, Mass., 1941), p. 131; cf. *idem, English Politics in the Early Eighteenth Century* (Oxford, 1956); *idem*, 'The Idea of Party in the Writing of Later Stuart History', *JBS* 1 no. 2 (1962), 54–61.
[80] *Ex. inf.* Mr John Brooke.

the subject since the late 1960s has dissociated himself from Walcott's analysis.[81] The denigration of that scholar's work became almost ritualistic, and one suspects that he was sometimes condemned unread. Yet it should be acknowledged that he was a pioneer of the detailed investigation of parliamentary politics in these years, and among the first deliberately to work towards an alternative to Trevelyan's two-party teleology. Nevertheless the framework of interpretation on which he chose to deploy his research has not survived further enquiry, and any early-Stuart attempt to use Namierite techniques before the Civil War must now take account of the reinstatement of party in 1689–1714.

So far has that reinstatement gone that it now seems more credible largely to explain Court and Country issues in Whig and Tory terms. Professor Walcott's metaphor now seems more than ever misleading, Dr Hayton suggested:

> If we are to retain the interpretation of 'Whig and Tory' and 'Court and Country' as different sets of points on the political compass, the least that should be done is to alter their arrangement. Rather than view them as competing polarities, the line from Court to Country cutting across that from Whig to Tory at right angles, we should set the two alignments much closer together ... But perhaps it would be wiser to throw away the compass altogether ... it may be better to treat 'Court and Country' separately from 'Whig and Tory', as something quite different: 'another level of political consciousness' has been one suggestion.[82]

To Professor Hexter in 1958, accepting Walcott's account of political practice in William III's reign, it seemed that what had been wrongly diagnosed by the Old Guard as the 'rise of the gentry' in the early seventeenth century was in reality an hiatus, a 'power vacuum', a time of gentry independence after the end of their feudal organisation as the magnates' armed retainers, since 'the magnates had not yet found their vocation for commanding solid phalanxes of borough members sitting in Parliament for the rotten and pocket boroughs that the magnates controlled'.[83] By the 1980s, the accumulation of new scholarship had made it impossible to accept the second part of this argument as an account of parliamentary politics after 1688. The discrediting of the Walcott model may have encouraged early-Stuart scholars to seek analogies in the earlier period for the real (though lesser) magnate influence in the later. On the other hand our better understanding of the ideological basis of party in the

---

81  Cf. the work listed in Clark, 'Decline of Party', p. 503 nn. 1–3, plus, importantly, W. A. Speck, *Tory and Whig: The Struggle in the Constituencies, 1701–15* (London, 1970), and Horwitz, *Parliament, Policy and Politics in the Reign of William III*.

82  Hayton, 'The "Country" Interest and the Party System, 1689–c.1720', p. 65, quoting Frank O'Gorman, *The Rise of Party in England: The Rockingham Whigs 1760–82* (London, 1975), p. 495.

83  Hexter, 'Storm over the Gentry' (1958), in *Reappraisals in History* (London, 1961), p. 148, citing Walcott, *English Politics in the Early Eighteenth Century* (1956).

decades following the Exclusion Crisis has encouraged us to look for more momentous causes of the prominence of issues in the events of the 1640s than gentry indiscipline alone.

The reinstatement of party in the reigns of William III and Anne was not undertaken as a challenge to the Old Guard, however. Rather the contrary. With near unanimity, the historians who worked on those years saw their contribution as highlighting a contrast between English society before and after 1714: a transition between an open society, a vigorous and undeferential electorate, an ideologically articulate struggle over principles; and a closed society brought about by 'the crushing of the electorate', political dissent stifled by single-party government, issues at a discount in a secularising, somnolent oligarchy. Scholars such as Holmes, Dickinson and Speck (whose achievements for the period before 1714 are not here disputed) rested their case by linking it to the account of Walpolian oligarchy classically formulated by J. H. Plumb.[84]

Within this perspective, it seemed quite acceptable that Namierite analysis should apply to the parliamentary alignments of the first two Georges, and the able application of this pattern to the 1740s by Dr J. B. Owen in *The Rise of the Pelhams* (1957) was long unquestioned either by Namierites or the Old Guard. So deeply rooted was this belief that remarkably little attention was paid to a formidable achievement of scholarship which, in fact, demolished it. In 1970 the volumes of the *History of Parliament* covering the years 1715–54 were published, edited by Romney Sedgwick.[85] Their effect was seismic: tall structures were levelled to the ground; many illusions the earth opened and swallowed up. But the earthquake occurred in a desert area: there were few or no travellers to gauge and report its effects.

Not only did Sedgwick and his collaborators, especially Dr Eveline Cruickshanks, argue that the traditional parties of Whig and Tory survived during the reigns of the first two Georges: the survival of a Tory

---

[84] J. H. Plumb, *The Growth of Political Stability in England 1675–1725* (Harmondsworth, 1969; first pub. 1967), pp. 26, 54–7 for a dismissal of electoral deference and gentry leadership as proposed by Namier and Walcott. Both authors have since been substantially vindicated on this subject by the work of D. C. Moore, John Vincent, Norma Landau, Frank O'Gorman and others. Plumb's theory of the Civil War is supported by reference (p. 32) to, among other works, W. B. Mitchell's *The Rise of the Revolutionary Party in the English House of Commons 1603–29* (New York, 1957), one of the texts since discredited by early-Stuart revisionism. Cf. Plumb, *op. cit.*, p. 187: 'The seventeenth century had witnessed the beginnings and partial success of a bourgeois revolution that came near to changing the institutions of government. In this, however, it never succeeded. The Revolution of 1688 and all that followed were retrogressive from the point of view of the emergence of the middle class into political power. Socially and economically they continued to thrive, but not politically', etc., etc.

[85] Romney Sedgwick (ed.), *The History of Parliament: The House of Commons 1715–1754* (2 vols., London, 1970).

parliamentary party of over 130 MPs had been observed by Owen and accepted even by Plumb.[86] But, though they accepted it, they dismissed the fact as an interesting anomaly. Plumb continued (four pages later) to write of 'the destruction of the Tory party', and Owen adhered to a Namierite factional model of parliamentary alignments. Court and Country swamped Whig and Tory, most historians believed. What made Sedgwick's volumes explosive was Dr Cruickshanks' argument, which made it impossible so to brush Tory survival aside: that the Tories were heavily involved, at different times, with Jacobitism and that the latter was a powerful and lasting force in politics.

This claim did not rest on the military ability of the English gentry to effect a restoration from their own resources: Dr Cruickshanks explicitly acknowledged the insuperable practical problems in the path of any such attempt, obstacles which proved decisive in 1715 and 1745. Yet, as she pertinently observed, Professor Underdown had shown how the same military realities and a ruthless persecution of Royalists by a determined central government had ruled out a spontaneous restoration in the 1650s.[87] Nevertheless, 1660 revealed the wide basis for a restored monarchy once military intervention from elsewhere (in this case, Monck's army) had made the initial breakthrough. Stuart allegiance in the reigns of George I and George II, as during the 1650s, had therefore to be gauged by other means.

Such an argument, if true, shifted the centre ground in historical debate. Tories had traditionally been pictured as a small anomaly within a system defined by Locke, or latterly as hardly distinguishable from opposition Whigs within a Country opposition sharing a neo-Harringtonian idiom of discourse. In both scenarios, Jacobites had consequently appeared as a tiny fringe of extremists with no place in a world of Whig practicalities. Now, pursuing Dr Cruickshanks' insight, historians went on to confirm not only that the Whig v. Tory alignment was the overriding axis on which parliamentary groupings were to be understood, but also that that alignment corresponded to an ideological polarity which overrode and subsumed the economic–reductionist polarity of Court and Country. Dr Cruickshanks did not examine ideology directly, however, and not all these implications were immediately apparent. What with hindsight appears as a self-confidently revisionist campaign began, in the 1970s, as a cautious

---

[86] J. B. Owen, *The Rise of the Pelhams* (London, 1957), pp. 66–7; Plumb, *Political Stability*, p. 169.

[87] David Underdown, *Royalist Conspiracy in England 1649–1660* (New Haven, Conn., 1960). Professor Underdown's excellent study was perhaps neglected since, as he warned, the reader would search his pages 'in vain for yet another set of generalisations (based on insufficient evidence) about the status of the gentry, whether Royalist or parliamentarian, rising or declining' (pp. x–xi). Social-change explanations still dominated the field.

and technical exploration of the complexities of early-Hanoverian high politics.

One line of enquiry was opened up by Dr Cruickshanks' pioneering work on the Tories. Dr B. W. Hill offered a framework of interpretation from the 1690s to the 1740s not merely in terms of party but of a party *system*. Even into the 1730s, the emergence of a 'Country' opposition was prevented by the antipathies of Tories and opposition Whigs on central issues. Those observations led Dr Hill to conclude that parties survived after 1714 not only because of their wide electoral base in the country, especially in the county and larger urban constituencies (again a line of argument stemming from the localist researches of the History of Parliament group), but also because of the persistence of those burning issues of principle, dating from the Exclusion Crisis and the Revolution, which had been the staple of political conflict under William III and Anne.[88]

The Old Guard or Old Hat establishment was willing to accept B. W. Hill's first argument about Tory strength in the provinces, but resisted the second, on the survival of a Whig v. Tory nexus.[89] The thesis of the 'secularisation of politics', explored above, continued for many historians to obscure the lasting vitality of politico-theological issues, especially ones focussing on the Church and the dynasty.[90] Clearly, parliamentary politics to 1742 at least had now to be conceived in party terms. But subsequent events, especially those which led to an armed rebellion, had yet to be explained. Was the '45 a last, despairing, romantic, hopeless gamble? Or was it the mishandled (but still extremely dangerous) culmination of widespread resentment against Hanoverian rule? Was Tory parliamentary cohesion to be explained in self-sufficient terms as the result of efficient party machinery, or in relation also to an alternative dynastic option? It was this problem which Dr Cruickshanks' work in the Stuart papers finally solved, making intelligible the manoeuvres which led to the fall of Walpole and the restoration attempts of 1744 and 1745 in terms of Tory responsiveness to Stuart appeals.[91] Secondly, work had been proceeding concurrently on the Whig party after the '45, and the extension of a

[88] B. W. Hill, *The Growth of Parliamentary Parties 1689–1742* (London, 1976); by contrast L. J. Colley, 'The Loyal Brotherhod and the Cocoa Tree. The London Organisation of the Tory Party 1727–1760', *HJ* 20 (1977), 77–95, ascribed Tory survival to that party's rudimentary organisation (a thesis which was more welcome in Old Hat and Old Guard circles) rather than to the survival of a traditional ideological nexus.

[89] See Geoffrey Holmes' review, 'The Division of the House', *TLS* 27 May 1977, pp. 657–8.

[90] It is fair to say that Dr B. W. Hill did not explore these issues in depth; they did not attract the attention of historians, in the post-1714 period, until the mid 1980s.

[91] Eveline Cruickshanks, *Political Untouchables: The Tories and the '45* (London, 1979). A controversy had developed over the extent of popular Jacobite commitment: cf. Nicholas Rogers' articles listed in Appendix B.

Namierite analysis to inappropriate areas was challenged also for the 1740s. Dr J. B. Owen's detailed narrative of 1742–6[92] revealed, I argued, a political world dominated by a Whig–Tory polarity; parliamentary groupings indeed reordered themselves in this traditional pattern after the turmoil surrounding the fall of Walpole.

The question revisionists had then to pursue was: when and how far (if at all) did the parties of Anne's reign break down? To agree that the Tories disintegrated in 1714–16, leaving the Whigs without an identity other than that provided by their monopoly of the spoils of office, played into the hands of the Old Guard. No real emancipation from that old orthodoxy was offered, either, by a theory of Whig and Tory survival which was built around an account of their primitive organisation in the constituencies and in Parliament, though this is true enough as far as it goes.[93] A more adequate revisionism is one which places political action in a quite different ideological framework, and here again, in their rediscovery of religion, revisionists in both centuries explored similar territory. What reconciles the 1715–54 and 1754–90 volumes of the *History of Parliament*, and what reveals the compatibility of Namierite and revisionist interpretations, is the argument I sought to justify with a high-political narrative of the events of the 1750s: that political manoeuvre, in the context of the retreat of Jacobitism, broke up the historic parties of Whig and Tory and paved the way for the factionalised world of the 1760s, made familiar to us by Namier.

If so, we can answer with some certainty the question: do modern parties date from the Civil War or from the 1690s? The answer, I would suggest, is: they date from neither episode. In particular, if historians wish

---

[92] Owen, *The Rise of the Pelhams*. Dr Owen placed a Namierite analysis on these events, however, and it was this analysis from which I dissented in 'The Decline of Party, 1740–1760', *EHR* 93 (1978), 499–527. This does not mean that we can neglect Owen's work. My disagreement is with the analytical section of *The Rise of the Pelhams*; the narrative section contains by far the best account we have of the actual working of politics in the 1740s, and must be ranked with those other technically accomplished narratives (like Russell's of 1621–9 or Horwitz's of the reign of William III) which have provided a scholarly modern alternative to old orthodoxies.

[93] Linda Colley's *In Defiance of Oligarchy: The Tory Party 1714–60* (Cambridge, 1982) was written from 'a twentieth century liberal or socialist perspective' (p. 7) and quoted the Old Guard with approval; it took up Dr Cruickshanks' (1970) and Dr B. W. Hill's (1976) demonstrations of the survival of a Tory party at Westminster and added much valuable detail, particularly for the organisation and operation of the party at constituency level. Dr Colley stopped short of accepting Dr Cruickshanks' views on the central role of Jacobite allegiance, however. Since I disagree with several of the main theses of the book (see my review article 'The Politics of the Excluded: Tories, Jacobites and Whig Patriots, 1715–1760', *Parliamentary History* 2 (1983), 209–22), I am happy to add that it also contains much of interest.

to treat Victorian parties as the paradigm, it is to the world after 1832 that we must look for their emergence.[94]

### Patronage and clientage: the survival of 'Old Corruption'?

These qualifications with which later historians have surrounded Namier-ite analysis of patronage structures might have warned early-Stuart revisionists against too much enthusiasm about what they seem in the mid 1970s to have regarded as a new toy. As in some of Walcott's work, the ingenious tracing of putative patron–client relationships is apt to be taken further than the evidence warrants. The concept can be a useful corrective to a model of an overriding two-party system, or of nineteenth-century economists' models of man as an atomised, independent individual, but the early-Hanoverian evidence points to the survival, indeed the flourishing, of such patronage relationships even in a world in which Whig and Tory identities and tactical parliamentary groupings were clear-cut.

The hierarchical ideology of order may indeed mesh with peer-led factions of politicians; but this did not prevent the existence from 1688 to the 1750s of an ideological polarity caused largely by a schism within a common world view – a debate over the proper application of shared values. To seem to treat patron–client relationships as a sufficient expla-nation of political conduct, especially where they cannot be reconstructed in detail, or are reconstructed inaccurately, invited a crushing reply: and this Hexter, Hirst[95] and Hill[96] provided for the earlier period. Courtiers, admitted Hexter, were an exception: in a system without an overriding ideological polarity most material rewards flowed from the Crown, and this gave 'Court' a definition and a continuity which 'Country' could never attain on the basis of private patronage alone.

'It has not yet been proved that there was a rigid client–patron

[94] J. C. D. Clark, 'A General Theory of Party, Opposition and Government, 1688–1832', *HJ* 23 (1980), 295–325; *idem, The Dynamics of Change: The Crisis of the 1750s and English Party Systems* (Cambridge, 1982); cf. Marie Peters, '"Names and Cant": Party Labels in English Political Propaganda c. 1755–1765', *Parliamentary History* 3 (1984), 103–27; B. W. Hill, *British Parliamentary Parties 1742–1832* (London, 1985); though cf. two reviews: the present author's, in *EHR* 101 (1986), 440–2; Ian R. Christie's, forthcoming in *Parliamentary History*, and Professor Christie's article, 'Party in Politics in the Age of Lord North's Administra-tion', *ibid.* 6 (1987), which finally disposes of the myth of a Tory party surviving 1760 as the new party of government.

[95] Hexter, 'Power Struggle, Parliament, and Liberty', pp. 15–22, and Derek Hirst, 'Unanim-ity in the Commons, Aristocratic Intrigues, and the Origins of the English Civil War', *JMH* 50 (1978), 51–71, a critique of Christianson and Farnell; 'what bound men together in opposition to James and especially Charles was an adhesive more powerful than favour, hierarchy, or the patron–client relation', inferred Hexter. But the revisionist point is to doubt (though arguments on patronage structures are a weak way of doing it) whether men were so tied at all until a late date.

[96] Hill, 'Parliament and People', pp. 105–15; cf. Rabb, 'The Role of the Commons', pp. 72–4.

relationship in the early seventeenth century, of the sort that Namier described in the mid-eighteenth', observed Christopher Hill,[97] and though this is true for the earlier period, the Hanoverian revisionist must protest that it is equally the case in the eighteenth century that patronage alone was very rarely either a sufficient or a rigid determinant of political behaviour.[98] Patronage and clientage, condescension and deference were reciprocal and balanced relationships which imposed obligations on both sides: to treat patronage as synonymous with subservience is at once to destroy the *political* character of that link. Professor Rabb usefully pointed to scholarship on the eighteenth-century electorate[99] to correct early-Stuart revisionists' too-enthusiastic use of this analytical device.

Historians of the eighteenth century have indeed advanced much further in their investigation of the themes of deference and clientage, and early-Stuart historians could profit from a greater knowledge of this now-extensive literature. Too often, they seem to have had only the haziest idea of what had been done or, indeed, of what Namier's contribution really was. 'The Namier method seems to me appropriate only to periods in which no serious issues divided the political nation', Hill added;[100] but this was almost never the case. It is indeed part of the familiar patronising denigration of 'the eighteenth century', which in reality extends its damaging effects to the years 1660–1832, to suppose it an era of somnolent oligarchy, devoid of issues, its politics a matter of intricate but sterile manoeuvre conducted in the language of place, patronage and perquisite. But however essential these assumptions are to the conventional model of the Old Guard, the Hanoverian revisionists could not accept them.

If the politics of *both* 1604–42 *and* 1714–60 can be usefully (but not exclusively) analysed in terms of structures of patronage and clientage, then we can better appreciate the strength of the political order in the later period, and appreciate its powers of survival between 1640 and 1660 despite the more bizarre political phenomena which those decades witnessed.[101] In this context the Restoration becomes more easily explicable, and the events of 1688–9 assume greater importance as a response to problems

97 Hill, 'Parliament and People', p. 106.
98 Cf. especially J. B. Owen, 'The Survival of Country Attitudes in the Eighteenth-Century House of Commons', in J. S. Bromley and E. H. Kossman (eds.), *Britain and the Netherlands* 4 (The Hague, 1971), 42–69; *idem*, 'Political Patronage in 18th Century England', in P. Fritz and D. Williams (eds.), *The Triumph of Culture: 18th Century Perspectives* (Toronto, 1972), pp. 369–87. On the basis of this work, Dr Owen rejected the Court v. Country explanation of 'the Great Rebellion', as he chose in revisionist fashion to call the events of the 1640s.
99 Rabb, 'The Role of the Commons', p. 74, referring to a paper by Frank O'Gorman, since published as 'Electoral Deference in "Unreformed" England: 1760–1832', *JMH* 56 (1984), 391–429.
100 Hill, 'Parliament and People', p. 107.
101 Christianson, 'Causes of the English Revolution', pp. 67–74.

earlier left unsettled,[102] not the defence of a bourgeois order against counterrevolution. If few members of the Long Parliament desired to overturn the social order, the same is true of the members of the Convention Parliament of 1688–9; and if we can avoid intoxication by the more extreme rhetoric which surrounded those events, the exceedingly conservative nature of the social order which succeeded need not be stressed. It may also be possible to explain the long survival of what Old Hat orthodoxy persists in calling the 'unreformed' parliamentary system. Within this new perspective, 'Old Corruption' was a set of practices and their attendant norms, not a set of weaknesses and contradictions.

Despite much sophisticated scholarship, there remains a widespread belief that the early Stuarts presided over a ramshackle, anachronistic, inherently non-viable regime, long in decay, which met its inevitable nemesis in 1640–2. The same assumption still pictures Hanoverian England bumbling its way to necessary and inevitable reform in 1830–2, though here more historians can still be found who are willing to give such beliefs an academic dress. The scenario is merely shifted from a conflict between Crown and Parliament to a conflict between Parliament and People, but though the names are different the plot is curiously similar. Yet if Neale's research on Elizabethan Parliaments actually made untenable this view of Stuart government by showing the long antecedents of what were once seen as new problems[103] it might be suggested that Sedgwick's and Namier's volumes of the *History of Parliament* showed the long viability of the 'unreformed' system despite the 'weaknesses' which allegedly compelled the Reform Bill.[104]

The strength of kinship and patronage networks as sufficient explanations of MPs' voting behaviour should not be exaggerated, as J. B. Owen has shown for the 1740s and James J. Sack for the 1820s. Yet the existence of increasing numbers of division lists in the early decades of the nineteenth century allows accurate measurements to be made of the correlation between peers' voting in the House of Lords and their clients' voting in the House of Commons, especially over the crucial issues of Catholic Emancipation, the repeal of the Test and Corporation Acts, and parliamentary reform. It was on such issues in the 1810s and 20s that Dr Sack detected increasing conflict between patrons and clients. 'This may

---

[102] Cf. especially J R. Jones, *The Revolution of 1688 in England* (London, 1972).

[103] G. R. Elton, 'A High Road to Civil War?' (1965), in *Studies in Tudor and Stuart Politics and Government* (2 vols., Cambridge, 1974), vol. 2, p. 166.

[104] It will be important to discover whether a similar conclusion emerges from Roland Thorne (ed.), *The History of Parliament: The House of Commons, 1790–1820* (5 vols., London, 1986), which had not been published when this work was written. The persistence of ancient patterns, and the ability of old practices to adapt to new needs, is suggested by Peter Fraser, 'Party Voting in the House of Commons, 1812–1827', *EHR* 98 (1983), 763–84.

herald a growth in issue-orientation in the House of Commons in the place
of more traditional and automatically functioning kinship and patronage
groups', he suggested. 'There was some ideological imperative working
within the seemingly most deferential section of the pre-1832 House of
Commons.'[105] If the explanations which other historians have offered of this
'ideological imperative' are correct, one might suggest that similar statistical studies of correlations between Lords' and Commons' voting, extended
into the 1840s, would show the much reduced and continually weakening
power of patronage: the effective end of that nexus of patron, client and kin
which parliamentary historians have traced from the early-Stuart period.
But this is a suggestion for future research to test.

The old thesis that economic divisions generated the parties of the Civil
War is not one that now commands much confidence. Yet the general
thesis that economic divisions and stresses gave rise to parliamentary
parties in the eighteenth century and, in 1832, to parliamentary reform can
be much more exactly tested for this later period, when the survival of
pollbooks and the long continuity of Whig and Tory, or Whig groupings, at
Westminster allows meaningful calculations to be made. It is the *absence* of
voter preference based on social stratification which is remarkable in the
eighteenth century, and, instead, the continued predominance of religious
affiliation as an index of voting behaviour.[106] Christopher Hill's model of
an urban-bourgeois revolt against gentry hegemony, and sympathetic
historians' desire to rescue the thesis by relocating it in 1688, 1714 or the
1780s, are flatly contradicted by recent work on the eighteenth-century
electorate.[107]

This research was not quickly assimilated by political historians,
especially in respect of the 1832 Reform Bill. Theories of parliamentary
reform and social change were still related with a gratifying simplicity.
Professor Cannon offered as a reason for the emergence of 'liberal and
democratic ideas' in the 1640s: 'Social and economic change was strengthening the middling ranks of society and rendering an absolutist and
patriarchal government increasingly inappropriate.' Consequently, the
House of Commons was displaying a 'new mood of assertiveness' even by
the end of Elizabeth's reign.[108] It was an assertiveness somewhat muted

105 James J. Sack, 'The House of Lords and Parliamentary Patronage in Great Britain,
    1802–1832', *HJ* 23 (1980), 922, 927, 930.
106 Cf. the important work of J. A. Phillips, chiefly *Electoral Behaviour in Unreformed England*
    (Princeton, 1982), discussed by the present author – somewhat critically in 'Eighteenth
    Century Social History', *HJ* 27 (1984), 773–88, and more appreciatively in *English Society
    1688–1832*, chapters 1 and 6.
107 Cf. the work discussed in Clark, *English Society 1688–1832*, chapter 1.
108 John Cannon, *Parliamentary Reform 1640–1832* (Cambridge, 1973), pp. 20–1. Professor
    Cannon rightly noted (p. 22) 'the link between religious nonconformity and reform' from
    the 1640s to the 1820s; but the argument of the book proceeds without significantly

after 1660, however. By the 1760s, though, a 'marked increase in the size of many towns' and the 'rise in the number and importance of the middling classes of society' produced a similar political response. The rising middle classes allied with the declining country gentry to demand an end to their exclusion.[109]

At least, they ought to have done so, but evidently didn't. A solution was at hand in a later decade, however, when Paine provided 'the missing link between parliamentary reform and social and economic progress'. Even this was premature, we later learn, because reform 'waited not upon tranquillity but upon urbanisation', which evidently happened to a sufficient extent not in the 1640s, the 1760s, or the 1790s but at some later time. Unfortunately, the 1801 census shows that, apart from London, 'the towns were still of modest size'.[110] Change was at hand, however. By 1812, Westminster politics was reflecting the 'extraordinary expansion of the economy that had taken place since the later 1780s': the rich were getting richer, the poor getting poorer, and, all the while, 'an even greater danger to the unreformed system was the rapid growth in influence of the middle classes'. Contrary to earlier suggestions, they had in fact 'played a relatively small part in any of the previous reform agitations'; but now, at last, 'perceptive politicians realised that they were a powerful force waiting to be harnessed'.[111]

A slump in *c.*1815–19 seemed to be their opportunity. It was not to be, however, since from 1820 economic recovery and growing prosperity paradoxically had the opposite effect of *reducing* pressure for reform.[112] Nevertheless, the growth of the towns saved the day once more: by the end of the 1820s 'a majority' of MPs 'realised the need' to grant them separate representation,[113] and Macaulay duly defended the Reform Bill as a safeguard against revolution 'by bringing over to the side of security and stability the power of the middle classes'.[114] Lords Grey and Holland agreed: the middle class almost unanimously wanted the Reform Bill, and could not be resisted.[115] A similar measure would soon have been inevitable, in any case: 'If it is legitimate to postulate the same economic

drawing on this insight. More relevant to Cannon's model is Harrington's *Oceana*, 'a major contribution to political thought, which expounded the relationship between property and political power, and advocated an agrarian law, manhood suffrage and the ballot', etc., etc.

[109] *Ibid.*, pp. 47–8, 52. As a result, in the 1760s, 'For the first time for decades fundamental and profound questions were raised in British political life' (p. 61). Revisionists have, of course, since discovered not a few such issues in the decades before 1760.

[110] *Ibid.*, pp. 120, 142.

[111] *Ibid.*, p. 165.

[112] *Ibid.*, pp. 184–5.

[113] *Ibid.*, p. 189.

[114] *Ibid.*, p. 215 (Professor Cannon's paraphrase).

[115] *Ibid.*, pp. 245, 250, 252.

developments without the political changes, one can hardly see the old regime surviving the acute recessions of the 1840s'.[116]

The flexibility and usefulness of this pattern of argument is sufficiently apparent from these examples; but, of course, the continued repetition of the same explanation refutes itself. Professor Cannon's justly influential study provided the best statement of a certain case, yet the invocation of these familiar and seldom-examined nostrums was all the more remarkable because of their coexistence with an insight which, in fact, revealed their obsolescence: 'Catholic Emancipation was the battering ram that broke down the old unreformed system'.[117]

Professor D. C. Moore had pursued a somewhat different revision of the received account of 1832 through a close examination of the provisions and working of the Act. Equally, though, it was a critique of the Old Guard and their allies:

> As a rule, the first Reform Act has been considered in the context of that historical model often associated with James Harrington's *Oceana*, according to which changes in the balance of economic power inevitably produce concomitant changes in the balance of political power. In much the same way that Harrington attributed the defeat of Charles I to the growing wealth of the gentry, most historians have attributed the first Reform Act to the growing wealth of the new middle class or classes. In their attempts to define the dynamics of the Act they have focussed their attentions upon industrialization, Radical agitation, and the ostensible Whig belief that 'concession to a sustained popular demand ... [is] the wisest policy for a governing aristocracy'. And then they have gone on to discuss ... the sort of measure which might be explained as the product of such phenomena. But that measure was never drafted. To account for the measure which was drafted another model is required as a means of organizing a somewhat different set of causal phenomena.[118]

Such a critique met with much stronger resistance for the late eighteenth and early nineteenth centuries.

'Progress would seem to depend on deliberately abandoning the notion that the reigns of the first two Stuarts not only led to war but were somehow certain to lead to it', wrote Professor Elton in 1965, and though much progress was made in removing that teleology in the next two decades it is too soon to say that a similar revision has been effective for the years before 1832. If a civil war was inconceivable in 1640, it must be added that a massive measure of reform was inconceivable in 1827. In both cases convulsion and conflict generated alignments and ideas of inevitable processes which have been read back into the preceding era: yet the received orthodoxy is seriously undermined by the discovery that practical

[116] *Ibid.*, p. 253.
[117] *Ibid.*, p. 191.
[118] Moore, *The Politics of Deference*, p. 189. He quoted the *Oxford History of England*.

political activity in the 1820s did *not* revolve around the question of the parliamentary franchise. Electoral behaviour, as Dr J. A. Phillips' work has shown, had much more to do with religious motivations and affiliations than it did with the pursuit of secular democratic goals.[119] An examination of the course of *events* in the decades before 1832 fully bears out that analysis: the Reform Bill is tactically as well as substantively intelligible only in its relation to the repeal of the Test and Corporation Acts in 1828 and Roman Catholic 'Emancipation' in 1829: here again, revisionists in both centuries have reached similar conclusions.[120]

Without a due attention to the religious element in society's rationale, the characteristic values, structures and practices of England's ancien regime are likely to strike the historian as 'bizarre and anomalous' for failing to conform to the sociologist Max Weber's criteria of bureaucratic rationality. Nevertheless, even within a positivist vision, a modern historian has been correctly led to diagnose the phenomena sometimes labelled 'Old Corruption' as 'genuinely indicative of a pre-modern, non-Weberian conceptual mode, which lacked at least an element of the modern notions of merit, individual responsibility, and organizational rationale and which, furthermore, must be taken at least partly at face value.'[121]

Measured by financial criteria – the system of patronage, nepotism, high salaries, perquisites, fees, sinecures and pensions on which radicals like Wade and Cobbett dwelt – the ancien regime survived until 1832 and demonstrably disintegrated thereafter. But why, if these abuses were so

---

[119] The strong correlation in parliamentary voting in the 1780s and 1790s between support for electoral reform and for attempts to subvert the Anglican establishment is demonstrated by Grayson Ditchfield, 'The Parliamentary Struggle over the Repeal of the Test and Corporation Acts, 1787–1790', *EHR* 89 (1974), 551–77; cf. *idem*, 'Dissent and Toleration: Lord Stanhope's Bill of 1789', *JEH* 29 (1978), 51–73.

[120] Clark, *English Society 1688–1832* chapter 6, 'The End of the Ancien Regime, 1800–1832'; G. I. T. Machin, 'Resistance to Repeal of the Test and Corporation Acts, 1828', *HJ* 22 (1979), 115–39. Interestingly, this line of revisionist argument may be said to have derived from an historian who later became a pillar of the early-Stuart anti-revisionist establishment: cf. J. H. Hexter, 'The Protestant Revival and the Catholic Question in England, 1778–1829', *JMH* 8 (1936), 297–319.

[121] 'If historical research into modern British history is to advance beyond those frames of reference which normally mark its conceptualisation, it is surely just to these bizarre and anomalous – and hence, ignored or camouflaged – trends and tendencies to which the historian ought to turn': W. D. Rubinstein, 'The End of "Old Corruption" in Britain 1780–1860', *P&P* 101 (1983), 59, 68. I had unforgivably missed Dr Rubinstein's most important article when finishing *English Society 1688–1832*; I am pleased to see that we both attach great importance to the impact of the Reform Bill in terminating a particular social order, though for different reasons. I had sought to trace the structure and disintegration of the pre-modern conceptual mode which Dr Rubinstein inferred but did not describe. Dr Rubinstein argues for the existence of a social nexus embracing peers, bishops, lawyers and the military by uncovering the vast incomes which they continued to be able to draw from the system until the 1830s.

evident, were they so resistant to criticism?[122] It seems more persuasive to analyse 'Old Corruption' as the survival of practices, still perfectly viable but now denounced by a body of men entertaining a wholly new ideology; practices dating from Elizabeth's reign or even earlier.[123]

'Perhaps the most important pre-modern and non-rational survival was the unreformed House of Commons itself', added Dr Rubinstein. Most discussion had indeed focussed on the question of parliamentary reform. Why did the 'unreformed' system last so long? One answer to that question was provided by the realisation that the forces which undermined the system were not the ones which the Old Hat and Old Guard orthodoxy had focussed on. The idea of 'one man one vote, one vote one value' was in reality a rare one in English history, and particular explanations are needed to account for its occurrence among minorities of 'advanced' intellectuals. Dissent, not Democracy, broke down the old order. Secondly, it had been conventional to write of 'the unrepresented condition of the new manufacturing towns . . . Such growing commercial centres as Manchester, Birmingham and Sheffield lacked direct representation altogether.'[124] This traditional rhetoric had hindered an understanding of how the system actually worked, and distracted attention from the well-known fact that the inhabitants of those towns voted in their county elections: that they *were* directly represented, and that each Birmingham elector's votes counted for exactly as much as a rural Warwickshire elector's votes. In such a system democracy was not obviously a panacea, and was difficult to sell as one.

A better appreciation of the nature of the system seems likely to be provided by asking a question more familiar in early seventeenth-century scholarship. What did Parliament *do*? Did the system *work* efficiently, however lacking in uniformity were the franchise and distribution of seats? Hanoverian parliamentary historians still had something to learn from their early-Stuart colleagues. Virtually all of the scholarly discussion of the 'unreformed' Parliament was conducted on the assumption that the members of the House of Commons were there to represent (and, imperfectly, did represent) 'the people', but that the members of the House of Lords represented only themselves. Yet any functional analysis of the passage of

---

122 My main reservation about Dr Rubinstein's valuable investigation is that it appears to take up and apply the radicals' category, 'Old Corruption', rather than to criticise it – to explain why so many men patently did *not* subscribe to it. It will not do simply to label the practices of the ancien regime 'irrational'. Rationality is an attribute of means, not of ends.

123 As Dr Rubinstein is aware, citing analogous work on the sixteenth and seventeenth centuries: Joel Hurstfield, 'Political Corruption in Modern England: The Historian's Problem', in *idem, Freedom, Corruption and Government in Elizabethan England* (London, 1973); Linda Levy Peck, 'Corruption and Political Development in the Early Modern State: The Case of Britain', in A. S. Eisenstadt (ed.), *Before Watergate: Problems of Corruption in American Society* (New York, 1979).

124 Dickinson, *Liberty and Property*, pp. 225–6.

private and public legislation reveals that peers took a large and effective part in representing interests, localities and individuals despite the absence of a democratic mandate. Indeed, peers made better lobbyists: by their superior social standing they could usually command more weight at Court and with ministers than could most backbench MPs.[125]

Nevertheless, Members of the lower House might also take a leading part in parliamentary business, as Dr Langford has suggested, however few their electors: popular access to MPs might depend more on the location of MPs' estates and place of residence than on the location and franchises of their constituencies. A functional study of Parliament's role as a channel of local interests and a point of contact between the subject and the sovereign should examine both Houses together, mapping the geographical incidence of peers and MPs (and perhaps even bishops) and tracing their role in the daily conduct of business.[126] Such a picture would give us a much more rounded appreciation of the effectiveness of Parliament before 1832 than the traditional Whiggish and socialist histories of parliamentary reform, focussing as they do almost wholly on the rather peripheral questions of the Commons franchise and the distribution of seats. Provincialism still has much to contribute to our understanding of ancien-regime England, especially in curing its later cousin of its 1960s preoccupations with the counting of cotton factories in Manchester or the delineation of drains in Birmingham.

---

[125] Cf. Michael W. McCahill, *Order and Equipoise: The Peerage and the House of Lords, 1783–1806* (London, 1978), pp. 90–112, 168–208 and *passim*. Dr McCahill's most useful case for the continuing importance of the Lords would have been strengthened had he reformulated the Old Hat assumption that 'For centuries the Commons had been the aggressive partner of the constitution, the critic, the innovator' (p. 212).

[126] This re-examination has been begun, for the House of Commons, by Dr Paul Langford (preliminary results of his research presented in a paper read to the Cambridge Historical Society on 26 February 1985). I would extend Dr Langford's important analysis to the House of Lords also. Cf. Hermann Wellenreuther, *Repräsentation und Grossgrundbesitz in England 1730–1770* (Stuttgart, 1979).

# 8

# CONCLUSION

We have long known that English history is a fragmented subject. Yet the segregation of these two centuries has not been quite complete: the same currents of thought have flowed through both, and a few individuals have sought a more extensive vision. Among the most interesting contributions to debate have been made by those who, initially specialising elsewhere, have offered new views of a neighbouring period, as with Professors G. R. Elton and J. G. A. Pocock. To the present author, despite his insistence on the need to treat 1660–1832 as a thing-in-itself, it seems that much good might yet come from a closer integration of seventeenth- and eighteenth-century parliamentary, social and intellectual history. They must, however, be integrated in a new way. One of the most basic effects of the revisionism discussed here is to render untenable the teleological rearrangement of the English past into an account of the inevitable unfolding of Whig-gradualist or of revolutionary change, whether constitutional or economic. Partly this was brought about for the early-Stuart period by detailed studies of parliamentary business, partly by the removal of an earlier prop entailed in Professor Elton's insistence that 'We need to see the sixteenth century in terms of its own experience, not as the prehistory of a later revolution.'[1] It was a lesson which was being applied to the eighteenth century too, by similar means.

The means employed were not, indeed, identical. Hanoverian revisionists could have learned much from their Stuart colleagues. One of the shortcomings of *The Dynamics of Change* was its failure to attend more closely to the House of Lords, and although I am still not clear that such a study would be particularly revealing, the attempt should have been made. Secondly, detailed accounts of the fast-changing manoeuvres of Westminster tend to give one the impression that the localities are a changeless backdrop where time stands still; a longer chronological reference than 1754–7 would have showed more of the important respects in which local

[1] Elton, in *HJ* 16 (1973), 207.

political phenomena *were* being transformed in mid-century in ways importantly analogous to those I sought so inadequately to chart at Westminster. I remain unrepentant, however, in my refusal to treat Court and Parliament as an epiphenomenal world and in my belief that a sufficiently rigorous study could reveal enough of the political autonomy which that methodological position requires.[2]

It seems, then, that it is the high-politics historians rather than the earlier Provincials among the Stuarts who were the natural allies of the Hanoverian revisionists. Namierism, and Provincialism, were ways of shifting the ground of debate; most Hanoverian revisionists, by contrast, were willing to confront Old Hat teleology on its own ground and on its own issues of Westminster politics, the constitution, religion and political ideology. Diversions, even if successful, had distracted attention from the extent to which the main Whig case had remained standing; but a new challenge to the old orthodoxy in 1660–1832 can be projected back to the decades before 1660, and without the aid and encouragement supplied by some unexamined assumptions about Hanoverian England, the Old Guard (and even Old Hat) account of the early Stuarts looks decidedly weaker. Early-Stuart revisionists were equally slow in drawing on the work of their later colleagues; and the attempt to link these two areas will, one hopes, absorb much more academic effort.

Some outlines are already evident. How powerful was Parliament in the seventeenth and eighteenth centuries? From a picture of a strong institution enclosing clearly defined parties we have moved to a view of a weaker, less purposeful institution in which parties had difficulty in sustaining their integrity when dynastic issues were absent: in this respect the period from the Exclusion Crisis to the 1750s displays a very different pattern, clear Whig v. Tory distinctions being induced by conflicts over dynastic and religious questions which neither the Civil War nor the Glorious Revolution had settled.

A new account of the absence, or presence, of parties has its effect also on the familiar teleology. A clash of parties, Cavalier and Roundhead, led to the defeat of the first, it was once thought, and the ascendancy of the second, devoted as it was to parliamentary supremacy. The clash of Whig and Tory between 1689 and 1714, it was formerly believed, led to the elimination of the second and the domination of the monarchy by Parliament under the first two Georges. It was the clash of Grey's (libertarian) Whigs with Liverpool's and Wellington's (reactionary) Tories in the years to 1832, historians previously supposed, which ensured

---

[2] I would not wish to devote much effort to justifying my first book, though I still adhere to its central arguments. Since we can all do better, I believe historians are more wisely employed in criticising their previous work than in defending it to the letter.

the primacy of the Commons in Victorian England. It seems that the successful struggle for parliamentary supremacy, like 'the secularisation of politics' or 'the rise of the middle class', can be observed in *any* seemingly self-contained period; but look forward to the next such period, and the battle seems always in need of winning again. It may or may not be that this scenario applies to *one* such period; it is highly implausible that it applies to them *all*.

The Provincials, too, have scored some important gains, though at the risk of implying that these familiar phenomena apply to *no* period.[3] Christopher Hill, at least, ceased to urge the 'rising gentry' thesis, though without actually disowning it.[4] As far as the gentry are concerned, early-Stuart county studies firmly disprove the idea of their long-standing division into two clear-cut sides, or of a gentry-led initiative to seize sovereignty in response to the classic Whig issues of taxation and representation. But if the Provincials have been at their most effective in showing what did *not* happen, it is the high-political historians who have been more successful in showing us what *did*.

Certainly, we would wish to progress beyond the Old Hat methodology which treated great constitutional–libertarian issues as if they had a life of their own, and as if their modern forms were the achievement of long-standing, purposeful endeavour. Equally we now dispense with the Old Guard assumption that such claims of principle were merely manifestations or reflections of 'underlying' economic change. It was indeed curiously patronising in some quarters to presume that only the gentry elite comprehended the issues and that the common man reacted by contrast to material imperatives – the fluctuations of wages, wheat prices or relations of production, and to the emerging class interest which these things were held to generate. A fuller understanding of the county community reveals a very considerable degree of popular awareness of theoretical matters – but an awareness largely focussing on questions of religion, and in a social context defined by shared ideas of hierarchy and deference.

Old Guard and Old Hat historians had generally adopted a model of a revolutionary society, animated by a bourgeois or a constitutionalist dynamic, confronting a conservative or reactionary regime. The earlier work of the revisionist school tended simply to reverse this, postulating a conservative society structured by Provincialist introversion or unanimous

---

[3] The problem is that the much-maligned 'Whig interpretation' contains a grain of truth. It responds to a set of perfectly real malaises: but it defines them wrongly, through its use of anachronistic categories, and so offers a false diagnosis.

[4] 'Premature' is now his word for it: Hill, 'Parliament and People', pp. 101, 103, 118: 'I suspect that in this respect Tawney was no more a Tawneyite than Marx was a Marxist or Namier a Namierite.' Such remarks signal a hauling-down of colours.

Calvinism, rudely challenged by an Arminian, absolutist royal power.[5] Each scenario had something to commend it, but both shared the implausible assumption that one major element in the nation stood still in the midst of flux. Further reflection shows us that this immutability is a characteristic not of human affairs but of historians' arguments: it was the result of accepting (consciously or unconsciously) only one side's definition of what the *status quo* really was.[6]

A more plausible approach is to accept that *all* elements in society are subject to continual change, decay and renovation. Appropriately, then, a more rounded account is beginning to emerge which accords a greater parity of esteem to the perceptions both of the defenders and of the enemies of the political order: in the early-Stuart period we see Royalist innovators as well as religious rebels (initially in Scotland and Ireland)[7]; in the early-Hanoverian period we see an equally new dynasty as bureaucratic centralisers, and we appreciate the force and the relevance of the Jacobite critique. Revisionism helps us not only to see each field in sharper focus and truer perspective; it also redresses the balance between the two eras. Both groups of revisionists are sceptical about historians' traditional agreement on 'the special importance of the Stuart century for the political and constitutional history of England'.[8] As J. H. Hexter explained it, 'the most important lesson of all' was that 'what was ultimately at stake in England in the early decades of the seventeenth century was liberty, not only the liberty of seventeenth-century Englishmen but our own liberty'.[9] It was to the revolutions of 1642 and 1688, declared Lawrence Stone, that 'England owed its peculiar eighteenth-century economic, social, political, legal and religious configurations, all so very different from those of the major continental European states. The key code word used by contemporaries to describe the difference was "liberty".'[10] It was this unexamined category, 'liberty', which was offered as a standard to which all historians

[5] Cf. J. H. Elliot, 'England and Europe: A Common Malady?', in Conrad Russell (ed.), *The Origins of the English Civil War* (London, 1973), p. 250.

[6] I am indebted for this idea to Robert W. Tucker and David C. Hendrickson, *The Fall of the First British Empire: Origins of the War of American Independence* (Baltimore, 1982). Arguments like theirs about government policy in the reign of George III could valuably be developed for the reign of Charles I also.

[7] Having argued the importance of the relations between our four nations – Wales, Ireland, Scotland, England – I acknowledge that I have said almost nothing about that question here. I hope to discuss it at length, for the period *c.* 1600–1850, in a future book.

[8] Kevin Sharpe, 'Introduction. Parliamentary History 1603–1629: In or Out of Perspective?', in Sharpe (ed.), *Faction and Parliament*, p. 1.

[9] J. H. Hexter, 'Power Struggle, Parliament, and Liberty in Early Stuart England', *JMH* 50 (1978), 47. I should add that I do not deny the *importance* of the early-Stuart period (or the great ability of the historians who have written on it). What I find implausible, both in point of substance and of method, is a claim of its *special* importance.

[10] Stone, in Pocock (ed.), *Three British Revolutions: 1641, 1688, 1776* (Princeton, 1981), p. 96.

should rally: to question its exact meaning was made to seem tantamount to denying its desirability. Revisionist scholars thus looked particularly sinful in subjecting the idea of England's *special* inheritance of 'liberty' to academic scrutiny. Yet in an age of European integration, they were encouraged for a variety of reasons to question the Whig assumption that English society, in Stone's senses, *was* profoundly different from its continental neighbours.

The Old Hat historians, and especially Professor Hexter, had a point in arguing for the 'hourglass theory' of representative institutions: proliferating in the middle ages, threatened and squeezed into a narrow channel from the end of the sixteenth century to *c*.1688, broadening out again thereafter. But the revisionist historian protested against the covert substitution which turns this into the history of liberty *per se*, as if 'liberty' were a thing unchanging in itself which men succeed in enjoying only in greater or lesser degree, and which only representative institutions can secure.[11] This is, in truth, an American perspective.

The English have always lacked that universally diffused belief, which I find in all groups of American students I teach, that their political system is a *democracy*, and that it is premised upon democratic values.[12] The English experience has for so long, and to so great a degree, been a matter of rulers and ruled, hierarchy and deference, obedience and allegiance: looked at in secular terms, the triumph of Whig values was really about the replacement of one set of patrician rulers by another, slightly different, set. English scholars do not feel that, in being appropriately sceptical about politicans and their platitudes, they are putting at risk some precious but fragile inheritance, the achievement of early-Stuart self-sacrifice.

Because of the circumstances in which their republic was founded, Americans still translate 'representative institutions' as 'liberties'; apart from a handful of polemicists, the English make no such easy association.[13] Their inheritance is a most complex one, in which the residual values of an

---

[11] J. H. Hexter, 'The Birth of Modern Freedom', *TLS* 21 Jan. 1983, pp. 51–4. This analysis seems to imply that 'liberty' exists only in the form of 'freedom *from* . . .'; the implication of my argument in this book may be that it exists only in the form of 'freedom *to* . . .'.

[12] Hexter's 'gradual imprinting on the collective consciousness of Englishmen of the awareness that their liberties required the survival of representative institutions' (p. 54) is much more true of Americans. Some of my English pupils are conservative, some radical, a handful might even be called disaffected: but almost none of them are instinctively democratic in the modern American sense. English understandings of liberty have always had much more to do with the rule of law than with democracy; in England, the second of those things has not been a precondition of the first.

[13] Hexter, *ibid.*, p. 54, blames the prevalence of Marxist analysis for English scholars' remarkable neglect of early-Stuart parliamentary history in the years *c*. 1920–70 compared with the superb and extensive work of their American colleagues. There are other reasons, too; and we might valuably reflect on the even greater neglect of the parliamentary history of *c*. 1714–60.

ancien regime co-exist with and subtly modify apparently quite contradict-ory values. The American inheritance, superficially and structurally similar, was transformed in essence and impact by rebellion in the 1770s. Consequently, rhetoric about English democracy has had much practical value as a way of cementing an American alliance;[14] as an academic analysis, the revisionist historian finds it of only limited use. Englishmen and Americans are deeply attached to their liberties, as is only right; but those liberties, extensively and superficially similar, are in important ways profoundly different. These basic differences between modern Englishmen and modern Americans[15] have been rather obscured than elucidated by the Old Hat and Old Guard historiography of the seventeenth and eighteenth centuries.

It may be that some early-Stuart revisionists have been premature in seeing a consensus emerging from revisionist studies:[16] considerable difficulties remain over the working of aristocratic clientage and the relation between 'localist' and 'high-political' revisionisms. Nor should the attachment of large numbers of historians to quite different assumptions be underestimated. Progress has been irregular, and slower in the later period. Professor Rabb identified the common ground he considered had emerged:

No historian of the period should again repeat the simplifications that marked the Gardiner/Notestein interpretation. The relentless unfolding of a grand plan; the clear-cut constitutional and ideological divisions; the coherence of both 'oppo-sition' and 'court'; and the exclusive concentration on events at Westminster – and even there only in the House of Commons – no longer command support ... It is now clear that developments were more sporadic than Gardiner or Notestein allowed; that divisions were often as much within men's minds as between men; that the consequences of foreign policy, especially of war, influenced domestic affairs more than has been realised; and that overblown usages like 'tyranny' and 'party' are both inapprorpriate and misleading.[17]

If we could leave the argument there, we might record a large measure of agreement. Professor Rabb, like Professor Hexter, chose however to defend a methodology which entailed that the points listed above were essentially dilutions of the traditional interpretation, not reconstructions of its frame-work. Did the events of the 1620s *lead to* those of the 1640s? It 'seems more misleading than helpful to break up chronology so severely, to contextua-

---

[14] Twice in the present century have Englishmen and Americans been confronted with the most momentous need to declare that they believed in the same ideals. The element of truth in this claim has allowed the attendant rhetoric to swamp much else of importance.

[15] To understand these differences is to understand the peculiar problems faced by modern American historians in explaining ancien-regime England.

[16] E.g. Paul Christianson, 'Politics and Parliaments in England, 1604–1629', *Canadian Journal of History* 16 (1981), 107–13.

[17] Theodore K. Rabb, 'Revisionism Revised: The Role of the Commons', *P&P* 92 (1981), 60.

lise every occurrence so totally, that the larger movements of history vanish'. Detailed political narrative results in 'an atomisation of history'. 'Unless there is some shape to the past, some connection among its bewildering mass of relics, there is no point in studying it.' The suggestion that epic events can arise from 'largely accidental' causes is to 'reduce human motivation to the trite and the mechanical'.

To the eighteenth-century historian, all this seems distressingly reminiscent of the debate between Namier and Butterfield. It echoes, too, the reception given to other detailed narratives, including Cooke and Vincent's *The Governing Passion*. Both sides seem only to draw apart with continued debate. Professor Rabb wishes 'to speak, if not of a steady crescendo, then of a fitful but fairly high road to civil war. The progression, slow and drawn out, was not inevitable, but it *was* a progression.' If this were only an empirical observation, all might yet be well. But Professor Rabb describes this progression as 'the basic dynamic' which 'has given meaning and an overall pattern to the reigns of James and Charles I',[18] and we are brought face to face once more with a most profound disagreement, and one not yet reconciled within scholarly debate.

To a large extent, the debate is one between generations; it will be resolved in the way all such debates have to be settled. Indeed, its general outlines have come into sharp focus only at a moment when the arguments of certain historians suddenly seemed no longer to be eternal truth, or even modern scholarship, but voices from the past − a surprisingly remote past.[19] It is less remarkable that the young of today find a gulf opening up between themselves and the mental world of their seniors if we recall the seniors' years of birth: E. J. Hobsbawm (1917), R. H. Hilton (1916), H. R. Trevor-Roper (1914), Christopher Hill (1912), J. H. Plumb (1911), C. B. Macpherson (1911), J. H. Hexter (1910), George Rudé (1910). Beside them, Lawrence Stone (1919), Raymond Williams (1921) and E. P. Thompson (1924) seem almost modern.[20]

It is understandable, however, that socialist or liberal doctrine should seem vital and important to men who are themselves contemporaries of the Russian Revolution or of Mr Asquith, and that they should find it interesting and important to engage in debate with such historic figures as R. H. Tawney (1880), Wallace Notestein (1878) or G. M. Trevelyan (1876). In no sense is seniority a reproach; the same process overtakes deserving and undeserving alike. But the historian's own historical

---

[18] *Ibid.*, pp. 74–8.

[19] For an analysis which treats this cohort of scholars (and Maurice Dobb, 1900–76) as a clearly defined school of thought, see Harvey J. Kaye, *The British Marxist Historians: An Introductory Analysis* (Cambridge, 1984).

[20] To make this point reminds us of the profound contrast between such men and other historians of similar vintage who demonstrably update their outlook.

location must be diagnosed if any of us are to imagine that we can transcend it in even the smallest degree. It would, perhaps, be wrong to conduct this debate as if agreement over fundamental issues of method could be secured by argument: we should aim at something less morally satisfying, but more attainable, and less dependent on the organisation of the historical profession on the 'adversary system' so beloved of the English. The debates discussed here produced some real gains in knowledge, but too often they have only reinforced differences of principle which have been clearly perceived as such by most of the participants. It is a comforting doctrine that 'Controversies among historians commonly arise from misunderstandings',[21] but not, alas, a true one.

[21] G. R. Elton, in *British Studies Monitor* 3 (1972), 16.

# APPENDIX A

## Newman's eighteen Theses on Liberalism

### (see pp. 102–3 above)

From J. H. Newman, *Apologia Pro Vita Sua* (ed. Martin J. Svaglic, Oxford, 1967), pp. 260–2:

1. No religious tenet is important, unless reason shows it to be so.

   Therefore, e.g. the doctrine of the Athanasian Creed is not to be insisted on, unless it tends to convert the soul; and the doctrine of the Atonement is to be insisted on, if it does convert the soul.

2. No one can believe what he does not understand.

   Therefore, e.g. there are no mysteries in true religion.

3. No theological doctrine is any thing more than an opinion which happens to be held by bodies of men.

   Therefore, e.g. no creed, as such, is necessary for salvation.

4. It is dishonest in a man to make an act of faith in what he has not had brought home to him by actual proof.

   Therefore, e.g. the mass of men ought not absolutely to believe in the divine authority of the Bible.

5. It is immoral in a man to believe more than he can spontaneously receive as being congenial to his moral and mental nature.

   Therefore, e.g. a given individual is not bound to believe in eternal punishment.

6. No revealed doctrines or precepts may reasonably stand in the way of scientific conclusions.

   Therefore, e.g. Political Economy may reverse our Lord's declarations about poverty and riches, or a system of Ethics may teach that the highest condition of body is ordinarily essential to the highest state of mind.

7. Christianity is necessarily modified by the growth of civilization, and the exigencies of times.

   Therefore, e.g. the Catholic priesthood, though necessary in the Middle Ages, may be superseded now.

8. There is a system of religion more simply true than Christianity as it has ever been received.

   Therefore, e.g. we may advance that Christianity is the 'corn of wheat' which has been dead for 1800 years, but at length will bear fruit; and that Mahometanism is the manly religion, and existing Christianity the womanish.

9. There is a right of Private Judgement: that is, there is no existing authority on earth competent to interfere with the liberty of individuals in reasoning and

judging for themselves about the Bible and its contents, as they severally please.

Therefore, e.g. religious establishments requiring subscription are Antichristian.

10. There are rights of conscience such, that every one may lawfully advance a claim to profess and teach what is false and wrong in matters, religious, social and moral, provided that to his private conscience it seems absolutely true and right.

Therefore, e.g. individuals have a right to preach and practise fornication and polygamy.

11. There is no such thing as a national or state conscience.

Therefore, e.g. no judgements can fall upon a sinful or infidel nation.

12. The civil power has no positive duty, in a normal state of things, to maintain religious truth.

Therefore, e.g. blasphemy and sabbath-breaking are not rightly punishable by law.

13. Utility and expedience are the measure of political duty.

Therefore, e.g. no punishment may be enacted, on the ground that God commands it: e.g. on the text, 'Whoso sheddeth man's blood, by man shall his blood be shed.'

14. The Civil Power may dispose of Church property without sacrilege.

Therefore, e.g. Henry VIII, committed no sin in his spoliations.

15. The Civil Power has the right of ecclesiastical jurisdiction and administration.

Therefore, e.g. Parliament may impose articles of faith on the Church or suppress Dioceses.

16. It is lawful to rise in arms against legitimate princes.

Therefore, e.g. the Puritans in the 17th century, and the French in the 18th, were justifiable in their Rebellion and Revolution respectively.

17. The people are the legitimate source of power.

Therefore, e.g. Universal Suffrage is among the natural rights of man.

18. Virtue is the child of knowledge, and vice of ignorance.

Therefore, e.g. education, periodical literature, railroad travelling, ventilation, drainage, and the arts of life, when fully carried out, serve to make a population moral and happy.

There was little that was uniquely Roman Catholic in his list: even theses 14 and 15 were widely denied within the Church of England. As in other matters, Newman carried over to Rome a large measure of entirely mainstream Anglicanism.

# APPENDIX B

# The recent debate on Jacobitism after 1714

Over the years much scholarly (and very much more unscholarly) history has been devoted to the subject of Jacobitism. A new phase in the scholarly discussion of the question was opened in 1970 by the volumes of the *History of Parliament* edited by Romney Sedgwick, *The House of Commons 1715–1754*. Dr Eveline Cruickshanks' research on Tory MPs, and her section of the Introduction on 'The Tories' (vol. 1, pp. 62–78), committed those volumes to the argument that 'the available evidence leaves no doubt that up to 1745 the Tories were a predominantly Jacobite party, engaged in attempts to restore the Stuarts by a rising with foreign assistance' (Preface, vol. 1, p. ix).

Such a thesis generated a controversy among parliamentary historians, most of whom were not yet reconciled to the idea of a Tory party surviving after *c.*1715, let alone to the idea of its owing its survival to dynastic ideology and related tactical options. Dr Eveline Cruickshanks restated her position in *Political Untouchables: The Tories and the '45* (London, 1979), and a claim that the disintegration of the Jacobite option underlay the conflicts and organisational disintegration of the 1750s was a theme of my own *The Dynamics of Change* (Cambridge, 1982) and earlier articles. Linda Colley meanwhile was working out an argument that Tory survival after 1715 was to be explained chiefly in organisational terms, initially in her article 'The Loyal Brotherhood and the Cocoa Tree: The London Organisation of the Tory Party, 1727–1760', *HJ* 20 (1977), 77–95, and more fully in *In Defiance of Oligarchy* (Cambridge, 1982). I reviewed the debate to that point, with suggestions of my own, in a review article: 'The Politics of the Excluded: Tories, Jacobites and Whig Patriots 1715–1760', *Parliamentary History* 2 (1983), 209–22. Though covering a slightly earlier period, Daniel Szechi's *Jacobitism and Tory Politics 1710–14* (Edinburgh, 1984) should be noted. The susceptibility of the subject to quite different historical reconstructions is ably shown by A. J. Youngson, *The Prince and the Pretender: A Study in the Writing of History* (London, 1985).

Other genres of scholarship were meanwhile contributing to the debate, including regional studies. Rupert C. Jarvis' careful research, embodied in *Collected Papers on the Jacobite Risings* (2 vols., Manchester, 1971–2), had been unduly neglected, and S. W. Baskerville's Oxford DPhil thesis of 1976, 'The Management of the Tory

Interest in Lancashire and Cheshire, 1714–47', had few imitators. Such themes were more often pursued north of the Border, as in Bruce Lenman's *The Jacobite Risings in Britain 1689–1746* (London, 1980) and *The Jacobite Clans of the Great Glen 1650–1784* (London, 1984), continuing a long tradition of Scots scholarship more recently including, for example, Rosalind Mitchison's 'The Government of the Highlands, 1707–1745', in N. Phillipson and R. Mitchison (eds.), *Scotland in the Age of Improvement* (Edinburgh, 1970), and Elizabeth K. Carmichael, 'Jacobitism in the Scottish Commission of the Peace, 1707–1760', *Scottish Historical Review* 58 (1979), 58–69.

South of the Border, scholarly studies of the reactions of local communities to the '45 can be traced in F. J. McLynn, *The Jacobite Army in England, 1745* (Edinburgh, 1983); W. A. Speck, *The Butcher: The Duke of Cumberland and the Suppression of the '45* (London, 1981): and a series of articles by Dr Nicholas Rogers: 'Aristocratic Clientage, Trade and Independency: Popular Politics in Pre-Radical Westminster', *P&P* 61 (1973), 70–106; 'Popular Disaffection in London during the Forty-Five', *The London Journal* 1 (1975), 5–27; 'Resistance to Oligarchy: The City Opposition to Walpole and his Successors, 1725–47', in John Stevenson (ed.), *London in the Age of Reform* (Oxford, 1977), pp. 1–29; 'Popular Protest in Early Hanoverian London', *P&P* 79 (1978), 70–100; 'Riot and Popular Jacobitism in Early Hanoverian England', in Cruickshanks (ed.), *Ideology and Conspiracy* (Edinburgh, 1982), pp. 70–88; 'The Urban Opposition to the Whig Oligarchy, 1720–60', in M. and J. Jacob (eds.), *The Origins of Anglo-American Radicalism* (London, 1984), pp. 132–48. A particular controversy can be followed in Pat Rogers, 'The Waltham Blacks and the Black Act', *HJ* 17 (1974), 465–86; E. P. Thompson, *Whigs and Hunters: The Origin of the Black Act* (London, 1975; Peregrine edn, Harmondsworth, 1977); Eveline Cruickshanks and Howard Erskine-Hill, 'The Waltham Black Act and Jacobitism', *JBS* 24 no. 3 (1985), 358–65.

For Wales, see P. D. G. Thomas, 'Jacobitism in Wales', *Welsh History Review* 1 (1962), 279–300, and Philip Jenkins, 'Jacobites and Freemasons in Eighteenth Century Wales', *Welsh History Review*, 9 (1979), 391–406. The history of Irish Jacobitism in the period after 1714 is almost *terra incognita*, but see two articles by F. J. McLynn: 'Ireland and the Jacobite Rising of 1745', *The Irish Sword* 13 (1979), 339–52, and '"Good Behaviour": Irish Catholics and the Jacobite Rising of 1745', *Éire–Ireland* 16 (1981), 43–58.

SOCIAL AND INTELLECTUAL

For England, the exploration of the social, political and cultural nexus of Jacobitism was taken up by Paul Chapman, 'Jacobite Political Argument in England 1714–1766' (Cambridge PhD thesis, 1983), and Paul Monod, 'For the King to Enjoy His Own Again: Jacobite Political Culture in England 1688–1788' (Yale PhD thesis, 1985). Dr Chapman sees a collapse of popular Jacobitism in the 1720s; Dr Monod traces its importance until a much later date. I attempted a small contribution to such questions, *inter alia*, in *English Society 1688–1832: Ideology, Social Structure and Political Practice during the Ancien Regime* (Cambridge, 1985). Three articles by F. J. McLynn should be consulted: 'Jacobitism and the Classical British

Empiricists', *BJECS* 4 (1981), 155–70; 'Issues and Motives in the Jacobite Rising of 1745', *EC* 23 (1982), 97–133; and 'Jacobitism and David Hume: The Ideological Backlash Foiled', *Hume Studies* 9 (1983), 171–99.

## RELIGION

Church historians were generally not forward in the debate, though special mention should be made of the contributions of Dr G. V. Bennett: 'Jacobitism and the Rise of Walpole', in N. McKendrick (ed.), *Historical Perspectives* (London, 1974), pp. 70–92; *idem*, *The Tory Crisis in Church and State, 1688–1730: The Career of Francis Atterbury Bishop of Rochester* (Oxford, 1975); *idem*, 'English Jacobitism, 1710–1715: Myth and Reality', *TRHS* 32 (1982), 137–51; and John Findon, 'The Nonjurors and the Church of England 1689–1716' (Oxford DPhil thesis, 1978).

## DIPLOMACY

Diplomacy, espionage and strategy proved much more fertile areas, in the wake of Paul Fritz's pioneering 'The Anti-Jacobite Intelligence System of the English Ministers, 1715–1745', *HJ* 16 (1973), 265–89; *idem.*, *The English Ministers and Jacobitism between the Rebellions of 1715 and 1745* (Toronto, 1975). Eveline Cruickshanks' *Political Untouchables* attended to the diplomatic dimension of the '45, and a fully researched account was provided by F. J. McLynn, *France and the Jacobite Rising of 1745* (Edinburgh, 1981); see also his article 'Voltaire and the Jacobite Rising of 1745', *Studies on Voltaire and the Eighteenth Century*, 185 (1980), 7–20. The moribund field of early-eighteenth-century diplomatic history has now been revivified by such works as Jeremy Black, *British Foreign Policy in the Age of Walpole* (Edinburgh, 1985).

## CULTURAL

One of the pioneers in the recovery of Jacobitism was a student of English literature: Dr Howard Erskine-Hill. See his *The Social Milieu of Alexander Pope* (London, 1975); *The Augustan Idea in English Literature* (London, 1983); and a series of articles, including: 'Literature and the Jacobite Cause: Was There a Rhetoric of Jacobitism?' in Cruickshanks (ed.), *Ideology and Conspiracy*; 'Alexander Pope: The Political Poet in His Time', *ECS* 15 (1981–2), 123–48; 'Under Which Caesar? Pope in the Journal of Mrs Charles Caesar, 1724–1741', *Review of English Studies* 33 (1982), 436–44; 'The Political Character of Samuel Johnson', in Isobel Grundy (ed.), *Samuel Johnson: New Critical Essays* (London, 1984). Dr Erskine-Hill's views thus constituted a critique of Donald J. Greene, *The Politics of Samuel Johnson* (New Haven, Conn., 1960), which had drawn its political framework from J. B. Owen, *The Rise of the Pelhams* (London, 1957) – for which, see above, pp. 152–4. Dr Erskine-Hill and I had been independently working on Johnson: cf. my briefer treatment of the same theme in *English Society 1688–1832*, pp. 186–9.

COLLECTIONS

The papers read at the Jacobite Conference of 1979, organised by Dr Cruickshanks, are published as Eveline Cruckshanks (ed.), *Ideology and Conspiracy: Aspects of Jacobitism 1689–1759* (Edinburgh, 1982), with an editorial Introduction reviewing the current state of the debate. For the proceedings of the 1987 conference, see Eveline Cruikshanks and Jeremy Black (eds.), *The Jacobite Challenge* (Edinburgh, 1988). Jeremy Black (ed.), *Britain in the Age of Walpole* (London, 1984) collects essays by eight authors, with an editorial Introduction which places the Stuart threat squarely back on the agenda for the historian of Walpole's era: the '45 was 'the greatest crisis that affected the eighteenth-century British State', contends Dr Black.

# INDEX

*English Society 1688–1832: Ideology, social structure and political practice during the ancien regime*

'Jonathan Clark ... has taken on some of the most distinguished historical writers of recent years – Christopher Hill, E. J. Hobsbawm, J. H. Plumb, Lawrence Stone, E. P. Thompson ... every now and then – and not that often – a work of history is written that really does break the moulds of received interpretation; a work that is a seminal study of great importance and originality. Clark's book is of this order ... impressive, decisive, and extremely scholarly ... a work of enormous distinction.'

E. R. Norman, *The Spectator*

' ... impossible to fault ... invariably interesting ... an original and distinctive view of the eighteenth-century world ... liberal and Marxist historians of ideas ... had better raise their game before the next encounter.'

Alan Ryan, *London Review of Books*

'In one of the most impressive books on the eighteenth century to appear in recent years Jonathan Clark has produced an important and persuasive revision of most historical views of the period ... Anyone interested in the eighteenth century will find this an exciting book to read. Its significance is not however restricted to those interested in the period. Clark's revisionism demands the consideration of all those working on early and late modern English history and will ensure an expectant readership for his next book, *Revolution and Rebellion*.'

Jeremy Black, *History Today*

'This is a remarkable, even a sensational book, which will cause much fluttering in academic dovecotes ... This is a far-ranging piece of revisionism, lucidly, elegantly and temperately argued, and though Clark is driven to reject the work of just about every historian working in this field, living or dead, he manages to discharge this task with remarkable tact and good manners ... It is a book which ought to be required reading for anyone interested in eighteenth-century men, manners and literature.'

John Kenyon, *The Observer*

' ... written with élan and precision ... always clever ... never dull, silly or routine ... Every reader will argue with many things in this book. But it is as brave, as exciting a book as I have read on the eighteenth century this decade. It breaks the mould of Hanoverian politics.'

John Morrill, *The Times Higher Education Supplement*

*The Dynamics of Change: The crisis of the 1750s and English party systems*

' ... a challenge for the heavyweight championship of eighteenth-century English historical scholarship.'

W. A. Speck, *Historical Journal*